Holy Hell

A Memoir of

Faith, Devotion, and Pure Madness

GAIL TREDWELL

Copyright 2013 by Gail Tredwell

All rights reserved. This book may not be reproduced in whole or in part without written permission from the author.

Published by Wattle Tree Press
Maui, Hawai'i

ISBN-10: 0989679403
ISBN-13: 9780989679404

Cover illustration and design by Lisa Desimini
www.lisadesimini.com

For Irene Ada Tredwell
My real mother

Leona,
Thanks you for your dedicated service
Gail ♡

ACKNOWLEDGEMENTS

I would like to express my heartfelt appreciation to the friends and family who showered me with their love and support during my transition back to a "normal" and balanced life. Without you, the journey would have been far more arduous. Thank you.

I also want to thank the friends (who prefer to remain anonymous) who read the manuscript in its various stages of development and offered their invaluable insight and suggestions. Oodles of gratitude to the one friend who held my hand and journeyed with me to the darker realms, places that I was unable to face on my own. You are amazing.

Special mention goes to Lisa Desimini, my brilliant cover illustrator and designer. Thank you for your creative vision, patience, and amazing talent. You are an absolute gem to work with.

And last but by no means least, I want to thank Paul Wood (writer, teaching artist, and co-author of Lurigancho—another, very different true story of escape). Paul was my tireless, cool-calm-and-collected, genius editor. Thank you so much for believing in the importance of my story and for nurturing my talent as a writer.

Gail Tredwell

While all the incidents described in this book are true, the names and identifying characteristics of some people have been altered in an effort to honor their privacy. The stories are based on many years of diary writings and the best of my recollection. All dialogue is as close an approximation as possible to actual conversations that took place. This memoir isn't the definitive account of Amma; it is my own remembrance.

CONTENTS

1. Who am I? · 1
2. All aboard · 13
3. Turning a new leaf · 30
4. Arunachala and I · 40
5. Becoming Gayatri · 59
6. The anklets · 74
7. An ashram is born · 84
8. Amma's children · 96
9. Days of bliss · 106
10. The operation · 117
11. The recuperation · 130
12. Our mother, our guru · · · · · · · · · · · · · · · · · · 146
13. Dishonorable discharge · · · · · · · · · · · · · · · · 155
14. Something's cooking · · · · · · · · · · · · · · · · · · · 167
15. The plot thickens · 177
16. I need a break · 194
17. My guru, my girlfriend · · · · · · · · · · · · · · · · · 208
18. Growing pains · 220
19. To be or not to be? · 234
20. Man in heat · 244

21. The dawn of doubt · 255
22. The meltdown · 267
23. Shattered dreams · 282
24. The great escape · 297
Epilogue. My own two feet · 318

Twenty-two year old Gayatri

ONE

WHO AM I?

I stand in front of the mirror emotionless as a corpse.
Who on earth is looking back at me? Do I know this person? There's a faint resemblance to someone I might have known a long time back, but now I'm confused.

This woman's skin is sallow. Her hollow and sunken eyes are set in such deep black circles they would make a raccoon envious. Her scraggly hair hangs loosely over her shoulders, so she tucks it behind her ears. Then out of habit she starts to tie it into a bun, but refrains.

I take a long hard look at the figure's never-ending forehead and the thin strands of hair pathetically trying to cover that scalp. I'm distracted for a minute as I look around the room to take another glance at the flowers on my bedside table. So pretty, so perfect their colors, so sure of themselves.

I try not to look at the lifeless heap of orange robes slumped in the corner. But their painful presence is too hard to miss.

My thoughts drift to the San Ramon ashram just ten minutes from where I am hiding. Thunderbolts of anxiety attack my body when I imagine the mayhem that is occurring—now that they know I have run away.

I wonder if they have found my note and have actually given it to Amma?

In an attempt to distract myself from such an excruciating train of thought, I focus on the fragrance in the room. It's coming from a candle that's also trying to make its presence known. My room looks perfect, so warm and comfortable, with a bed covered in a pretty pink and white quilt. I'm tempted just to lie down and accept the bed's embrace. But I resist.

How strange it feels to see myself no longer wearing a sari. Twenty years later. Clad again in Western clothes. The bare skin at my neckline stares rudely at me. I shudder at the sight of my breasts. Even though a knitted top covers them, I feel exposed and improper. Turning sideways I take a real good look at their shape, as if seeing them for the first time. My dress ends just below the knee, so I look at my legs, then at the freckles I haven't seen for a very long time. On my left shin I see the big brown spot, the birthmark I've had my entire life but completely forgotten.

I have just turned forty-one, but somehow the image looking back at me is much older. I'm perplexed. I'm having an allergic reaction to the person I'm looking at.

The phone rings, snapping me out of my trance. I quickly step away from the mirror admitting to myself that maybe I don't recognize this person… but it is me… not a stranger… and I have to accept it.

I rush to the phone. But it stops after just one ring.

I wait with my mouth agape, eyes fixed on the plastic object. It starts ringing again, but then stops. I begin to shake inside and feel faint. I reach for a nearby table for support. If the phone rings once more, then I know it is my friend and my code to pick up.

It does.

Holding the phone to my ear, I dare not speak until I know who is on the other end.

"Gayatri, are you there? It's me, Tara."

"I'm here." I reply faintly. "I was afraid to talk until I was certain it was you."

"My mum just called telling me you had run away and was extremely upset. I didn't let on I already knew, for I would have had a lot of explaining to do. She said the ashram has gone crazy, and Amma is visibly devastated. It seems they've sent out search parties to all the hotels in the region and the airport thinking you're flying off to your sister in Germany. They're actually having a devotee over there call her as we speak. They have people combing the hills in San Ramon, and they've even made surprise visits as far away as Santa Cruz to some old-time devotees you were close with."

This news shatters my nerves. I have to sit down before I collapse. It hasn't been even twenty-four hours since I ran away.

Tara goes on to say, "Balu intends to stay in California until you are found. Everyone else, though, is going back to India on Tuesday as planned."

Part of me is tickled to know that I am just ten minutes from the San Ramon ashram, yet they are searching as far away as Germany. I am being kept up to date via Tara who is in Paris, and she is receiving the inside scoop as it unfolds from her mother who is a member of the San Ramon ashram.

Before I ran away, I didn't know how I was going to react. Once I entered my hiding place, would I break down and start screaming hysterically? Would I roll around the floor in agony?

But here I am, relatively calm.

Numb is probably a better word.

I have known Tara for many years. Two months ago when we were on tour in Paris with Amma and her whole entourage, I decided to share a little of my grief with her. I felt comfortable doing so for a couple of reasons. Firstly, because in her youth her parents had been followers of another guru but had left that ashram disillusioned. So she was no stranger to scandal. Secondly, even though her parents were ardent devotees of Amma, she wasn't.

Sitting in the dark outside the program hall far away from anybody else's ears, I shared with Tara a few of the secrets I carried. As I uttered the words, abusive, manipulative, secretive, and sex to her a chilly gust of wind rushed by. Tara, who was dressed in her corporate attire having arrived straight from work, gazed intently at me. I was frozen in terror at having shared such information for the first time. I stared at Tara awaiting her reaction. She gently brushed aside the fine brunette strands of hair that were resting on her cheeks.

She looked at me. "Gayatri," she said. "You have to leave. You have to get away."

I gasped and fell into shock. This was the first time I had heard such words out loud and not just from within my own mind. This was the first time someone had actually affirmed my greatest fear—maybe I should leave. Maybe I will actually leave. And this left me staring at the ultimate dreaded question.

How can I?

Here I am though, just two months later, successfully out of the ashram with Tara on the other end of the phone. Our next assignment is to call my dad in Australia. I don't want him to worry or panic in case he gets a phone call from the ashram fishing for information and saying that his daughter is missing.

"Dad, it's me. Gail." Actually I don't know if I refer to myself as Gail now. I just hope he will figure out it is me from the thick Indian accent I have acquired over the years.

"Dad, I have to tell you something. I have left. I ran away from the ashram."

"Jesus, really? I thought you were going to be with them for the rest of your life."

"No kidding. So did I, Dad. But things changed."

"Oh well, I'm glad. Actually, I'm really happy and relieved. Are you okay? Do you need anything? Can I send you some money?"

"No. I don't know what I'm doing yet. I'm safe though. I have a couple of friends helping me. I'm just going to hide out for a few days until they've all gone back to India, then I will probably fly over to Hawaii. Dad, my friend is on the other line and using her company's phone, so I'd better not talk long. I just wanted you to hear the news from me. I love you and will talk again soon."

"Bye, Gail. Take care. I love you, too," says my dad as he hangs up.

Tara's voice says, "Gayatri, I should get back to work. I'll call you tomorrow to see how you're doing and give you an update."

"Okay, bye," I reply in a frail voice.

Holy Hell

In a daze, I go and sit on the living room couch, then lie down and eventually curl into a ball not knowing what else to do. I am consumed with so much fear that I have all the blinds closed. I am afraid to peek outside.

The night before this, when I arrived at the house, I kept clutching a dark blanket around me so as not to reveal even one speck of my orange robes. Unrealistically I feared that one of the neighbors might see me and report my whereabouts to the ashram. My entire world revolved around Amma and the ashram, so I stupidly assumed everyone knew me. I was terrified that Amma would have me dragged back against my will and that I would be severely punished. I was particularly fearful because of all the secrets and inside information I carried. I knew I was an absolute threat to the continuation of her holy charade.

Now I open my eyes and look across the room.

My stomach churns when I see my laptop computer sitting on the kitchen counter, one of the few possessions I smuggled out ahead of time. There will be tons of email from people reaching out, begging me to return. To read them will create more pain than I can bear. I also fear that the ashram will somehow be able to track my whereabouts if I log on.

The house where I am hiding has been arranged by Maya, a friend who helped me escape. It belongs to an Indian man, an old colleague of hers who is away in New Delhi. So I am all by myself. Even though he is far away in India, India is definitely in his home. His place is filled with the aroma of the many spices I have come to know so well over the years, the spices that permeate one's being and linger with a haunting presence—chili, turmeric, cumin, coriander, mustard seeds, even stinky old asafetida. Gazing down from the wall are the familiar faces of Ganesh and Durga, Hindu deities I too have grown fond of. His home is made up of the typical mixture of Western comfort and Indian tradition. My mind is simultaneously immersed in thoughts of faraway India and the chaos I have created at the ashram nearby.

Out of nowhere the central heating kicks on with a thump. I almost jump out of my skin.

I feel hunted.

A short while later I hear a key in the front door. Is this some relief, some company, or perhaps some news? I sit up in anticipation like a refugee hoping for a chunk of dry bread and water.

It is Maya popping in briefly on her lunch break. She looks tired and slightly frazzled. Most likely from not sleeping the night before and the stress of harboring an ashram fugitive.

"I've brought you some food. How are you?" she asks not waiting for an answer. "You were right," she says tearing open a package of frozen food and throwing it in the microwave.

I sit numbly on the couch, watching her run around.

"Guess what happened this morning. My house was searched. A couple of devotees made an unannounced visit thinking you might be there."

Shaking my head in nervous disbelief, I speak for the first time. "I knew they would be desperate to find me, and that you would be on their extensive suspect list. That's why I asked you to return immediately to the program last night and make yourself seen. I was hoping it would protect your involvement and keep me safe from them."

"I hear it's a terrible scene back at the ashram," says Maya as she plops down on the couch next to me. "The swamis are a mess, and Amma is apparently crying hysterically outside her room."

I am thinking to myself—Well yes, I'm sure she is devastated. But I bet it's a different picture when she's not in public. I have witnessed her wrath and heard what she has to say about people who leave the ashram. I have seen her shift with the snap of a finger and turn her anger into tears of sorrow whenever a newcomer enters her room.

Maya opens the microwave, puts the food on a plate, and hands it to me. "I'll pop in again briefly after work, okay? Now don't you worry. Everything will be all right. Nobody suspects a thing. Got to go."

She closes the front door behind her, leaving me once again with my thoughts, and my fears.

I start imagining how Robyn, my sister, is feeling about getting a phone call out of the blue asking if I am there with her. She, of course, knows nothing of my whereabouts or even that I have left. But I'm sure she will be delighted and will probably thank them for the good news.

I smile and chuckle. Robyn was never a fan of Amma.

Robyn visited me in India in 1983 during the very early days of the ashram. At that time, another Australian woman named Saumya, who had recently joined the ashram, was planning a short trip back to Sydney to settle some affairs. Robyn just so happened to be living in Sydney at the time, so I gave her address to Saumya thinking they could meet up. As it turned out, they flew to India together. During the flight, Saumya was describing to Robyn about life in the ashram. She proceeded to share stories of how Amma would hit and kick me, then throw me out of her room for several days at a time. I was shocked when Robyn told me this, and I couldn't understand why Saumya would be sharing such information. At the time I was protective of Amma, and I accepted such treatment as part of my training as her nearest and dearest disciple. Was Saumya hoping Robyn would try to convince me to leave? Or was she so wrapped up in her envy of my close relationship with Amma that she didn't realize the impact of what she was saying?

My sister swore that if she ever saw Amma lay even one finger on me, she would kick her in the butt and say what she actually thought of her.

I whispered, "Don't let anyone hear you talking like that."

In those days, early in my long years of experience with Amma, I considered myself to be very happy. I felt that the ashram was my new and true family.

Robyn stayed only a few days and couldn't get away fast enough. Since that visit, I assumed she has always worried for my sanity and safety, certain that I had joined a cult.

The most recent visit with my sister happened just one month ago, toward the end of Amma's European tour. Robyn had taken the overnight train from where she lived in northern Germany and come to Munich to spend a day with me. Our host drove me to the station to greet her, and we waited on the platform a few minutes for the train to arrive. I remember experiencing a mixture of excitement and nervousness. Even though Robyn was my sister, she was also somewhat of a stranger. I had seen her only twice in the twenty-plus years that had passed since I left Australia for India.

Suddenly there she was, my little sister, strutting down the platform in her blue jeans and jacket. I noted her self-confidence, how comfortable she seemed with herself. We both had the recognizable Tredwell family face, but we were such different people. She came running up to give me a huge hug. As she came closer, I had to stare. Bouncing up and down with each stride was something I'd never seen on her before—a big pair of boobs.

"Robyn, where the hell did you get those from?" I asked pointing at her breasts.

Without batting an eye she replied, "Oh, I woke up one fine morning, and there they were. It was as if they grew overnight." Staring at the same region on my body she continued, "Didn't you know it's part of being a Tredwell, and something that happens when you turn thirty?"

"No, I had no clue."

To be honest, I rarely thought about family, for my only world was Amma and the ashram. Family seemed so far away and from a different lifetime.

I hooked my arm around hers, and we headed back to the house. As always, I kept most of my emotion under wraps. It was against ashram policy to be attached to family.

In the afternoon, we went out for a stroll, to have some alone time and the freedom to talk privately. We headed out, my sister in her blue jeans and me in my bright orange sari. I always managed to turn heads whenever I went out in public. In India, it was because of my white skin. In the West, it was because I wore a sari. So I was more or less used to attracting negative attention. I wasn't quite sure how Robyn felt, but she didn't show any discomfort, if there was any.

"So, how's life? Are you still happy living in the ashram?" she asked with a smug look on her face.

"Yes, I'm all right," I lied.

Robyn looked at me with one eyebrow raised and said, "Well, you look like shit if you want my opinion."

Breaking down, I confessed. "Well, actually I'm not all right. I'm not at all happy. I don't know how much longer I can go on like this. At the same time, I don't know how I can leave."

"People do leave unhappy marriages, you know. They have to start life over and find themselves again. So what? It's nothing you aren't capable of doing. You would be just fine. Of course, you aren't married, but you get my drift."

"Oh, Robyn, it's not that simple. I have poured my entire heart and soul into this organization for twenty years. It's much stronger and more complex than any marriage. I just don't know—how can I leave? It would create so much devastation."

With a stern look on her face, Robyn cut me off. "Just ask yourself this, are you happy? Can you not think of yourself for once? They'll survive. Life will go on without you. But will you survive? Remember the saying—nobody is indispensable."

"But I don't know what I would do. Where would I go? How would I survive? I don't have any money, or a career. I feel ill at the thought of staying, but even more so about leaving."

I had to sit down. The mere discussion of this topic was exhausting. We found a sidewalk café and chose a lovely table in the corner set against a trellis of miniature roses. Robyn took a deep breath, let out a sigh, and placed her hand on mine. "You know, I have never liked Amma and this whole guru thing. What do you get out of this life?"

Searching for a suitable answer, for myself as much as for Robyn, I said, "But there is such a spiritual atmosphere. How can I isolate myself from that?"

"Bullshit. That's pure projection," she scoffed. "People feel what they hope and desire to feel. Spirituality is everywhere. You don't have to suffer and sacrifice your entire life away like this. Look at you, you're miserable and lost. What's so spiritual about your state?"

"Robyn, I hear what you're saying, and I know you are coming from a place of love and concern. I just don't think I'm ready. Can we change the subject? I don't have the strength to talk or even think about this anymore."

We never discussed the topic again. The rest of our visit was spent enjoying our time together and talking about her life. The next morning we parted ways. She returned to Bremen, and I continued with the tour, but now with even more confusion and doubt about my life in the ashram. Her words of advice and encouragement, although hard to accept, became like drops of water on the seeds of change that were already sprouting inside me after talking to Tara.

Now I smile as I imagine how proud she must feel to know that I have run away.

My first day as a free woman outside the ashram is almost over. I get up from the couch and go to my bedroom where I curl up once more in my ball-like position, but this time with the added solace of a warm and cozy bed. I feel relieved to know that Amma and her entourage will be heading back to India in the morning. I can't wait to hear that they are on their way. I feel certain that those few thousand miles between us will alleviate some of the pressure I am feeling.

I strongly object to the fact that Balu, Amma's head swami, is staying back with the intention of finding me. No way in hell is this going to happen. I am escaping from him, too.

I feel I should get a message to Amma and the ashram and tell them they should quit searching for me. But there is nothing I can do at this hour. I have to sit tight and trust that I will find out more in the morning from Tara, my Paris correspondent.

My dry and burning eyes are pleading with me to go to sleep. My body is starting to surrender to the pleasing comfort of the soft mattress and the sweet-smelling blanket snuggled against my skin. I can't fight any longer, nor do I feel a need to. I decide to say goodnight to the first day of my new life. After twenty years of sleep deprivation, I go out like a light.

Holy Hell

The following morning greets me with a slight sense of relief and calm. I can't say what the weather outside is doing. My only world is the one I am living inside the house. I can hear the occasional car drive by, and I wonder who is inside the car and what kind of life that person leads. Is he married and off to work? Is it a mother driving her children to school? Are these people happy, depressed, or somewhere in between? What is life like on the "outside?" I am free now to create my own world and find out for myself. That thought is equally exciting and nerve-wracking. Thankfully, the phone starts to ring. I pray that this is Tara, pray she is bringing me the good news that *everyone* has headed to the airport. I wait with the impatience of a child eager for a candy bar, and it feels like an eternity before the phone completes its set of rings. First set of rings… silence. Second set of rings… silence. When the phone starts ringing again, I quickly pick up.

"Gayatri, I have some good news and some bad news. They're all leaving for the airport in a couple of hours, but Balu is still planning on staying back. My mum said she wasn't sure but thinks he will probably leave on Thursday, so it would be just two more days."

Hearing this news is good. But it also stirs thoughts of the devastation that is going to occur in India once Amma returns without me. I know the Indian girls will take it really hard, for I am like a big sister to them, and this breaks my heart. There are nearly two hundred girls there now, and I love and care for them so much.

"Tara, I need to get a message to the ashram before they leave for the airport. I'm hoping it will put their minds at ease so they'll stop trying to track me down." I am also hoping it will encourage them *all* to head home.

In a perplexed voice, she replies, "But nobody knows I'm in communication with you. It's probably best that I stay undercover for now."

"Yeah, you're right. I'll have my sister do it. Tara, can you call Robyn so I can dictate a message to her? Then she can call the San Ramon ashram and pass it on."

"Great idea. I will try and get her on the line and call back in half an hour or so."

Here is the text of the message that I conveyed to Amma and her inner circle through my sister:

November 23, 1999

    I want everybody to know that I am safe and that my head is on my shoulders, but my decision is firm. It took me several years to reach this decision, but it is one hundred percent sure. It is the most painful and scary thing I have done. I am not leaving for worldly life, but to pursue my spiritual life in a more peaceful and loving environment.

    I am sorry to have caused so much pain to people, but I had to come to terms with reality and truth.

    I harbor no bitterness or revenge, only pain.

    I am praying to God for forgiveness for any pain and sorrow I have caused to the ashram.

    I want to pause here and turn the clock back twenty-one years. I wish to take you back to an era of innocence, hopes, and dreams, to a time when I was an impressionable, fun-loving, free-spirited young woman at the tender age of nineteen. This also happens to be the time when I first fell in love—with God.

TWO

ALL ABOARD

"Hurry up," yelled Franco as Sylvie and I scrambled along the train platform. By no means was this an easy task, for there were hundreds of people bumping into one another and running every which way. Travelers say chaos is one of the charming characteristics of India. But I suspect that this is something they tell themselves in order to survive. Early on I learned not to resist, just to go with the flow, otherwise your life will become pure hell. India is not a country with which you can ever have a mediocre relationship. You must love it or run for your life.

Eventually we found our carriage and allowed the pressure of the crowd to line us up in front of a door. Pushing and shoving is an accepted way of life in India. A queue is a rare phenomenon. The population has developed this manner of conduct into quite a fine art. Nobody pushes with their hands. They use their whole bodies, and this makes the contact somehow less personal, and honestly nobody thinks about it twice.

I watched my friends disappear into the train, and for a split second I panicked. Then miraculously I found myself standing before a door. Without delay I grabbed onto the clammy railing, and with one gigantic heave, propelled myself forward, yanking my bag free from the bodies it was wedged between down below. As I made my way through the carriage, I chose to ignore the unabashed stares and eventually found the right compartment. It was a second-class sleeper and would be our home for the next three days. In the late seventies second-class meant no air conditioning, no seat padding, and no door to your individual compartment. The right side of the carriage was lined vertically with additional benches. This arrangement guaranteed a complete lack of privacy for the occupants and a constant stream of people shuffling up and down the narrow corridor to the bathrooms.

I flung my bag onto the corner of the top bunk where it would be safe from roaming hands. Excited, I sat down by the window to watch the flurry of activity transpiring outside. Women carried baskets of food in one hand, dragged a child along with the other, and somehow rested an infant securely on one of their maternal hips. Men loaded with suitcases and rolls of bedding hurried by. The more affluent folk carried nothing. Trailing closely at their heels with the most graceful gait, porters dressed in bright red jackets balanced stacks of luggage ever so elegantly on their heads. Most women were gaily clad in vibrant colors, and every facet of the rainbow was whizzing before my eyes.

Children selling peanuts, roasted chickpeas, and other oddities hurried through the train making frantic, final pleas, trying to convince everyone to buy from *them*. The whistle blew, and I could see the uniformed station agent wave his green flag, so I knew our departure was imminent. The commotion on the platform began to ease. People became stationary with their gaze glued to the train windows. The hubbub inside amplified. Family members who had extended their goodbyes a little too long struggled through the obstacle course of bodies and luggage to reach the exit before it was too late. With a long, final blow of the whistle, the train began its forward motion. Like fleas jumping off a large beast, the little entrepreneurs loaded with their baskets of wares leaped off at the last second. I watched in awe how each one of them managed to land upright despite the building momentum of the train. We were leaving the north of India and Kashmir with its beautiful

Holy Hell

lakes and the breathtaking Himalayas for southern India, with Madras as our final destination.

Without saying a word, the three of us grinned at each other and started to chuckle—our way of saying, "Thank God, that's all over."

I had met Sylvie and Franco two months earlier while having dinner at a café in Srinagar, the main town of Kashmir. From our first meeting we became good friends and travel companions. Sylvie was German, with a pleasingly plumpish baby face, peaches-and-cream complexion, and hair that looked as though she'd been shocked with a thousand volts of electricity. She had recently been experimenting, trying to create Rastafarian dreadlocks, but had failed miserably. Franco was Italian from Genoa, a strikingly good-looking young man, the personification of tall, dark, and handsome.

When I met them, I was living on one of the many houseboats on Dal Lake, in the center of town. Because I was recovering from a bout of hepatitis, I had been alone in bed for a couple of weeks with nobody to look after me. Many nights I sadly gazed out the window across the water to other boats from which I could hear laughter, music, and people enjoying each other's company. Thousands of miles from home and clueless as to where the boyfriend I had ditched a month earlier had gone, I was feeling lost, vulnerable, and terribly alone in the world. Physically ill and mentally depressed, I had cried out many a time, "I want my mommy." These outbursts shocked me because when I'd left home two years previous—at age seventeen—my relationship with her was somewhat strained.

Despite the lack of privacy, the inability to bathe, and the stench of the bathrooms, I loved riding the trains in India. Dusk, my favorite time of day, was approaching, so I got up and stumbled down the corridor to the open doorway of the carriage. With a steadfast grip on the railing, I embraced the wind in my face as the scenery rushed before my eyes. India is such a vast and spacious country once you are out of the cities. Apart from the occasional village, it is just miles and miles of uninhabited land. All this open terrain seemed a shame in light of the overpopulation and deprived conditions I had witnessed in the cities. With heartfelt emotion, I thought to myself, *Oh India, you are such a land of extremes, but I think I'm falling in love with you.*

My feet had first touched Indian soil in Calcutta on March 21, 1978, after my boyfriend and I had traveled for six weeks through Southeast Asia. I was excited about visiting India, but at the same time nervous. Fellow tourists shared many a tale of the extreme poverty, beggars, lepers, disease, and theft they had witnessed. With great fervor, they told horror stories of their bags being sliced open by thieves when they walked down the street and of hooks coming over the door to steal their belongings when they went to the bathroom. I really didn't know what to expect, but felt I needed to experience this country for myself. Despite all the grave and negative warnings, the minute I arrived in India, I felt very much at home. I was captivated by the simple lifestyle, richness of color, density of delightful aromas wafting through the air, and the down-to-earth joy of the people, despite their poverty.

From childhood I always had an interest in the occult. I was fascinated by Ouija boards, ESP, and fortune-telling. So the country's undercurrent of the supernatural and its inexplicable mystical allure also had me intrigued.

My boyfriend wasn't interested in spending more than a few days in any one place, nor in getting to know the local people. All we did was visit tourist sites, stay at tourist bungalows, and socialize with other tourists. Our original plan, the Aussie thing to do in those days, was to spend a few weeks traveling through Southeast Asia and cut across the Middle East to Europe, with England as our final destination.

Our opposing ideas of what "traveling abroad" meant began to put a strain on the relationship. By the time we arrived in India, we were no longer a couple, barely friends, and determined to part ways once we reached our next stop, Nepal.

However, something strange overcame me once I landed in India. Overnight I felt possessed with such inner strength and confidence that I told him to beat it. Even though I was only nineteen and all alone in a strange country, I felt safe and self-assured. At the time I didn't realize that this was only a fleeting moment of bravery.

Holy Hell

It was getting dark, and my thoughts returned to the moment. Before heading back to the compartment, I took one long, last look toward the landscape that was rapidly disappearing into the golden sunset. I grinned and thought of how happy I was. Suddenly a speck of coal landed in my eye, snapping me out of my infatuation. We were on a steam train, and I realized we would be covered with soot by the time we got to Madras. I giggled and wondered if I would still be able to see my freckles by then.

When I arrived back at the compartment, I discovered that Sylvie had bought dinner for us all, a simple meal of two chapattis (unleavened flatbread) with some curried potato and peas. I had already been more or less a vegetarian ever since leaving home at age seventeen, but now I was quite strict as to what I consumed. Eating *anything* in India felt scary enough without adding meat to the equation. After dinner, we decided to try to get some sleep, as there wasn't much else to do. Franco took the bottom bunk, for he was less likely to get groped during the night. Sylvie and I each took one of the top bunks. I spread my thin travel mattress over the three-foot-wide wooden bench, arranged the clothes inside my backpack to form a makeshift pillow, made sure my passport and money were safe, and lay down. I had a bird's-eye view down the aisle and could see that most people were settling down for the night. Even though I didn't know the language, I could tell that many passengers were amused to have us on board. *What is it that makes us such a spectacle?* I wondered. *Is it the way we dress? The color of our hair and eyes? Perhaps it's our mannerisms, language, or the awkward way we ate the food with our hands?* But the gawking and idle conversation were harmless. The staring was so transparent that one couldn't really be offended by it.

"Sweet dreams," I said, giving my pillow a final thump.

"Same to you," my friends replied in a tangle of Italian and German accents.

I lay there for a while, silently observing the behavior of the families below. They had such a down-to-earth and practical way of caring for one another. The roles were distinct—women were the caregivers, men the protectors. The rocking of the train had a soothing effect, and I soon found myself struggling to keep my eyes open. Ensuring once more that my valuables were safe, I allowed myself to drift off to another world.

Several hours later my eyes opened. Much to my amazement, I realized that I had had a good night's sleep. Despite the hard and narrow bed I lay on, I felt refreshed. Grabbing my toothbrush, toothpaste, mug, and thin cotton towel, I crawled down and made my way to the bathroom to freshen up as best I could. Thankfully, there weren't any mirrors. I didn't need one to see how dreadful I looked and to guess how much worse I was going to look by day three. I laughed at the sign on the wall written in both English and Hindi. "Please do not use the latrine while stopped at stations." No need for a sign when you can see the train tracks through the hole.

When I returned, Franco was sitting up but not quite awake. Sylvie was sound asleep. In between stretching and yawning, Franco said, "See outside, how different it looks. We're probably right in the middle of India."

"It looks like we are in a desert," I replied.

Sylvie stirred and sat up only to bump her head on the ceiling of the train. "Sheiser!" was her first word for the day.

Throughout the day, at each and every station, vendors jumped onboard and rushed through the carriage selling snacks, tea, and coffee. You could hear them crying, "Chai, chai, coppee, coppee." Later in the day, an old man with a small bag carefully tucked under his arm began making his way through the carriage. I couldn't quite tell what service he offered until I witnessed him sit down next to someone, pull out a long piece of metal, and start cleaning the person's ears.

Sylvie excitedly shrieked, "I've heard about these fellows. They supposedly clean out so much wax it's almost unbelievable."

My adventurous spirit kicked in and I announced, "I'm going to give it a go. Why not?" Without hesitation, I signaled him over.

His eyes lit up like a flickering neon light, and I could almost see the rupee signs in them. Unable to contain his excitement, he exclaimed, "Madam, twenty rupees."

Holy Hell

I was accustomed by then to marketplace haggling and to the inflated prices people always wanted to charge the Westerners. So I firmly objected, "No, ten rupees."

Back and forth we went until we mutually agreed upon fifteen, which was still probably too high, but what the hell. He asked me to sit cross-legged facing him. Grabbing me by the ear, he turned my head to the side and began cleaning. He kept showing me these huge clumps of wax, and if I wasn't seeing them with my own eyes, I would never have believed such a story. Suddenly I felt something wiggling at my crotch. *Oh no, what's going on?* I couldn't turn my head, for I had a piece of metal in my ear. But I could faintly see through the corner of my eye that it was his big toe. *This can't be intentional. The old fellow mustn't realize where his toe is. It must be a nervous twitch.* I will never know for sure, but I have a sneaky suspicion he knew darn well what he was doing.

Eventually the novelty of the train ride wore off. It had been three long days and nights. We were bored, tired, dirty, and coated with tiny flecks of coal in our hair and all over our sticky skin.

The final morning greeted us more favorably. We were in Tamil Nadu, just two hours from our destination. The scenery once again was green with acres upon acres of flourishing paddy fields. Bullocks harnessed with yokes were plowing the earth as water gushed ferociously from bore wells. It was amazing to see the difference, not only in the countryside, but in the people too. I noticed the darker-colored skin, different attire, and women and children wearing flowers in their hair. The air was sweet and slightly humid. I liked what I was seeing and couldn't wait to explore another region of this wonderful country.

Delighted to have our feet on solid ground, we staggered out of the station onto the main street. Instantly, we were swarmed by a group of men wearing khaki shirts and shorts, the uniform of an auto rickshaw driver. Without a doubt, we were the preferred clients. They zeroed in on us like a bunch of pesky mosquitoes. We weren't feeling picky, nor did there seem to be a first in line, so we maneuvered our way through the crowd and hopped into the nearest vehicle. Immediately the bright yellow and black little three-wheeler began whizzing precariously through the tangled streets of downtown Madras.

The three of us were squished together on the one little seat with luggage crammed under our feet and piled high on our laps. We were hanging on for dear life, yet laughing and giggling at the same time. We wove around buses, cars, trucks, pedestrians, bicycles, bullock carts, cycle rickshaws, and cows. But what really caught my attention and had me gasp in horror was the sight of men on scooters with their wives riding side-saddle behind them, their saris flapping in the wind, holding on with just one hand because the other was clutching a child in their laps. The cows had me intrigued as well. Without a care in the world, they walked across the street and stopped right in the middle whenever they liked, almost as though they knew they were sacred.

Upon arrival at our hotel room, I flopped down onto one of the beds, where I landed with a thud. I was so tired, I'd forgot that these rooms never came with a spring mattress, just a thick cotton pad on top of a wooden board. My gaze started to wander around the room. *What is it with this country? Why is every hotel room painted the same ghastly bright blue? And why does every one have a ceiling fan that squeaks?* I got up from the bed and with my wobbly train legs went to open the windows. I unhooked the wooden shutters and pushed them open through the metal grids—a fixture you're guaranteed to find on every window in India. I thought it would be nice to let in some air, but fresh it was not. The dense humidity intertwined with the stench of exhaust fumes was like a punch in the face.

Lying back down on the bed, I got caught up in a daydream. I noted feelings of excitement and happiness, but also an unsettling aloneness. Something was missing but I couldn't quite put my finger on it. From a very young age I had felt I was different. I was sensitive and mildly intuitive. I tried my best to fit in but often felt out of place and awkward. I never wanted to lead a life that society considered normal. I wasn't interested in spending years at school earning degrees, getting married, having children, and living the happily-ever-after dream. Nor did I envy my girlfriends who still lived at home with their parents, worked at the same job they didn't

Holy Hell

like, and continued seeing the same boyfriend who they knew was far from perfect for them. I wasn't going to let fear of change hold *me* back.

There had to be more to life than this, surely.

I was in pursuit of happiness and some meaning to life. But I had no clue what any of my yearnings meant, and I most certainly didn't label myself as spiritual. Somehow I believed that the answer to my quest lay overseas because Australia and my childhood had disappointed me so far.

Ours was not a tightly knit family. The sweet and sentimental sign that reads "Home Is Where The Heart Is" was nowhere in sight at our place.

My parents didn't seem to have the most loving relationship either, which I'm sure contributed to the tension we kids felt at home. I don't recall my folks ever seeming happy together, and there was never any display of affection. I trust that there had been affection at some stage. Otherwise, they wouldn't have married, nor would the four of us children have come into existence.

My mother was a wonderful homemaker. She took great care of us and performed all the "duties" expected of women in those days—all the cleaning, laundry, ironing, cooking, sewing of our clothes, and knitting of our sweaters. Unfortunately, the one major aspect of mothering she was unable to express was love. I don't have one memory of ever being given a hug, and I certainly had never heard the phrase, "I love you." Without a doubt the cause for her inability to convey such basic human emotion was her own upbringing. Her mother had been born out of wedlock, which in those days was considered quite shameful. So my grandmother came into the world unwanted, branded as damaged goods, and treated as such. In turn, she raised my mother with the same bitter feelings, for that was all she knew. History then repeated itself with me, I suppose.

We were your average working class Australian family, living in the suburbs of Brisbane, eating a staple diet of steak, potatoes, and boiled-to-death vegetables. When asked what my religion was, I replied, "Christian of course." I assumed everyone with my skin tone was Christian. I thought that God was this really old man with a really long beard who sat on a really big throne high up in the sky. I attended Sunday School at the nearby Methodist

Church. I thought Jesus was cool and loved singing, "Jesus loves the little children, all the children of the world. Red and yellow, black and white, all are precious in his sight, Jesus loves the little children of the world."

Once the Bible story segment was over we got to play games, so I didn't mind. However, once I graduated and was expected to go to church, I refused. That was not fun. It was downright butt-numbingly boring.

One morning my Dad came into my room.

"Get out of bed, get dressed, and go to church," he ordered.

"You and Mum never go, so why should I have to?" I protested from underneath my bedding.

My father exited my room in silence. What could he say to that? I never went to church again. Instead, I filled my Sunday mornings with activities way more fun—roaming the neighborhood with my girlfriends, going to the local swimming pool, or experimenting with growing up as we hid behind the mulberry bush at the local park, puffing on a cigarette with our heads spinning as we coughed and giggled.

"Hey, Gail, the bathroom is free," Sylvie called out, releasing me from my thoughts.

Upon entering the bathroom, I noticed the usual stinky mothballs—India's version of sanitizing air fresheners—sitting in the drain hole. Showering wasn't an option. So, I settled for a bucket bath and re-surfaced soon after, a clean and fresh young woman ready to hit the town.

The first thing we wanted to do was find a nice restaurant. As we walked down the street, my senses were on fire. We were in T. Nagar, a part of Madras filled with jewelers, fabric stores, spices, and handicrafts. On every street stood vendors whose baskets overflowed with bundles of freshly strung jasmine flowers. The fragrance was intoxicating. Sylvie and I drifted like hypnotized bees toward these wondrous scents. A woman at one flower stand tied our teenage locks into ponytails, then looped the delightful jasmine strands through our hair. Such a simple gesture, but her actions were as fragrant as the flowers themselves. I began to notice that women of every age adorned themselves with these luscious blossoms. The flowers found their place on the soft, innocent, and hopeful heads of toddlers, likewise on the coarse, gray, and wise heads of crinkled old women. I was impressed that the culture placed no age limit on such a custom. Every woman had the right to adorn herself.

We walked past restaurants until we found one that read "Vegetarian Cuisine." The place looked clean, and the alluring aromas permitted no second thought. As soon as we sat down, a barefoot young boy—who if I weren't mistaken hadn't bathed for a couple of days—rushed over and wiped our table with a dirty rag. He flung the rag over his shoulder then with the same hand plunked a few steel tumblers down and poured water from a beat-up jug. Shortly after, a tall, dark, and not-so-handsome man with a protruding belly came to our table. He was clad in a white dhoti (India's version of sarong) and grubby white T-shirt. His skin glistened with sticky sweat.

"Namaskaram. What can I get for you?" he asked in proper Indian English.

I didn't need a menu. I already knew what I wanted. We placed our orders, and within five minutes we had our meal of choice staring back at us. In front of me sat a large, crispy, thin rice pancake called nai roast, alongside coconut chutney and sambar, a soupy split-pea and vegetable dish. For a minute or two, absolute silence descended upon our table as our voracious taste buds burst with delight. I was savoring every bite when unexpectedly something exploded in my mouth. Suddenly I felt giddy. My heart began to race, and water began flowing from my eyes and nose like a dam overflowing in monsoon season.

"Are you all right?" Sylvie enquired.

"Oh... no... I think I just ate a chili," I squealed in distress.

Throwing caution to the wind, I reached for the tumbler of water—the one that normally went untouched. I was desperate to extinguish the fire that was raging inside my mouth. I didn't know whether to laugh or cry, so decided to do both. After a few gulps of water, a couple of deep breaths, and many long sighs, I slowly regained normal consciousness.

"What would you ladies like to do for the rest of the day?" asked Franco.
"I know where I want to go," I said with a residual sniff.
"Let me guess. Hmm, could it be the beach?" Sylvie replied with a grin, nodding her head at the same time.

We devoured the rest of our food and, after studying our little guidebook, headed on our way. As we were waiting for the bus, I noticed an old man with an assortment of secondhand books spread out on the pavement. Although I wasn't much of a reader, something tickled my curiosity to take a look. One book in particular stood out, maybe because it had no cover, maybe not: *Tales of a Pilgrim Soul* by Suddhananda Bharati. I flipped through the pages, was intrigued, and so paid the two rupees. With one eye glued to the bus stop, I scanned the other books but saw they were either corny romance novels or textbooks. I dashed back to the bus stop, and just as I was showing them my latest acquisition, the bus arrived. I tucked the book inside my bag and boarded.

"Crowded" nowhere near described the state inside. There was barely standing room, and the conductor was screaming something at us that we understood to mean, "Move in farther!" Before I knew it, there I was, wedged between a bunch of Indian men. The female folk were all at the far end of the bus. Reassuring myself that this would be only a short ride, I grabbed the sticky railing on the ceiling and held tightly onto my shoulder bag in fear of getting pickpocketed. After a few minutes I felt something. *Oh no. This can't be happening again. I'm not going to play sucker this time.* Letting go of my bag, I furiously grabbed hold of the mysterious wandering hand, dug my nails in as hard as I could, and then twisted with all my might. Eventually I heard a tiny squeal that betrayed the identity of the hand's owner. I cast him a look of scorn, imagining that I were one of those Hindu goddesses endowed with the power of wrath and turned him into a pile of ashes on the spot. I managed to instill some fear, I guess, because he jumped off at the next stop. The rest of the ride was uncomfortable but uneventful.

We got off the bus, walked a block, and suddenly we were standing before the beautiful, big blue ocean at Marina Beach. Something inside me lit up, and Franco noticed.

"Wow, you look so happy. You look different. Your eyes, they're really bright and blue."

I loved the ocean, always had, so I guess it was showing. We strolled along the shore, and I smiled with delight as the occasional wave wrapped itself around my ankles. After a while, we sat in the sand and silently absorbed the scenery and salty air.

When we weren't out exploring the town, I was immersed in my new book. This was the first spiritual book I'd ever read, and it contained basic and practical information on how to lead a devout life. It discussed the importance of yoga, meditation, conscious living, and doing well to others. It also explained the principals of karma (how we reap the fruits of our actions) and reincarnation. Although I was reading these topics for the first time, everything seemed to make perfect sense, as if I were merely refreshing my memory. The more I read, the more curious I became, especially when it mentioned that one can attain a state of perfection and pure bliss while living in the world. This all sounded so cool. I was eager to learn how to meditate and do yoga.

The next place we chose to visit was the magnificent temple town of Kanchipuram. By then, I was starting to feel a little weak. I had no appetite. This had me worried, for I knew too well the symptoms of hepatitis.

Shortly thereafter, I found myself in an Ayurvedic clinic diagnosed with a mild relapse of the illness. I was ushered into a back room where they administered a wonderful enema and asked me to drink a tumblerful of the most bitter, disgusting, vile, horrendous gunk I had ever tasted in my life. They promised to cure me if I came back for three more doses. I really had to think about that one. Alone, I went back to our hotel to rest and to disappear into a woeful state of self-pity. I was saddened by this turn of events, and I worried if it meant I should return to Australia. I was not at all ready for that, not when the main intention behind my travel was to find happiness. Certainly, I had yet to discover the magic formula for happiness. Once again I was feeling depressed, overcome with worry, and desperately unwilling to return to Australia, to the unfulfilled life I had left behind.

A while later I was awakened by the creaking of the door and realized I must have dozed off.

"Hey, Gail, how are you feeling?"

Sitting up, all I could do was let out a pathetic moan.

"Come on, cheer up. It's only a relapse. Just go back and drink the medicine, and you'll be fine," Franco reassured as he stroked my head.

"That's easy for you to say. I don't know which is worse." Yet I knew I had no choice but to brave the vile concoction three more times.

Sylvie grabbed me by both hands, dragged me off the bed, and sweetly said, "Come on, stop sulking. It will be dark soon, and we really should visit the temple."

I got up, rinsed my face with the tepid pipe water, combed my hair, and headed to the temple with my buddies.

We stepped through the elaborately carved, towering temple entrance as the sun was bidding farewell to the day. This was perfect timing, for the evening ceremony had just begun. Immediately I was enraptured with the ambience and drama. Members of the temple were feverishly bashing on drums and large cymbals while an Indian clarinet player kept in tune. Incense and frankincense teamed together for tug-of-war with the fragrance from oodles of jasmine flowers. Before me stood the statue of a giant elephant, Ganesh, the hindu god and remover of obstacles. The statue was covered entirely with silver plating. If it hadn't been made of stone, it would have buckled from the weight of the adornment of jewels and flowers around its neck. Before this deity, a priest waved a brass lamp containing the glowing, golden flames of burning camphor, and he chanted in perfect synchronicity with the arc of the lamp. I stood there dazed by the stimulation of my senses.

Suddenly my attention was drawn to the people around me and to the intensity and passion of their focus. Men, women, and children of all ages and castes were pouring their hearts out with undivided fervor and devotion before the deity. It was at that moment my jaw dropped. And on its downward spiral it bumped my heart and sent my feelings flying. I broke down. *Oh my God, now I know what's missing in my life. I am missing the connection to a higher power. It's God that I've been missing.*

Preferring not to make a scene, I ran until I found a dark corner where I could have my meltdown in private.

On the ancient stone steps of the Kanchipuram temple, worn smooth by millions of bare feet, my heart cracked open like a seed in the moist earth. I began to wail uncontrollably. From the depth of my being I cried out, "Where are you? Where are you, God? It's you that's missing in my life. I need to find you and feel you in my heart always. Please send me someone to teach me yoga and meditation." This outburst continued until I was too weak to cry anymore. I sat steeped in silent, somber peace. I'd just experienced my first heartfelt entreaty to God and somehow felt that I had been heard.

Eventually my friends, who'd been searching for a while, found me all alone in the dark, slumped against the wall.

"What's wrong?" they asked.

Through the dim light I could see the concern on their faces. But how could I explain what had just happened? How could I explain the transformation taking place within me?

I got up, brushed the dirt off my bum, and signaled, let's go. Not only did I not have the words, but I was literally unable to speak. I followed my friends back to the hotel and didn't utter a peep for the remainder of the evening. The exhaustion from this experience, coupled with my mild case of hepatitis, swiftly escorted me off to a deep slumber.

In the morning Franco was determined to know more about what had overcome me the night before. By then my emotions were settled, but I was reluctant to go into much detail about my spiritual experience. I merely said, "Franco, you remember when we were in Ladakh and we had that really magical experience? Well, it was something like that."

With a bewildered look on his face he replied, "I'm not sure I understand."

During our prior stay in Kashmir, we'd decided to take a ten-day trip to Ladakh, a mountain kingdom nestled between the Himalayan and Karakoram ranges at the top of India bordering Tibet. The journey required a two-day bus ride up treacherous mountains to an elevation of 11,500 feet.

The narrow road was open only a few months of the year. The rest of the time, it was either buried in several feet of snow or too hazardous from the melting ice.

Those mountain peaks were like nothing I'd ever seen. Their colossal stature had me spellbound, not just because of their size but because they caused me to contemplate their creation. Peering out the bus window, my eyes were unable to see their base. Looking into the distance, I could see other vehicles like tiny ants making their way up higher still. My heart pounded as we came around corners, just to have to back up to let another vehicle pass. I clutched the seat in absolute terror as I saw the tires inches from the edge, knowing that the only outcome if we went over was death. It was on this bus ride that I had my first awakening to the power and presence of an Almighty God.

That journey had been broken by an overnight stay in the town of Kargil. Everyone lay on mattresses spread around the floor of a dumpy hotel. Within a short while, I heard a slapping noise. Suddenly, like a symphony orchestra in full tempo, all the people in the room were slapping themselves crazy, myself included. Then one of the travelers in the room screamed, "Bedbugs!" That was a first for me.

Realizing sleep was not going to be an option, my two friends and I grabbed our shawls, scarves, and beanies and headed out into the crisp night air. The dark sky sparkled with a myriad of stars, which I imagined were winking at me. Suddenly, I was wide awake and full of excitement to be in this remote region of the planet. In the distance, we could hear what sounded like a river, so we allowed our ears to guide us in that direction. Within a few minutes, we were gazing at a rapidly running stream. It bounced over boulders and glistened in the moonlight like a diamond necklace. We continued to stroll by its side until we were almost knocked over by the full moon, which rose above the hill directly before us. All three of us froze in our tracks and stood in silent awe gazing at its luminosity. It felt as though I had stumbled into Heaven, high up on this deserted road in the middle of nowhere.

"Franco? Do you remember that magical night?" I asked.

Holy Hell

He nodded and said, "Yes."

"Well, something like that happened to me yesterday."

Whether he understood my inference as to the spiritual significance of my experience, I'm not sure. But that was the best explanation I could give him at the time.

We stayed a few more days in Kanchipuram so that I could ingest my medicine from hell, and as promised I soon felt strong enough to hit the road.

We discussed where to go next and decided upon the holy town of Tiruvannamalai. According to the guidebook, the town had an ashram. Instantly my mind was flooded with images of scrawny old men with long beards lying on beds of nails and of yogis with limbs twisted like pretzels immersed in meditation.

We caught a bus from Kanchipuram to Vellore, then another on to Tiruvannamalai. Our driver, as normal, drove like a maniac. I started to feel agitated from the blaring music, abrasive wind, and reckless traffic. That's when I remembered the wise words a fellow traveler had offered when I first arrived in India: "There is a great deal of sound pollution in this country, but you mustn't resist. You have to allow the noise to flow right through you. Otherwise you will suffer."

I quickly put her words into practice and was able to endure the rest of the journey. After being on the road a few hours, I saw a town in the distance, also a solitary mountain that seemed to have popped up out of nowhere. As we drew closer to this mountain, I saw the towering pillars of a gigantic temple standing at its feet. I sensed there was something very special about this place and the mountain. *I wish we could stop here instead. I would love to check this place out.*

Just as I was thinking thus, the conductor cried out, "Tiruvannamalai!"

THREE

TURNING A NEW LEAF

The bus dropped us off in front of the magnificent temple right in the heart of this small town. Immediately I noticed there were fewer cars and no auto rickshaws. The quietness was a pleasant change. The only form of transport to take us the few miles to Ramanashram was cycle rickshaw or horse-drawn wagon. Naturally we gravitated toward the horses.

The carriage looked like an old gypsy wagon—a canvas canopy suspended over two large wooden wheels. There were no steps. The driver pushed down on the rear of the cart to enable a less embarrassing boarding. We threw our luggage up to the front, then on all fours crawled in one by one. Within a couple of minutes we were out of town making our way through the village, which consisted of small concrete homes and mud huts with thatched roofs. Bare-bottomed children were running around everywhere merrily playing with each other, their only clothing a piece of red cord tied around their hips. Nearby, a dog was scavenging in the gutter until it was chased away by a couple of pigs who seemed to run the place. I also noticed patties made out of cow dung stuck to the sides of the houses—once dry, they are used as fuel for cooking, I later learned. It was a dry, dusty, and dirty little town, but very much alive.

The carriage began to slow. The driver called out to the horse, pulled on the reins, and then came running around to announce we had arrived at our destination. Once more, he lowered the back of the wagon, and we slid out with luggage in hand. Across the street, I saw a freshly painted brick wall. Above the entry was an arched metal sign, which read "Sri Ramanashram." Inside standing guard were a couple of giant old trees surrounded by a neatly swept dirt courtyard. A building to the right looked like the office, and toward the back of the property up a few steps, a temple. I smiled when I caught sight of the mountain towering just behind, as if it were keeping a watchful eye on everyone. We began to make our way through the front gate when we were besieged by beggars. They all wore tattered clothing. Some had deformed limbs, while others were clearly suffering from leprosy. One old woman came rushing up, looked me right in the eye, and pitifully began crying, "Ma, Ma, Ma," rubbing her belly and making a dreadful face. Just as we were reaching into our bags to pull out a few coins, we heard a commotion like a stampede of cattle. Our act of surrender had triggered another horde of beggars to come hobbling and rushing toward us, waving their arms and crying out. Hastily we dropped the money into the nearest begging bowls and dashed through the gate into the safe confines of the ashram.

Franco and Sylvie went into the office to see if there were any rooms available. I waited outside. I wanted to do some people watching. I was anxious to find out what kind of unique human beings frequented an ashram. I got quite a shock when I saw regular folk roaming around. My misconception—that an ashram was frequented only by old, bearded, skinny yogis—went up in a puff of smoke. However, I did notice something rather special on the faces of most of the people. There was serenity to their way of being and a sparkle in their eyes, and I suspected that this radiance was caused by their spiritual practice. I wanted to experience whatever it was they were experiencing, to feel that same peace within myself. I quickly clamped down on my emotions, realizing this was not the time or the place to have another outburst. As an added precaution, I went inside the office to see what was going on.

Looking around, I saw several pictures of an exceptionally gentle-looking bald man with the most penetrating eyes and saintly aura. I presumed he was the head of the ashram, for there were oil lamps lit in front of his image. I noticed a photo of the mountain and felt of surge of excitement when I read the inscription below: "Holy Mountain Arunachala." *My suspicions were right. The mountain is special. I just knew it.*

I also noticed the not-so-saintly eyes of the man behind the desk, who was giving us a critical once-over as he explained that they had limited accommodations and that all the rooms were reserved.

"Why don't you try across the street?" he suggested with a strained smile. "Several homes have been turned into guest houses. You shouldn't have any problem finding somewhere else to stay."

I suspected we were being judged on our attire, for I noticed most of the Western women were wearing saris or at least had all their limbs covered. Part of me wondered if he felt we weren't spiritual enough to stay at the ashram. I didn't know what to make of this character and felt disappointed we couldn't, or weren't worthy enough, to stay there.

As we stepped outside the office, a gentle-natured man dressed in orange robes seemed to sense our plight. He suggested we try Saraswati Nilayam, a house across the street just a few minutes away. We grabbed our luggage and made our way back out the front gate. This time, we were prepared. Like race horses with blinders on, we galloped through to avoid being hassled by beggars a second time.

Eventually I would learn how to walk casually by, smile, and say "another time" without too much guilt.

We crossed the street and walked down a dirt lane lined with tall trees until we reached the house. We opened the gate and entered the compound to see an exceptionally large, family-style concrete home complete with water well and lovely gardens. There was also a cute little hut with thatched roof to the side of the well. This caught my eye immediately. I heard the gate creak once more, so I quickly turned to see a man coming in on his scooter. Just as I wondered who he was and that he must have been right behind us, he parked his vehicle and came over. His complexion was jet black, in perfect contrast with the bright white, crisp, long-sleeved shirt and dhoti that he was wearing. I surmised he was from a wealthy family by the thick, gold-link chain around his neck and chunky gold rings on his fingers.

"Hello, my name is Balakrishnan. I am owner of this fine property," he said, reaching out to shake hands with Franco as he acknowledged both of us women.

"Nice to meet you," we courteously replied.

"Do you have a room we could rent?" I asked.

"Certainly. This was my family home, but now I rent rooms and live in town with my wife and children. Please come. I will show you which is available."

While talking to us, he gave a swift backward flick of his heel. The dhoti rose from his ankles into the air. Without even looking, he retied it in half to sit at knee level. "Wow, that's impressive," I mumbled to myself and made an exaggerated face commending his technique.

He showed us a large room on the side of the house. "This will cost thirty rupees a week. Okay for you?" he asked with slight apprehension.

The price was more than reasonable, so we happily accepted his offer. He then proceeded to show us around the property.

"Here is the water tank where you can fill your buckets. I come daily to pump water from the well. Actually, that is why I am here now. You have very good timing," he joked, shaking his head in true Indian fashion. "If there is no electricity, which is often the case, you can use this bucket to draw water from the well," he said, pointing to a small, rusty metal bucket dangling from a rope.

I placed my hands on the edge of the well and peered in. My eyes traced down the sides of its moss-and-fern-covered interior and realized it would be quite a haul, for the water was at least a hundred feet down. Even though we had no kitchen, and the bathroom and toilet were outdoors, we were thrilled. Not only was it close to the ashram, but it also had a peaceful atmosphere with lots of trees and shade. We paid him the money, and he left us to do his chores—pumping water into the tank and irrigating the garden. There was electricity that day.

After freshening up, I headed back to the ashram. I was curious to know more. Wanting to dress more conservatively, I put on an ankle-length skirt and a short-sleeved T-shirt covered with a vest. I went back into the office and apprehensively approached the man seated behind the desk, hoping that my new attire would render him more accepting.

"I want to learn how to meditate and do yoga. Is there anyone here who can teach me?" I asked in earnest.

"Sorry, we cannot help you. But Bhagavan can," he replied emphatically.

"Oh, good. Where can I find him?"

"Just go to the meditation room and he will guide you."

"Thank you so much," I said and excitedly left the office in search of this Bhagavan fellow.

I found the meditation room and peeped inside expecting to see a wise old man teaching how to meditate. Instead, I saw a handful of people seated cross-legged on the floor with eyes closed, serenely meditating. *Where's Bhagavan? I thought the man in the office said he was teaching a class?* That's when I saw propped up on a couch behind an enclosure a large painting of the same saintly man in a reclining position. *Well, that's helpful. How is a painting going to teach me anything?* I was upset and disappointed, feeling all hope was lost of ever learning how to meditate. I moved away from the room and found a nice big tree to crouch up against, for once again I needed to weep. After a short while, a European lady noticed me crying and came over to ask what was wrong. After I explained my dilemma, she couldn't help but chuckle.

With a smile, she lovingly explained, "Bhagavan Ramana Maharishi left his body nearly thirty years ago, but he is very much alive in spirit. His presence can indeed teach you everything you need to know. All you have to do is sit in silence."

I wiped the tears from my eyes, feeling like quite a knucklehead. Her suggestion was a new and strange concept for me, but I was willing to give it a shot. Grabbing hold of those few words of encouragement, I tiptoed into the meditation room and sat in the corner on the bare, cold concrete floor with my knees up against my chest. I studied the other people and noticed they were all seated on individual little rugs. I suddenly imagined them as "magic carpets" that transported them to faraway realms, and I had to quickly cover my mouth so I wouldn't giggle out loud. Becoming serious once more, I tried to imitate their postures. I crossed my legs, put my hands gracefully in my lap, straightened my spine, closed my eyes, and thought, *Okay now what?* I only lasted about five minutes in that pose before I had to re-position my legs. Even though I'd already mastered the famous Indian squat, I wasn't used to sitting on my bum on hard concrete as rigid as a statue. But I wasn't ready to call it quits just yet and decided to give it one more try.

I looked around the room and had to acknowledge there was a distinct, peaceful energy permeating the space. I glanced over to Bhagavan's picture, looked him fair and square in the eyes, and in my mind said, "All right, you. Stop sitting there doing nothing and show me how to meditate! Okay, here we go." I resumed my position. "Come on, come on. Something has to happen." I sat there thinking and thinking and thinking. Finally, I gave up and left the room. Even though I hadn't really experienced anything, I was proud of myself for at least trying.

Before leaving the ashram, I went into the bookstore and purchased a copy of Ramana's *Life and Teachings,* then headed home to my friends. When I got back, they were both taking a nap. I quietly lay on my mattress and read a little of the Saint's life. The book explained that when Bhagavan was just sixteen, he had his first experience of enlightenment. In later years, he devised a technique called "Self Enquiry" in which you search inside for "I," the eternal witness. He taught that while you meditate, you must be watchful. When a thought arises, you ask, "To whom is this thought occurring?" The answer will be, "To me." You should then enquire, "Who am I?" He said the more you repeat this process, the quieter your mind will become, and eventually it will return to its source. This technique sounded very practical, so I thought I would try it next time I went to the ashram.

That evening we strolled into town to have dinner. After we returned, I dove back into my book.

"Gail, we're going outside to smoke a joint. Are you coming?" enquired Franco.

"No, thanks. I'm going to stay here and read," I said, turning my head ever so slightly.

"All right then. We'll be back shortly." He had an utterly bewildered look on his face.

Seeing his expression made me realize what had just happened. Dropping the book onto my chest, I thought, *I can't believe it. Did I just say no? Did I just turn down an opportunity to smoke marijuana?* Normally I was the first out the door, the one inviting everyone else to come smoke.

There was a good reason, though, for my change in behavior. As I lay there reading and pondering these new teachings, an incredible river of peace was flowing through my body. I was already on a high such as I'd never experienced before. I didn't need marijuana anymore.

In the morning, much to my dismay, Sylvie and Franco announced that they were going to leave the following day. They had only one week left on their visa, and they wanted to spend a few days in Goa before catching their flight from Bombay back to Europe. We had become quite close in the four months spent traveling together, and the thought of them leaving made me sad. In my heart, I felt Tiruvannamalai was where I needed to stay for a while, and being Australian I didn't need a visa. I could stay indefinitely if I wanted. There was so much transformation taking place within me—it was as though I was becoming a different person overnight. As much as it hurt to say goodbye, I had to accept the fact that it was time.

Before I knew it, the moment for us to part ways arrived. Carrying nothing but my heavy heart, I walked my friends back up the lane to where a cycle rickshaw was waiting. Seeing them seated together brought tears to my eyes.

"Auf Wiedersehen, Sylvie," I said, giving her a kiss on the cheek. Looking at Franco, "Ciao, my friend." I grabbed their hands and after a quick glance at the mountain said, "May you always be happy together. Hopefully we will meet again someday."

I watched the driver turn the rickshaw around, climb on his bike, and grab the handlebars. The muscles in his leg flexed as he pushed down on the pedal. They turned around, waved goodbye, and shouted, "Take care, Gail, our dearest Aussie friend!"

After a final smile and wave goodbye, I stood still and watched them slowly fade into the distance. There I was, on the side of the road, all alone once again. The reality hurt. As I headed back to the house, I pulled myself together by trying to find something to feel excited about. The first thing I needed to do was ask Balakrishnan if he had a smaller room I could rent long-term. It was on this day, in September of 1978, that I turned a new leaf and embarked on a fresh chapter of my life.

That afternoon I was excitedly moving my luggage into a small room at the front of the house. The room was only about eight feet wide by twenty feet long, but it had two windows and opened onto the porch. I spread out my thin mattress and covered it with a pretty sarong I'd bought in Bali. I unpacked my luggage, something I hadn't done in a very long time, and made my room as cozy as possible. Caught up in the thrill of making a home after seven months on the road, I decided to head into town to purchase some cooking supplies and to see what else I could find. A few hours later I returned with a kerosene wick stove, a stainless steel saucepan and frying pan, a couple of steel plates and bowls, rice, oil and vegetables. I also brought some ornaments I had found in front of the temple, two pieces of silk to place in the window sills, a lovely peacock blue sari, and, most importantly, a padlock to keep everything safe. I couldn't wait to learn how to wrap the six yards of fabric around myself just like an Indian woman.

In India, the social equivalent of an Australian pub, and more wholesome, was the local tea shop. It was the perfect venue to meet other Westerners, to enhance one's knowledge of spirituality, and to discuss philosophy, gurus, ashrams, and interesting places to visit. One could engage in highly intellectual debates over whether the path of devotion was superior to the path of advaita (non-dualism). Or one could just sit and listen, which is what I normally did. Not that I didn't have an opinion, but somehow I preferred being a silent witness. One day, though, I had to open my mouth when a chap blatantly contradicted himself.

He lectured: "I don't have a guru or belong to any form of religion. I recently went to a discourse in Madras and was taught that in order to achieve enlightenment, one must live without any beliefs."

"Do you believe that?" I cleverly asked.

"Why yes, I …"Then he frowned.

I didn't mean to be a smart ass, but somehow I felt compelled to point out that his words were merely an idea stuck in his head and not grasped on a deeper level.

Over the course of the next few days, I met some of the other residents at Saraswati Nilayam. There was a French Canadian couple living in the quarters at the side. They called themselves Iswari and Nataraj. The fact that they had been in India for quite some time was apparent in the way they dressed. She wore a sari with perfect grace. Her light brown hair, always neatly plaited, fell to her hips. Her countenance, although gentle, was a little dreamy at times, and she was lean with long, lanky limbs. For some silly reason, she reminded me of Popeye's sweetheart, Olive Oyl. Nataraj, on the other hand, was a strong person with an inflated ego to match. He had intense, piercing eyes, a huge nose, and a fit physique. He was a brilliant astrologer.

The next person I was to meet wound up playing an important role in my life by introducing me to the history of saints and Hinduism. I was at the tank by the well washing my pots and pans when I heard someone approaching from the far end of the compound. I looked up to see a short Indian man with dark complexion and with thick, curly long hair dangling over his shoulders down to his waist. He had a slight potbelly, a surprisingly friendly face, and eyes that smiled at me through iconic John Lennon style glasses. He didn't look like your typical Indian male, so I was curious. I wiped my hands on my skirt and went over to introduce myself.

"I'm Gail, and I recently moved into the front room."

"My name is Madhu." He spoke in what sounded like a French accent.

"Where are you from? You don't sound like you are from India."

With deep pride in his voice he replied, "I *am* Indian but was born in Reunion Island."

My facial expression must have revealed I had no clue where on earth that was because he responded right away with, "It's a French island in the Indian Ocean not too far from Madagascar. You should come over for tea sometime."

"I would love to," I replied joyfully.

FOUR

ARUNACHALA AND I

Every morning like clockwork I would visit the ashram and as per custom I'd walk slowly and meditatively around Ramana's samadhi (tomb) a few times, then sit on the side and meditate. Most days my mind was as fidgety as a monkey tied up in a patch of biting ants. However, on a few occasions, sitting there with my eyes closed, I felt as though someone was pressing a finger on my forehead, right between my eyebrows (spiritually known as the third eye). The first couple of times this happened, I had to crack one eye open to see if someone was standing before me, but no one ever was. On one such occurrence, my mind became absolutely still and absorbed within this spot on my forehead. In this state of peace and absence of thought, time became irrelevant and my usual awareness of physical discomfort vanished. Eventually my mind became aware of its surroundings, and the person named Gail returned. I got up from where I was seated. In a dreamlike state I floated out of the hall, taking a glance at the clock as I exited. I had to pause for a second. I found it hard to believe that forty minutes had gone by. I smiled to myself. *I think I just had a taste of what meditation is all about.*

Holy Hell

That afternoon Madhu invited me to his place to get acquainted. Upon entering his quarters the first thing I noticed was a small library of books. I made a mental note to remember to ask if I could borrow a few. After some general conversation he proceeded to tell me about a custom called giri pradakshina (mountain circumambulation) that was said to be of great spiritual significance. Then as though warning me he said, "It's about a ten-mile walk and takes roughly four hours. I usually start at four a.m. Would you like to join me tomorrow?"

"Um, yeah, sure," I replied half-heartedly, dreading having to get out of bed that early. But I was eager to learn the culture and enhance my spirituality. I thought, *If that's what it's going to take, then so be it.*

"I don't have an alarm clock. Can you wake me up a little before four?"

"It's a date."

"Great. I'll see you in the morning then," I said with a smile, feigning enthusiasm.

Getting up from my chair I asked, "Do you mind if I take a look at your book collection?"

"No. Go right ahead."

The first book that drew my attention was about Sarada Devi, the wife of Sri Ramakrishna, a famous saint from Calcutta. The next one was about Anandamoyi Ma, a female saint from north India. I asked if I could borrow them, and he happily obliged.

Once back in my room, I began flipping through the pages of Anandamoyi Ma's book and stumbled upon a few pictures of her. Even though the images ranged from her early twenties to her late seventies, her face in every photo emitted radiance and bliss. The mere sight of these images overwhelmed me with serenity and emotion. One photo in particular made my heart skip a beat. It was a picture of Gurudidi Priya, her devoted attendant. The woman was on her knees, with her body pressed up against Ma's. Her eyes looked upwards and were locked into Ma's distant gaze, while her arms were wrapped in loving embrace around her guru's knees. The love and devotion in this image made me weep, and the experience launched in me a subtle longing for such a connection. Immersed in these sweet thoughts, I drifted off to sleep.

Several hours later from the depth of slumber, I was disturbed by a rattling noise. I heard Madhu whispering through my door, "Gail, it's time to wake up."

Oh God, is it four a.m. already? It feels as if I just went to sleep. "I'm awake. I'll be ready in a few minutes," I groggily replied.

I peeled myself up off the mattress, got dressed, then went outside to brush my teeth and splash some cold water on my face to wake my brain a bit. Still half asleep, I sat in the courtyard on a little concrete bench staring into space. Within a few minutes, Madhu returned and asked if I was ready.

"Yes, just let me grab my shoes."

"No, you won't need them. Pradakshina is done barefoot, as a form of penance. The mountain is sacred, and you walk around it as you would a deity in a temple."

"Okay then, let's go," I said grimly, looking down at my poor feet and wondering how they would survive ten miles of road, dirt, and rocks.

Within a few minutes of walking, the fuzziness in my head disappeared, and I was amazed at how clear my mind felt. The morning air was quiet and cool. The only sounds were those of birds chirping as they excitedly greeted the new day and the faint creaking of a bullock cart in the distance. After a mile or so, we veered off the tar road and progressed along a dirt road through open, empty land. Dawn began to break, gradually unveiling the surrounding landscape and enabling me to see the mountain from various angles. We passed an occasional lonesome shrine, then a small temple with bathing pond. Before long, we approached a tiny village. Men rode by on bicycles, ringing their bells as they passed. Half-asleep children were squatting on the side of the road going potty while the four legged sanitation department waited impatiently nearby. Women with straw brooms swept in front of their huts. After sprinkling some water these women began drawing intricate designs with a white powder. Madhu explained that this was a tradition to invite and welcome all into the home, especially Lakshmi, the Goddess of prosperity. Symbolically, it also prevented evil spirits from entering.

Holy Hell

The dirt road continued a few more miles around the foot of the mountain. The silence was broken only slightly by the murmur of traffic from a distant highway. As we came around another bend, we found a shrine in the shape of a small tunnel. Without uttering a word Madhu closed his eyes, cupped his hands in prayer for a few seconds, and then crawled through the tunnel on all fours. I stood motionless, not understanding what he was doing, and giggled slightly at the sight of him wiggling his way through the hole. Once he was done, he explained that one should make a wish and then crawl through the shrine for it to become true. Gathering my thoughts, I paused for a moment to wonder what I truly wanted, then crawled through with, "I want devotion and to know God" fervently repeating in my heart. With a smile on my face and my prayer submitted to the "powers that be," we continued around the mountain.

I was clueless as to how much time had elapsed, so was pleasantly surprised when I saw the giant pillars of the temple in the distance. My thoughts immediately went to my feet, and I paused for a second to inspect their condition. Apart from them being very grubby, they were just fine. As we passed the temple, Madhu promised to take me on a tour later that week. I smiled with delight. We then walked the last couple of miles out to the ashram and were back at Saraswati Nilayam by nine. Even though I was a little tired and my feet a little tender, I was extremely happy to have been introduced to this wonderful ritual. From that moment on, I walked around the mountain twice a week remembering, of course, to crawl through the little tunnel with a spiritual prayer tucked away in my heart.

Later that afternoon I went to the local post office to see if there was any mail from home. I was feeling slightly anxious because I'd recently done something out of the ordinary and wasn't sure how my folks would take it. Instead of sending a pretty but rather vague and impersonal postcard, I wrote them a letter describing my unexpected love for India and stating that I might stay a while. (I did not foresee twenty-two years.)

It had been almost two years since I'd last seen my parents. At age eighteen I had packed up my possessions and, with a girlfriend, drove almost three thousand miles from Queensland's Gold Coast to Perth in Western Australia. It took us three days to cover the distance, and we literally drove until we felt sleepy, turned the ignition off, and then crawled into the back of the station wagon for a nap. A large part of that journey passed through the outback and across the Nullabor Plains, a vast, treeless, limestone plain that extends twelve hundred miles across South and Western Australia. About twenty-five million years prior to our visit that region had been the bed of a large sea. Now it was the world's largest single piece of limestone. There wasn't one bump, curve, or change of scenery to keep you alert, so many drivers fall asleep at the wheel. Crossing the Nullabor is considered quite an achievement. Roadhouses sell stickers saying, "I have crossed the Nullabor." So of course, I just had to slap one on the bumper of our car.

After living in Perth for a year, working a variety of mundane jobs and partying my nights away, I felt bored and decided to go overseas with my boyfriend. So I phoned home to deliver the news. Shortly thereafter I shipped a few boxes back to Brisbane and was gone. I don't know how my parents felt about this. I never gave them the opportunity to express an opinion, let alone sought their permission.

I asked the Tiruvannamalai postmaster if there was any mail for Gail Tredwell. Within a minute, he returned with an envelope and handed it to me. Immediately I recognized the handwriting. It was from Mum. So I dashed home to read her letter. My heart sank and I fell into shock as I read the contents. Without any sweet-talk, she got straight to the point.

"Your father and I are getting a divorce, and the house is up for sale."

I knew they hadn't been happy for quite some time. But divorce—how could they? That only happened to other families, not mine. But even more unsettling was the news that the house was going to be sold. The home where I grew up was going to have strangers living in it. The thought of other people sleeping in my bedroom and of a new family sitting together around the dining table made me cry. My foundation had just crumbled beneath me. Even though I was a free spirit traveling the globe without a care in the world, my wanderings had always emanated from a tiny dot on the planet—home. I suddenly felt lost and all alone, like a spider without a web.

The sadness remained intense for several days. But like any memory it gradually became less potent and faded with time.

A few days later I had an eye-opening experience of the fragility of life itself. I was peacefully strolling home down my lane when I was startled by the blood-curdling scream of a baby pig as it rushed by. The poor thing was being chased by a stray dog and literally running for its life. The pursuit ended near the entrance of my compound when the dog pounced on the tiny animal. I started to yell, "Stop! Leave the little thing alone!" I picked up a small rock and hurled it at the dog, to no effect. The attack was vicious. There was not a hope in the world for the creature. Then with the baby pig dangling from its jaws, the dog cast me a sly glance and dashed through the fence into the bushes. As I came through the gate, I could see the dog ripping the pig apart with its teeth and crunching on the bones and flesh. When we made eye contact, the dog covered its prey and growled. There was nothing I could do, so I took my shaking body and tear-filled eyes back to my room.

I tried to pacify myself by accepting the fact that such violence was merely a part of nature, the natural progression of the food chain for a desperate animal in India. Lying there though, I couldn't help but ponder the incident more. Just a few minutes ago this cute little pig, full of life, was running and squealing to save itself. Tomorrow it's going to be the excrement of a dog. Where did its life force go?

Getting even more carried away, I thought, *Oh my God, what if a similar thing happened to me? I could become a pile of poop too. Where would the person I call "me" go? What would happen to my life force?* I was undergoing major renovation. The many false perceptions I held and the many things I had taken for granted while growing up were all being challenged. The home that had provided shelter and security was up for sale. My parents were going their separate ways, shattering the family unit. The fragility of life itself had been displayed vividly before my eyes through the baby pig incident. These experiences left me raw and vulnerable with serious questions about life on earth. Now more than ever I sensed the need for a guru, someone to show me how to transform this emptiness I was feeling into a permanent state of peace and fulfillment.

I loved my simple life in Tiruvannamalai. I passed my time with daily visits to the ashram, walks around Arunachala, meditating, and reading. On occasion I'd also walk through the hills on a path that started from the far end of the ashram and out through a tiny gate. It was a gentle walk. The most intriguing part was that after I crossed the first hill and entered a tiny valley, every ounce of noise vanished. In an instant I was engulfed by incredible silence, a silence that echoed that quiet space within myself.

Slightly farther up the hill and across toward town was a tiny dwelling called Skandashram and Virupaksha Cave, where Ramana had spent many of his earlier years meditating. I liked spending time there to contemplate, meditate, or to simply sit and soak up the spiritual vibrations. Toward the end of the trail was a collection of gigantic boulders overlooking the town. From there you could gain a magnificent aerial view of the Arunachaleswara Temple sitting proudly upon twenty-four acres of land. I loved to sit there and watch the crazy commotion called daily life while feeling safely removed from it all. This vantage made me reflect on the books I had read. These books described a state of consciousness that witnesses life with complete acceptance. I was hoping one day to be able to lead my life from such a detached state.

Looking back now, I wonder how on earth this twenty-year-old could have acquired such lofty spiritual ideals. What made her run away from a relatively comfortable life in Australia to live almost penniless in a third world country? I strongly believe that I possessed a sincere longing to know God and to secure some meaning in life. On the flip side, I also believe that a part of this longing was my hunger to fill a void I felt inside. In my youth I had been a loyal friend and had gone out of my way to please. I never gave up on friendships even when the loyalty I displayed was far from reciprocated. I had one girlfriend in particular who was fine when it was just the two of us, but when another girl came into the picture, she would turn on me. One day the three of us were out having coffee and I briefly left the table for a bathroom visit. Upon return I began sipping my coffee, and the sight of that sent my friend and her accomplice into a fit of hysterical laughter. I later learned that the new girl had spat in my drink. Nevertheless, I forgave my "friend." When I left home at age seventeen and moved to the Gold Coast, I shared an apartment with this girl despite the mean streak she frequently displayed. Shortly after moving in together I gave her and another friend a ride back to Brisbane to visit family. The plan was for the three of us and some old friends from the neighborhood to go out that evening to the bowling alley. My friend said she would get a ride from her brother and we were all to meet at seven p.m. When I arrived, there was no sign of any of them. Thinking I had made a mistake, I drove to a different alley slightly farther away. Again, nobody. Feeling extremely sad, I went home in tears but sat up waiting for their car to pull into the driveway across the street. I wanted to give them the benefit of the doubt.

When I asked what had happened, I was told, "Oh, we changed our mind and went roller-skating instead."

In the morning when I explained to my mother why my face looked so long, she was furious. "I hope you are not going to give those little bitches a ride back with you?"

Despite my broken heart I didn't have it in me to be mean in return, let alone to stand up for myself. "Oh, it's okay," I pathetically responded.

"Let them take the bus. They don't deserve a ride after what they did to you."

I was not in the habit of listening to my mother, so ignored the sound advice she was offering. Growing up I experienced many similar incidents, and I sometimes felt so lonely and dejected that I would head to the nearby park and play on the swings as I shed tears. One day while sitting on the park bench I noticed a lonesome spider and felt an incredible affinity with the tiny creature. Between the numerous betrayals by my girlfriends, the fights with my mother at home, and the persecutions of a cranky old spinster who was my boss at work, I felt that growing up in Australia had left me scarred and seeking something greater. I believed that the solution to all my problems was hiding somewhere in this ancient land. I felt certain I would find the missing link to my life through my quest for God and a guru.

Another activity I enjoyed at Tiruvannamalai was cooking. Every few days I'd walk into town and purchase fresh vegetables and supplies from the market. The place was always teeming with women rushing around with baskets on their hips buying ingredients for their daily meals. The women drove hard bargains and argued ferociously over the price of the vegetables that the vendors had spread on the ground atop old rice sacks. Alongside the familiar potato, tomato, carrot, and eggplant were unusual varieties of greens, melons, and root vegetables. Behaving like a real pro, I too did my share of bargaining. I selected a bundle of string beans and handed them to the leathery-skinned man seated cross-legged on the ground. He picked up his scales, suspending them in mid air, and the two metal plates attached by chains began swinging to and fro. Placing the beans on one side, he added a metal weight to the other. Without giving the scales time to balance or make a clear determination of the actual weight, he demanded, "Madam, half kilo. You give ten rupees." And he tossed me a hopeful look.

"No. Too much rupees," I scoffed in my eloquent Indian English. "I give you five rupees, okay?" I knew that wasn't enough money, but in order to hit my target price, I had to play along with his little game.

"Madam, please," he begged. "You give seven rupees, best price."

I handed him the money, took the beans, and placed them in my tacky plastic-mesh shopping bag. As I began to walk away, he cried out, "You want potato, tomato? Today very fine one."

Without turning around I shook my head, waved my hand to gesture no, and walked off. My courteous days of smiling and saying "no thank you" were long gone. I no longer flinched with guilt, either. The vendors were merely pushing their luck, and they knew it.

Within a few weeks I began cooking and delivering meals to some folks in the community. One was a toothless, elderly Indian man who had been living at the ashram for over thirty years. In exchange he shared personal stories of his time with Bhagavan.

You might recall there was a cute little cottage on my property, the one by the well. Inside it lived an American man with a chronic illness. He was unable to eat the oily and spicy food. He had tried hiring an Indian family to prepare special meals for him, but they just couldn't comprehend that it was humanly possible to eat food without any chili. The man really seemed to be suffering, so I offered to cook for him as well. He gave me money to purchase the ingredients, but I refused to charge for my labor. After a few weeks he was still struggling from his illness and the rough conditions in India, so he decided to head home. As a token of appreciation, and much to my delight, he offered me the cottage with six months' rent paid upfront. There were also some supplies and a couple of simple furnishings such as a mattress and a chair. I was ecstatic, not just because it was the most desirable cottage in the whole of Tiruvannamalai at the time, but also because I was almost out of money.

A week later I moved my possessions from the little room in the main house to my adorable cottage. Compared to Western-style living it was still considerably small, but it contained a heck of a lot more space than I was used to. Inside was one large room with a shoulder-high dividing wall separating the kitchen from the living space. The kitchen had a couple of shelves, an elevated slab on the floor where I could cook, and a small enclosed area in the corner designed in such a way that I could squat to wash dishes and the water would drain outside onto the ground. An added bonus was the tiny covered entrance where I could sit and read. I was set for another six months. I had my few kilos of healthy red rice, several gallons of kerosene for my stove, and a four-inch-thick, lump-free mattress to sleep on. I was in heaven.

A few days later, as promised, Madhu gave me a guided tour of the Arunachaleswara temple. I was astounded by its splendor, history, and several-story-high towers covered with intricately carved sculptures. Despite the frantic commotion and relentless babble of the worshipers, there was an indisputably serene atmosphere lingering within the walls of this ancient place. Madhu was quite the storyteller and derived immense pleasure from dipping into his trove of knowledge of the Hindu faith. Whenever there was a festival taking place, he knew about it and made sure to invite me. For the most part, I was eager to participate, because I was intrigued by the mythology and esoteric meaning behind the idols and rituals. The only time I was slightly reluctant was when we needed to be at the temple by the crack of dawn or some such inconvenient hour.

One morning we arrived at the temple for the abishekam (sacred bathing ritual) of Lord Shiva at three-thirty a.m. I watched with ignorant curiosity as the deity was bathed in water, milk, yogurt, honey, clarified butter, and then rosewater. The idol was then dressed, ornamented, and worshipped with hymns and burning camphor. The statue was placed on a mini palanquin and carried by priests, who made their way out the front gate of the temple to the fanfare of cymbals, bells, drums, and other instruments. We joined the holy procession. Much to my astonishment, the parade kept growing by the minute as people rushed to join in. I noticed myself getting swept up in the emotion. I began to feel elated by the music, the shouting of the crowd, and the excitement in the air. Brass oil lamps were lit in front of shops while people holding offerings and flower garlands waited impatiently for the procession to arrive at their door. Even though these customs were absolutely foreign to me, I was drawn in and eager to understand this culture. In an attempt to fit in, I had worn my peacock-blue sari. However, with my lily-white skin covered in freckles, my blue eyes, and my golden hair, I'm sure I stuck out like a sore thumb. There I was, at age twenty, traipsing along in the middle of a Hindu festival in south India, something I would never have imagined myself doing just one year before. If someone had predicted this, I would have laughed.

A couple of months later it was time for a festival called Maha Shivaratri (Great Night of Shiva), which is principally celebrated by fasting and staying awake the entire night. Per scriptural traditions these penances are performed to gain boons to reach spiritual goals more swiftly. I was intrigued by the idea of doing penance in exchange for God's grace, so I decided to participate. After a successful day of fasting, I headed to the ashram just as dusk was settling in. I quietly entered the meditation room and sat in my favorite corner ready for the long overnight haul. I took a quick look around and was delighted to see Madhu among many others who, I assumed, were all observing the ritual.

Through the night whenever I felt my attention fading, I got up and walked around as I prayed for devotion and progress on my spiritual path. The night seemed as though it would never end, so at times I just sat there with my back propped against the wall. I was determined to stay awake and maintain a contemplative mood, to let God know that I meant business. Around ten p.m. I caught Madhu yawning and rubbing his eyes, so I had a sneaky suspicion he wouldn't last much longer. Sure enough, within a short while he leaned over, prostrated before the image of Bhagavan, and exited the room. Seeing him leave gave my ego a tiny boost.

As the night progressed, I noticed people starting to nod off. Their heads drooped, and then all of a sudden they bounced back into position like rubber balls off the floor. One by one most of them called it quits and crept out of the room, leaving just two other people to greet the new day with me. I wasn't quite sure when the ritual was officially over, and I wanted to do it right, so I waited for them to leave before I got up. With a huge grin on my face and feelings of major accomplishment, I made my way out the ashram at sunrise. I crossed the street and entered the tea shop. Holding three fingers in the air, I pointed with the other hand to a basket of food. Quickly realizing what I had done and that I was no longer in silence, I chuckled and proudly announced, "I want three iddlies (steamed rice cakes), chutney, and a chai, please." I was joyous to have successfully completed my first big penance and hopeful that my prayers would soon be answered.

A few weeks later, for some inexplicable reason, I fell into a deep state of silence and remained that way for several days. It all began one evening as I was strolling into town and felt as if I was walking in a blissful dream. My mind was quietly resting in my heart, my lips were gently sealed, and my tongue felt as though glued to the roof of my mouth. I found myself weeping and spontaneously meditating at times, which was so unlike me. I didn't want this wonderful experience to go away, so I stayed home to avoid interacting with people. A few days later a friend came to my cottage explaining that he hadn't seen me around and was checking to make sure I was okay. It was a rather awkward situation because I didn't want to be rude, but at the same time was feeling quite possessive of my blissful state. I answered him with smiles, hand gestures, and shakes of my head. Finally I thought, *Oh this is ridiculous.* Leaning up to his ear, I whispered, "I've been unable to talk and immersed in some weird state of bliss." With those magical words, the spell was broken. Regrettably I returned to normal.

My life in Tiruvannamalai moved along at a contented, peaceful, and happy pace. Before I knew it, one year passed. One afternoon as I was sitting on my verandah reading a book, I was disturbed by someone knocking on the door of the house across the lane. Whoever it was kept knocking incessantly and shouting, "Hello! Hello!" Finally, the uproar became so annoying that I thought, *For the love of God, what a clown. Isn't it obvious nobody is home?* That's when I heard the gate to my compound creaking open. *Oh no, here he comes.* If I were back in Australia, I probably would've run inside and hid till he left, fearing he was a Jehovah Witness coming to convert me. Believing this not to be the case, though, I got up from my chair and went to see who he was and what he wanted.

Before me stood a physically fit young Indian man dressed in a knee-length dhoti with a shawl wrapped around his bare torso and flung over one shoulder in the manner of an ancient Roman. A slightly cocky fellow, if my immediate impression was correct.

"Can I help you?" I asked, carefully masking my irritation.

"I hope so," came his reply in well-spoken English. "I'm looking for a man named Madhu and was told he lives around here."

Pointing to the far end of the property, I said, "He lives there in the rear unit but is away at the moment and won't be back for a couple of days."

"Oh, that's a shame. I was hoping to stay with him. I've come from Kerala to stay a few weeks to do some penance."

"Are you a friend of his?"

"No, I was given his name and address by a mutual friend in Madras. Oh, I've been so rude. Please let me introduce myself. My name is Chandru."

I could feel my guard coming down. He seemed like a nice enough chap, so I decided to invite him in for a cup of tea. During our conversation, he revealed that he was enrolled at Chinmaya Mission in Bombay where he was studying Sanskrit and ancient scriptures. He went on to say that he had a guru in Kerala. Her name was Ammachi (Mother). Without my asking, he began rummaging through his bag to find a photo of her.

Looking at the picture I exclaimed, "My goodness, she is so young. Why, she barely looks twenty years of age. For some reason I was expecting to see a crinkly old woman."

With a distinct air of pride in his voice he answered, "As a matter of fact, she just turned twenty-six."

I was speechless and kept staring at her photo. The young woman was dressed in a simple white blouse and ankle-length floral skirt. She was adorned with bell-shaped gold earrings, a stone-studded necklace, and a large nose ring. Her hands were modestly folded in her lap, and her powerful and piercing eyes looked straight into the camera, at which she was mischievously smiling.

Snapping out of it, I asked, "Does she have an ashram and a big following?"

"Actually, no. She still lives at home with her parents."

"Then how on earth did you hear about her, let alone determine she was your guru?"

"Three nights a week people flock to her for healing and blessings when she embodies Krishna and an aspect of the Goddess. She does this at her family shrine. The villagers think she's just an ordinary girl in a trance and have no clue as to her divine nature. Apart from myself, there are five or six other young men from neighboring villages who revere her as the Divine Mother."

"Interesting," I exclaimed. "But if there's no ashram, then how do you get to spend time with her?"

At last his enthusiasm waned. "That's a real problem," he admitted. "We love being in her presence, but her father is a real monster and chases us away if we hang around too long. He's afraid their family will get a bad reputation in the village."

I didn't quite know what to make of his story and his overzealous enthusiasm, but I was undeniably captivated by her picture. My interest and curiosity must have been obvious because he handed me a cassette recording of her singing devotional songs.

Getting up from his chair he said, "I'd better be off. I need to find somewhere to stay. I'll be back in a couple of days to see Madhu. Maybe I can tell you more about Amma then, too?"

"Sure, let's do that," I replied with mixed emotion.

After he left, I couldn't help but think, *Boy, was he on a mission. Very persuasive, and not much different from the Jesus-peddlers I used to hide from in Australia. Maybe he's out to convert me after all.* Nevertheless, I was happy to have met him and definitely eager to know more about this person he called Ammachi.

In the evening I went to Madhu's place to borrow his tape player. I'd always been fond of music and easily moved by its content. As a teenager, while listening to Carly Simon, tears would well as I gazed out my bedroom window pining for my heartthrob—my girlfriend's big brother's buddy, to pull up in his yellow VW beetle at the house across the street. But now, this love of pop music was on the threshold of being converted into love for Indian chants. I felt excited as I turned on the player. The recording was rather scratchy, but its contents were like nothing I'd ever heard before. Amma was leading the singing to the accompaniment of harmonium, tabla, tambourine, and hand bells. The voices of a few men and women followed until the chorus was sung in unison. Her voice touched my heart in an unexpected way, and within a couple of minutes I was an uncontrollable mess. I was sobbing so hard I became weak and had to lie down. I wanted to meet this woman and wondered if she was the guru I had been praying for. I barely slept that night and couldn't wait to see Chandru again to share my experience. I also became anxious for Madhu to return so that I could tell him about this wonderful new discovery.

For the next two days, I remained at home playing my tape over and over like a lovesick teenager. I couldn't wait to meet Amma but had no clue how or when such a meeting would take place. Finally, it was time for Madhu to return. I was sitting on my porch restlessly, keeping an eye on the gate. Eventually I heard it creak, and sure enough, there he was. I ran out to greet him and couldn't contain my joy.

"Madhu, oh my God, you won't believe what's happened since you were gone. This fellow showed up and told me about this guru of his. She's a woman, and she's really young, and he wants to stay here at the house with you," I babbled on and on without taking a breath.

"Oh, you mean Chandru?" he calmly replied, bursting my bubble.

"Yeah, but how did you know?"

"I ran into him on my way home and I've agreed for him to stay. He'll be over shortly."

Like a neurotic puppy I followed Madhu into his quarters and told him what I had learned about Amma. He was somewhat nonchalant. I couldn't tell if he was tired, not particularly interested, or simply annoyed. Assuming the latter, I left him alone and went back to my cottage to listen to Amma's tape once again. Later that afternoon, Chandru arrived and moved into the spare room at Madhu's place. Once he was settled, I excitedly told him about my experience and my eagerness to meet Amma. He seemed overjoyed to hear this. He said we could talk more after he completed his ten-day silent retreat. Realizing that he would be in seclusion, I offered to bring him lunch, promising not to disturb him but simply to place the food in front of his door at noon. He happily accepted.

A few days after Chandru completed his penance, he came home one afternoon with the news that he would be moving to a house at the top of the lane. He'd been offered a room in the home of an American named Neal. Chandru said he felt drawn to stay with this man, who went by "Nealu," because the man was ill and could use some assistance. I knew exactly who he was talking about. I had seen Nealu a few times at the ashram. We'd never spoken nor even made eye contact, for Nealu came across as serious and unapproachable. I'd watched him enter the prayer hall quietly and reverently lie face-down flat on the floor in full prostration. Then with what appeared to be an extreme amount of strain, he'd get up from the floor, bow his head, and exit. He was terribly lean and frail, had blindingly lily-white skin and a shaved head, and always dressed in traditional Hindu attire. I sensed he was a pure soul, very dedicated to his spiritual path, and I wondered if perhaps that was why he had no interest in socializing with other Westerners. That was my guess anyhow.

    I chose to continue delivering meals to Chandru and saw it as an opportunity to meet Nealu and try to get to know him. Whenever I arrived at the house, Nealu would be lying down, barely able to sit up. He was indeed quite ill. He suffered from chronic migraines, an ulcer, fatigue, and spinal damage. It took a while for him to open up to me, and I always felt slightly judged when I arrived with food for Chandru. I could sense him sizing me up, trying to figure me out, which made me uncomfortable and nervous. Through a later conversation with him, I learned just how strict a life he was leading. Uptight would be a better word for it. He said that one day, as he was making his way to the ashram, a Western woman had stopped him to make conversation. As they were parting ways, she'd put her hand on his arm. Her touch felt like a scorpion sting, he said.

    Struggling to keep a straight face, I thought to myself, *Goodness gracious, I think we need to chill out a wee bit here. I'm all for leading a pure and chaste life. But a scorpion sting? Give me a break.* By this time I too had made my own vow of celibacy. After reading the various books on Hindu saints and learning that even the married ones practiced celibacy, I assumed that the rejection of sexuality was part and parcel of spirituality. Without contest I adopted the belief that denial of human pleasure was essential in order to know God. In my ignorance I assumed all the Westerners in Tiruvannamalai were following suit. Later on, when I discovered a few were dating each other, I was in shock. It never crossed my mind to explore their philosophy or to wonder if sexuality and spirituality were truly at odds with each other, as I believed. Instead, I simply made another assumption. *These people are not as serious about spirituality as I once thought.*

I may not have been as uptight as Nealu, but my beliefs were as rigid.

Considering Nealu's strict monastic ways, I wasn't terribly surprised when a week later I was given the news that my lunch services were no longer required. This happened when I was strolling home down my lane. I saw Nealu and Chandru exiting the gate of my compound. At first I was excited, thinking it was a social call. I was about to invite them in for tea when Nealu began nudging Chandru.

"Tell her, tell her," he sternly ordered.

"Umm, because I am a spiritual aspirant it is better that I cook my own food."

My heart sank with disappointment, and my blood curdled with anger.

"Fine, whatever you want. Sorry if my food has polluted you in any way," I scoffed and stormed through the gate.

Nealu is such a jerk. How dare he doubt my intentions? I slammed the door to my cottage, dove onto my cushy mattress, and stewed for a while.

Chandru continued to show up occasionally at Madhu's house to share more stories about Amma. I was taken aback one day when he mentioned that Nealu was also becoming interested, and that they were planning to go spend a few days with her. Nealu wanted to check her out for himself, to gauge if she was indeed the real deal. He was rather intellectually inclined. Furthermore, he had already spent many years with a guru who had recently passed away, so wasn't in any rush for another. The day before they were to leave, Chandru came to say goodbye. I made him promise to tell Amma about me and how eager I was to come see her. He said that he had already written to her about me. I had never told him my secret yearning, for I felt that my ambition was too presumptuous. So I nearly fainted with his next words.

"I'm disappointed Nealu didn't invite you. Amma really needs an attendant, and I think you would be perfect."

I was over the moon to hear him say that. It was my heart's desire to serve a female guru like Amma, and I was starting to believe it just might come true.

Full of emotion I replied, "I don't want to go for just a few days. She already has my heart. When I make it to her side, I will stay forever."

The words had no sooner left my lips than I was overcome with the most horrible anxiety. *But will she accept me?*

FIVE

BECOMING GAYATRI

Chandru and Nealu had been with Amma two days now, and I found myself constantly wondering what they were doing, what the place looked like, and how Nealu was faring with his health, among other things.

With a huge grin on my face, I replayed the words Chandru and I had exchanged the day before they left. With a slight snicker he said, "I warned Nealu that Amma sees everyone as her children, that she may stroke him and put his head in her lap."

"That was very wise of you," I replied with a giggle.

Despite Nealu's strong opinions and occasional heartless behavior, he intrigued me with his abundance of inspirational stories. I was starting to look up to him, somewhat.

I could hardly wait for these two pilgrims to return so that I could hear what Nealu had to say about Amma. Even more, I was anxious to hear what Amma had to say about me. I was concerned that Amma might not accept a white woman, or might deem me too unpure to serve her. I also felt there was another strike against me—I had no money.

I was told Amma's family were poor, so I knew they would not be able to support me no matter how much service I offered. By that point, I was buying supplies with the money obtained from selling bottles and cans at the local scrap center. I got my greens by climbing a ladder onto the roof of the main house and plucking the tender leaves of the drumstick tree. All I had to offer was a small collection of silver jewelry I had acquired in north India, and the pair of silver anklets I wore all the time, the ones I often caught myself staring at, thinking how pretty they were.

Even though a major part of me felt that I was where I was supposed to be, this scraping for food caused doubt to creep into my mind. *Am I really meant to be in India, or am I being stubborn and stupid by hanging onto this dream of serving a guru and finding God? Should I just call it quits, go to the Australian Embassy, and have them ship me back?* Despite my high-strung mind, which seemed to thrive on worry, somehow I always managed to conquer these bouts of fear. Often all it took was a word of advice or a sign in the form of a gift.

Around the same time the soles on my sandals completely wore out. Filled with remorse, I ceremoniously placed them on the garbage pile at the back of our compound and was left with no choice but to go barefoot everywhere. Summer or not, I still had to make the occasional trip into town. So I made sure to go either in the early morning or late evening to avoid the scorching ground. That time of year was uncomfortably hot, intolerable for most Westerners, who usually headed home or ran for the hill stations. One morning at the ashram I ran into a European lady I had spoken to a few times. She looked utterly exhausted, and her hair was stuck in thin clumps around her face from the sweat pouring off her forehead. Her eyes were sunken and her cheeks so flushed she seemed to have rubbed them with beet juice.

She looked at me with a strained smile and confessed, "I need to get out of here. I was going to stay another month, but I'm afraid it just might kill me. I have a bag of items I won't be needing. Can I give them to you?"

I happily accepted her kind offer, thinking that beggars can't be choosers. Upon arriving home, I emptied the contents of the bag onto my mattress. Lo

Holy Hell

and behold among other things, there they were—a pair of sandals exactly my size. Everything I needed seemed to show up just at the right time, down to a pair of shoes. I was astounded by the serendipity and dug my heels even harder into India.

Before heading to Amma's, Chandru had suggested I choose an Indian name for myself. He said it would be a nice gesture and might help Amma relate to me. "Nealu," although not an Indian name, was easy enough to pronounce, had an agreeable Indian ring, and was derived by merely adding a "u" to the end of "Neal." I liked the idea of changing my name, but I didn't want just any old name. It needed to feel right. For that to happen, I believed it needed to reveal itself. A couple of days later I was in Madhu's place listening to some classical Indian music. As I sat relaxed in the chair with my head bouncing and fingers tapping to the music, I happened to glance over to his collection of cassettes. "Oh my God, there it is. There's my name," I shouted leaping out of the chair. I grabbed the cassette, and as my heart pounded, I read out loud "Gayatri."

Somehow, I felt in my heart that Gayatri was my name. All I needed now was the nerve to refer to myself as such and get the name to stick.

Slowly but surely time elapsed and Nealu and Chandru returned from seeing Amma. I was dying to try out my new name, so I jovially introduced myself as if meeting them for the first time.

Bowing, with my hands cupped together I said, "Namaskaram. My name's Gayatri. Very pleased to meet you."

To my greatest joy their faces simultaneously lit up—they loved my new name. From that moment onward they only referred to me as Gayatri. Along with the new name, a brand new persona was emerging. Gail, along with much of who she used to be, was about to become a thing of the past. One could almost say that my taking the new name of Gayatri was the equivalent of a death sentence for Gail.

As I suspected he would, Nealu returned head-over-heels and utterly smitten with Amma. He was convinced she possessed genuine spiritual powers and was eager to spend more time with her. I sensed a definite transformation in him, a softening of his ways. He went on to say that over the next month he was going to pack his possessions, close up his house, and head back to Kerala. Just as I was thinking I would like to make the journey with him, he asked if I was coming too. I couldn't believe my ears and was extremely touched, for it was the first time he'd openly included or accepted me in any way.

I was thrilled knowing my dreams were only a hair's breadth away from becoming reality, and my days of yearning and pining would soon be over. Each night I happily drifted off to sleep knowing that when I awoke, I would be one day closer to Amma's side. Coupled with my excitement was also a bit of sorrow to leave Tiruvannamalai, a place I'd grown to love. I cherished the friendliness and simplicity of the people. I smiled at the fond memory of little children running around with their brown bottoms exposed to the world. I loved how people's eyes sparkled when they smiled, whether they were flashing a set of brilliant white teeth or their lips were curled around their gums. Even though they were poor, they were happy. I knew I would miss the powerful and serene atmosphere of the ashram and temple, and especially my quiet walks around the sacred mountain. I was grateful for the many blessings and spiritual experiences bestowed upon me in this holy town. Yet I felt certain that it was time to move on. I believed I was sufficiently exposed to Indian spiritual culture and that I was ready for a life of service and surrender.

On January 14, 1980, the three of us headed to the train station. Nealu purchased our one-way tickets to Amma, and I embarked on what would become a twenty-year phase of my life.

Chandru had suggested this date because it meant we would arrive the following morning on the auspicious day of Pongal, a harvest festival celebrated across most of India, the equivalent of Thanksgiving. Even though I felt in my heart I would stay in Kerala, my mind was experiencing its usual array of doubts. I therefore decided to play it safe. I closed up my cottage but did not let it go, not just yet. I boarded the train carrying just one bag filled with clothes, books, some personal items, and my silver jewelry.

After a short ride, we changed trains at Viluppuram and commenced our overnight journey to Quilon, a town about one hour from Amma's village. During our travel, Nealu shared his typical insightful, inspirational, and spiritual stories. Then he made a rather unusual observation and comment. Discreetly pointing to a family on the train, he lectured: "Oh, the nature of maya (illusion). People so desperately want children and believe that they will bring much happiness into their lives. Little do they know. In actual fact, the joy one gets from children is as much as you get from biting into a chocolate-covered turd."

I couldn't believe my ears and struggled not to laugh too hard. I didn't want to ruffle Nealu's feathers, especially after he had been so kind to buy my train ticket, so I bit my tongue. I did, however, sit there thinking, *Goodness gracious dude, you've really got problems. You don't want children, I get it. Frankly, neither do I. But for heaven's sake, leave people alone.* For the rest of the journey he remained in good spirits, with less judgmental and far more uplifting tales to tell.

When I awoke the following morning, I noticed how green and lush Kerala was compared to Tamil Nadu. The air, although thick with humidity, was sweet and moist. As far as the eye could see, there were acres and acres of rice fields, jungle, and coconut trees. Like an excited child, I sat gazing out the window, taking deep breaths, inhaling the fresh air. Water was plentiful. The train rushed over several bridges suspended high above swollen rivers. For a brief moment, my mind flew back to my home in Australia where the familiar musty, leafy, perfume of bush creeks scented the air. In my childhood, especially on a sweltering summer's day, we frequently headed to the country to cool off in one of the many water holes at our disposal. Getting there was the most unpleasant part, for it meant being squished on the backseat of the car, along with my two brothers and little sister. Our elder brother, for whatever reason, gained immense delight in poking, jabbing, and annoying the living daylights out of us. After sufficient provocation, the inevitable always happened. The back seat turned into a boxing ring, with name-calling and fistfights. From the front seat Mum would turn around and tell us to be quiet. Her efforts had very little to no affect in controlling this unruly bunch.

No longer able to tolerate the racket, Dad would glare into the rear vision mirror and bellow, "Cut it out, you bloody brats, or I'll turn the car around and take you all home."

That usually kept us quiet for a little while. As soon as the cool air from a nearby creek came gushing through the windows, all tension subsided. If I were fortunate enough to be sitting by a window, I'd stick my head out and take a few long, exaggerated whiffs, as my heart filled with excitement. Within seconds of the vehicle coming to a halt, our bare feet hastily scampered across the smooth rocks, and with a mighty splash we'd enter the water. An alternate form of entry, if available, was to swing by a rope hanging from one of the trees. Running at top speed, we'd make the Tarzan call as we went flying through the air. We swam and played for hours on end, sometimes climbing on Dad's shoulders and using him as a diving board. All the while, Mum remained seated upon a blanket at the shore in her pretty floral sundress with legs elegantly folded to the side as she kept a watchful eye from behind her white-rimmed sunglasses. Only after being told repeatedly it was time to go home, would we finally obey. Then like water-logged sea creatures, one by one, we resurfaced from the depths. We giggled and stared with amusement at the skin on our fingers, which had puckered like prunes.

We pilgrims hopped off the train in Quilon and headed to a family's home that Chandru had pre-arranged so we could bathe and change into clean clothes. After we were all fresh, the family sat us down for a delicious home-cooked breakfast. But I found it hard to eat. I had butterflies in my belly.

We then caught a taxi for the remainder of the journey. My heart was pounding with excitement as my mind rehearsed different versions of this upcoming meeting. After taking a left off the main road, the taxi twisted and turned through narrow roads lined with trees, rice fields, and the occasional house. Eventually we came to the small town of Vallikavu, which took no more than one minute to pass through. The road grew narrower still. To the left was a canal containing disgusting water. Just as I began to screw my face up from the stench, Chandru laughed and said, "Don't be alarmed. It's low tide, and the smell is from coconut husks soaking in the water. It's a step they do before pounding them to remove the fiber, which is then turned into rope."

The stink was repulsive, and I had trouble believing it was coming from innocent coconut husks. But I dropped the issue. I had more exciting things to think about.

The taxi stopped. We had reached a dead end. Before us was a wide river waiting to be crossed.

Below to our right was a sun-dried old man standing beside a large wooden canoe waving his arms, beckoning us to get in.

I climbed down the concrete steps. Then with one hand holding my bag and the other lifting my sari, I stepped up and over into the canoe. The craft began rolling from side to side. I fumbled to keep my balance and stay upright. Quickly I leaned forward, placed my hand on the nearest plank, and sat with a thud. I clutched tightly onto the wooden beam and my bag of personal possessions and precious offerings.

Letting go for a second, I lifted the hem of my sari out of the yucky puddle of water dancing around my feet and wedged the fabric between my knees. Once we were all safely seated, the old man lifted a long pole from inside the canoe, dug it into the riverbed, and propelled us forward.

Amma lived in a tiny fishing village called Parayakadavu, which was situated on a thirty-mile-long peninsula that thrust between the ocean and this brackish river. Looking across the landscape, I failed to see any houses or sign of life for that matter. All I could see for miles and miles were coconut trees. As we drew nearer to shore, I finally caught sight of a congregation of women surrounded by water pots. They were squabbling and yelling at each other. Another thing I noticed was the absence of a landing. We were going to have to wade through the water. At times like these, I found wearing a sari to be quite the nuisance. Holding the sari up over my knees, I carefully stepped out of the canoe into the water just to feel slimy mud squish up between my toes. My body cringed when thoughts flashed through my mind of what else might be lurking therein.

We were in a remote fishing village, a place rarely frequented by the likes of us.

As we made our way past the women, the squabbling hushed. They stood in astonishment watching such strange-looking white people go by. Suddenly they began laughing and pointing at us, and cackling like a bunch of hens.

Chandru explained that this was the only water pipe in the village. So this was where I too would need to go for water. With this vital piece of information in mind, I politely smiled back. I didn't want to get on the wrong side of these women.

Children nearly peeing their pants with excitement came running and screaming, "Sayippu, madama! Sayippu, madama!" The translation was obvious: "White man, white woman!"

I could see there were only two types of dwellings in the village. One was a simple hut made of woven coconut palms with thatched roof. The other was a basic structure of plastered brick. The sandy lane meandered aimlessly through the village. Looking ahead, I could see that the path wound its way to the right, forced that way by the impassable presence of a swampy lagoon. Not knowing which way we were going, I was taken by surprise when Chandru suddenly turned left off the path between two homes. After a few more steps, I noticed a young man meditating in front of a small shrine. That's when it hit me.

We had reached Amma.

Instantly, my heart started to pound. I stood motionless in the sand, frantically looking around, expecting Amma to come rushing out from somewhere. Before me was a simple plastered home and shrine set amidst a dozen or so coconut trees, surrounded on three sides by swamp. There was a small cowshed on the far side of the property but no cow in sight.

Sensing our arrival the young Indian man who had been meditating came over to greet us. Straightaway I noticed his radiant face and that same sparkle in the eyes I'd seen in people of Tiruvannamalai. He was strikingly handsome with dreamy brown eyes and a thick head of stylishly groomed wavy hair. His nose was distinguished, his beard and moustache neatly trimmed, his skin a rich golden hue, and his build trim. In slightly awkward English with a heart-warming smile, he introduced himself as Balu.

He told us that Amma was at a nearby house taking a bath. But that she should be back soon.

Letting out a sigh, I plunked myself down in front of the temple. The suspense was killing me.

No sooner had I sat than a short, dark-skinned woman dressed in a bright green ankle-length skirt, white shirt, and head shawl came around the corner. She was beaming a huge smile and hurrying toward us.

It was Amma.

All of a sudden, Nealu and Chandru were face-first in the sand, doing full-length prostrations. I felt embarrassed and unsure if I was supposed to do the same. I didn't recall ever seeing women do that. Instead, I made my usual prostration, which was to kneel and bow. She gently tapped me on the shoulder. Then she grabbed Nealu and Chandru by the hand and sat them next to her in front of the temple. She looked at me and smiled, motioning for me to sit as well. Chandru introduced me to Amma, after which she uttered something.

"What did she say?" I eagerly asked, hoping for some incredibly profound or prophetic first words.

"She likes your anklets."

Shyly I slightly lifted my sari, looked at my ankles for a second, then smiled back at her. I hadn't known what to predict about this first meeting, but I certainly hadn't expected her to compliment my jewelry.

Nevertheless, her comment helped me relax and settle down a bit. Sitting off to the side, I was keenly studying Amma and her white smile, which shone in brilliant contrast to her deep complexion. Her slightly damp, thick, raven-black hair with its moderate waves hung gracefully over her shoulders. Even though she was short, and her hands and feet delicate, her build was solid and strong. I smiled with affection when I noticed how her ears stuck out slightly, and I remember thinking how cute they looked. The language barrier was frustrating, so then and there I became determined to overcome that obstacle as soon as possible. My heart and mind were racing with a wild mixture of emotions ranging from love, awe, excitement, and reverence, to fear, unease, and curiosity.

It never crossed my mind to exercise a little prudence, discernment, or the healthy application of doubt. She *had* to be the real deal. What else was I going to do—go back to Australia?

Shortly afterward, we were called into the house for lunch, where I was introduced to the rest of her family. Amma lived with her parents, three brothers, and two of her three sisters. (One sister was already married.) The house was very basic with three bedrooms, tiny shrine room, large dining room, a firewood kitchen, and concrete floors throughout. The dining room felt empty, occupied only by the lonely presence of a long wooden table and bench. The only furniture in Amma's room was a single bed, which was pressed against the back wall by a window, and a small metal trunk. A straw mat lay crookedly on the floor, and a few items of clothing were messily flung over a rope that stretched across the room. I was told Amma didn't spend much time in the house and rarely slept there. She much preferred to be outside at the foot of a coconut tree, or inside the temple or cowshed.

This being the holy day of Pongal, a small celebration was to take place that afternoon. A statue of Krishna had been brought out from the shrine and placed in the center of the verandah. A brass lamp had been lit before it. On top of a banana leaf, lay offerings—a mound of puffed rice, a large ball of brown sugar, and a few bananas. Some five or six devotees showed up, along with a small group of young women from the village, two of whom were Amma's cousins. Shortly afterward, to the accompaniment of harmonium, tambourine, and hand bells, they sang Hare Rama, Hare Krishna to various melodies. People took turns walking around the lamp and statue as they sang, using graceful bounding steps in time with the music. I was quite content sitting off to the side on a straw mat observing and singing along. That's when Chandru beckoned me to join. Never having liked the spotlight, I shook my head and waved my hand signaling that I was fine where I was. Amma disagreed. She turned her head, looked straight at me, and pointed to the stage.

"Shit," I mumbled to myself as I reluctantly got up.

It was the most dreadful experience. I felt ever so self-conscious as I strutted like a tin soldier around the lamp. Back in Australia at the disco, I had no problem letting my limbs fly. I used to shake my bootie for hours on end. But this was different. People were dancing from their hearts to the Lord's name. I wasn't used to this and most definitely was not about to fake it. After some twenty minutes of this torture, one of the girls from the village asked for my place. Breathing a sigh of relief I replied, "It would be my pleasure," and I slid off the stage back to my seat.

I was looking forward to the evening because Amma was going to be performing Krishna (a Hindu deity portrayed as a prankster, divine hero, and the Supreme Being) and then Devi (Divine Mother) bhava.

In the devotional traditions, bhava means the mood of ecstasy, also the channeling of emotional energies induced by the intensity of devotion to one's object of devotion. In Amma's case, I was informed, these manifestations had nothing to do with possession, when a spirit or deity temporarily takes over a body. Amma was supposedly in full control and manifesting these gods to enhance the devotion of the attendees, and for the good of the world. It was explained to me that Amma says she is like a tap and controls the amount of water, or in this case, spiritual power that is released. That she is only manifesting an infinitesimal part of her power during these bhavas, and if she revealed her full power, nobody could come near her!

I was informed that people would start showing up around five, so I decided to freshen up beforehand. I knew there was no such thing as running water, but my hosts indicated that I could find some water in clay pots at the rear of the house, by the toilet and bathroom. When I turned the corner, my jaw dropped in horror at the sight of the facilities. The so-called bathroom was nothing more than a shoulder-high enclosure made of woven coconut branches with gaping holes everywhere. Crows were scavenging in the dirt, lifting their tails, and pooping everywhere. One of them sat on the fence obnoxiously cawing and giving me dirty looks. Three grubby, chipped, and cracked clay pots lay sideways in the filthy sand. The toilet was an outhouse perched over the swamp at the end of a six-foot plank with an old rice sack hanging at the entry for a modicum of privacy. The Malayalam word for toilet is kakkoos, and the term seemed to fit this contraption perfectly.

I grabbed one of the pots, cautiously wiped the sand off its bottom, placed it on my hip like a true Indian woman, and made my way down the lane to the community water pipe. Much to my dismay the place was deserted except for an enormous quantity of pots scattered around. As it turned out, the water only flowed for a few unannounced hours during the day and late at night. Immediately I understood why the women had been squabbling earlier that morning. India had already taught me to lead a simple life with few luxuries, but this place really pushed me over the edge. Suddenly I longed for my water well back in Tiruvannamalai.

A girl who must have been watching my disappointment came out from the teashop, invited me in, and handed me a cup of tea. Without uttering a word—not that I would have understood anyhow—she grabbed my clay pot and promptly returned it full of water. Her welcoming and sweet gestures temporarily pacified my frustration, and I headed back to the house with a smile on my face.

In the bathroom, the overpowering stench of stale urine almost knocked me over. Trying not to cry I placed my pot of water in the sand. Inside was a large chunk of granite. I assumed I was supposed to stand on the granite to prevent the sand from splashing on me as I bathed. I thought it best to do an un-dress rehearsal by stepping on the rock to see what body parts might expose themselves to the world. The results were instant. *No way in hell am I going to stand in here naked.* I took off my sari and flung it over the front of the enclosure, careful not to place it in any crow poop. Holding my breath I squatted, took off my blouse, and tied my underskirt up over my breasts. Standing, I tipped the pot of water over myself thinking there has to be an easier way.

With the bathing ordeal complete, I sloppily draped the sari over my bare shoulders and around my wet skirt then swished my way to Amma's room, where she had told me to keep my things. After changing into a fresh set of clothes, I grabbed the straw mat that lay crookedly on the floor, gave it a shake, and then positioned it near the end of Amma's bed. I lay there for a while and soaked up the excitement of finally being in my dream position—at Amma's feet.

A while later the door pushed open. One of Amma's cousins entered the room. She began removing items from the solitary metal trunk that was pressed against the wall. I sat up and watched with curious delight. Out came a brightly colored skirt with shimmers of gold brocade, a sparkly yellow shawl, and a pair of ankle bells, also costume jewelry and a silver crown with peacock feathers popping out the top. From the adjacent room she yanked a dirty blanket off the bed, spread it on the floor, and then neatly ironed the skirt into four-inch pleats. She took a grubby comb and a tin of talcum powder from the sister's room, and then made her way to the temple with these various objects.

I decided to tag along, keenly observing each step, for it was my hope to be taking care of all this very soon. Amma's cousin displayed the jewelry, anklets, and crown on a knee-high wooden stool, and then she placed the clothes in the corner on top of a straw mat.

At five-thirty the singing began. Amma sat with her back against the right wall of the shrine with a small audience facing her. A slow and constant stream of people began to arrive from the village and nearby towns. Most of them, however, were not coming to see Amma.

They were awaiting her embodiment of Krishna and then of Devi.

After approximately one hour of singing, Amma stood and entered the shrine, signaling me to follow. Two of her cousins jumped up and came inside as well, closed the door, and bolted it. Amma changed into the sparkly skirt, ran the dirty comb through her hair, dusted some talcum powder on her face, placed a large spot of sandalwood paste on her forehead, strapped the ankle bells on, and she was ready for the next phase.

The girls opened the doors while Amma sat on the floor facing the Krishna statue soulfully singing a prayer. Within a couple of minutes she dramatically jumped off the floor, made her way to the back of the shrine where she stood facing the crowd, and placed one foot on the stool. Her entire body was vibrating. Her hands now formed mudras (symbolic or ritual gestures), and the bells around her ankles jingled excitedly, announcing the arrival of the god Krishna. With hands cupped in reverence and eyes overflowing with love, devotees cried out, "Krishna, Krishna."

The glittery shawl was draped around Amma's neck, and she was adorned with flower garlands, costume jewelry, and the silver crown. A multi-tiered lamp brimming with golden flames of camphor was waved before her, and the temple bells rang loudly. Her silver crown and many ornaments shimmered in the golden glow. The camphor slowly died in its final act of surrender. Then swiftly the first chords of the harmonium filled the air along with the delightful resonance of the Lord's name. Slowly Amma opened her eyes, bestowing a gracious smile upon everyone.

Congregated outside the temple doors, children were bubbling with excitement, pushing and shoving to be first in line. Glancing in their direction, Amma gave a gentle nod. Instantly the grubby bunch rushed into the temple, now on their best behavior. They stood patiently in line with their dreamy brown eyes fixated upon her. One by one they stretched out a right hand, into which Amma placed a tiny piece of banana. Like clockwork the little ones devoured the fruit, stretched their hands out again, and received a smidgen of sacred ash. Amma then placed one hand on each child's forehead, tilting his or her head back slightly to pour a few drops of holy water into an expectant mouth. In a flash of excitement the children turned and ran outside with giggly smiles on their faces.

I stood in the corner of the temple and watched with amazement as Amma began receiving the grown-ups. To the distressed she offered compassionate, loving smiles of consolation. She wiped tears from their eyes. Others, who were obviously ardent Krishna devotees, she greeted with mischievous smiles, laughter, and teasing pranks as part of Krishna's playful nature.

One such recipient was Amma's grandmother. This eighty-year-old woman stood in line with her bent knees, her lunged-forward hips, and one hand pressed at her waist to support her fragile body. Her sagging ear lobes each had a hole large enough to poke your little finger through. Her skin was

Holy Hell

deeply lined with wrinkles, yet her hair was shiny raven black without one strand of gray. Her eyes shined with love, and a toothless smile spread across her face as she waited eagerly for her turn. Amma used the glittery shawl draped around her neck to tie the old woman's hands together, keeping her captive for half an hour. Meanwhile, she repeatedly teased by pretending to pour water in her mouth, keeping the old woman with mouth gaping wide open. Before releasing her, Amma ripped a couple of large flowers out of her own garland and placed them through the gaping holes in those sagging ear lobes.

The woman exited the temple in a state of rapture, proudly showing her new ornaments to the crowd that was roaring with laughter.

Thanks to all this—the melodious devotional songs filling the air, the strangers transported by devotion, the stirring ambiance inside the temple—my heart was soaring through heavenly realms. I felt unbelievably happy. I stood quietly in the corner with tears of joy gliding down my face.

SIX

THE ANKLETS

After the conclusion of Krishna Bhava and a brief intermission, Amma returned to the temple to perform Devi Bhava (the goddess mood). This second transformation proved to be a very different and rather more intense experience. I was told that Amma was about to embody the fierce personality of Kali, the goddess of destruction of time, change, and death. I was also told she didn't like women touching her when she was manifesting these qualities. I found this prohibition odd. I couldn't understand why a so-called "divine mother" would be partial to the touch of men versus women. The warning set me in a not-so-relaxed mood, and I was nervous about what was to come—especially when I saw a trident and sword in the temple. After Amma enters her Devi mood, I was cautioned, she charges out of the temple to dance, and it's best to step outside at that time. Even though I didn't understand the logic or quite grasp what on earth they were talking about, I was absolutely fine with the idea of keeping a safe distance.

Amma sat on the floor of the temple once again. But this time she sang a prayer to the Divine Mother. As soon as she entered her Kali mood, the cousins fled, the doors to the temple slammed shut, and an Indian man assisted her as she donned a silk sari. He handed her the sword and trident and swiftly unbolted the door. Then, with amazing speed, Amma leapt out onto the verandah. I couldn't believe my eyes. She was dancing wildly to the music, twirling around and around, waving her sword through the air. I gasped in horror a couple of times when the musicians ducked as the sword came gyrating above their heads. Sparks flew into the air when her sword struck the ground or collided with the pillars a couple of times.

I felt a tap on my shoulder. It was the Indian man with a concerned look on his face shooing me out of the temple. As I looked outside, I thought, *You've got to be kidding. Go now and get myself decapitated?* Right at that moment though, Amma leapt off the verandah and headed towards the men who stood in line around the perimeter of the property.

"Oh, now I get it," I said out loud. Giving him a nervous smile, I dashed out of the temple and stood with the women who lined the opposite side of the property.

In almost drunken fashion, Amma made her way along the line of thirty men, tapping each of them on the shoulder with her sword. A few yards from where I was standing, a woman began shouting and making all kinds of weird noises. Her arms hung limply by her side, her entire body jerked uncontrollably, and her head rolled from side to side. Suddenly Amma came swirling across the courtyard, ran straight up to the woman, lunged the trident through her hair, and flung her to the ground. Amma's eyes were glistening but barely open. She began shouting angrily at the woman, and in between, I could hear her teeth grinding. Amma cried out for some sacred ash, which arrived with amazing speed. Taking a fistful of the ash, she ordered the woman to stand up. Then she threw the ash in the woman's face. I watched transfixed in terror. My eyes must have been popping out of my head.

I later learned that an evil spirit had possessed the woman, and that Amma was commanding it to leave. These theatrics were all very strange, but I found them fascinating, as though I were watching a real-life horror movie.

Once the exorcism was complete, Amma ran back onto the verandah of the temple, whirled around a few more times, then dashed inside. The doors slammed shut behind her. I quickly took a seat outside. Within a few minutes, the doors re-opened, and Amma was seated on the wooden stool. This time her face looked quite different. The playful and lighthearted facial expressions of Krishna had been replaced by the sultry and serious mood of Kali. Once again Amma was laden in costume jewelry and an even more elaborate silver crown. She held the sword and trident in her hands and, as before, her entire body was vibrating as the temple bells rang loudly.

The Indian man waved the burning camphor lamp before her, and worshipped her feet with flower petals as she sat with eyes closed and lips tightly sealed with a downward smirk. Eventually, she opened her eyes, handed the sword and trident to her attendant, threw a few handfuls of petals before herself, and nodded at the first man in line. I noted that no women entered the temple. They all stood in line outside, looking rather anxious, and waiting for Amma to give them the okay before daring to enter.

This time I wasn't standing in the temple shedding tears of joy but gratefully seated outside in a state of fear and awe.

I was happy and excited to have finally made it to Amma's side, but I still had two major concerns tormenting me.

Would Amma accept me?

If she did, how would I support myself?

Nealu and Chandru were aware of my plight and promised to ask Amma about my situation when the time was right. In my heart I had a feeling that the financially secure Nealu might wind up supporting me. All I needed (or so I thought at the time) was food and clothing. However, I barely knew him. As I said before, he wasn't the most warm-and-fuzzy person I'd ever met. So I let go of that idea.

A couple of days later I noticed Amma sitting on the far corner of the property at the base of a coconut tree talking to Nealu and Chandru. My heart began to race. I was on pins and needles wondering if their topic of discussion might be "Gayatri."

Holy Hell

I sat in front of the temple and keenly watched from a distance as my mind foolishly tried to imagine the gist of their conversation. After what seemed like forever, they got up. Nealu, spotting me in front of the temple, headed my way. Even though this man was frail, he walked tall with a graceful bounce to his step, and his face emitted an enormous amount of spiritual light.

With much elation in his voice he said, "Amma would like you to stay. In exchange for your services to her, I have agreed to support you financially."

Upon hearing these words, my heart skipped a beat. I was deeply moved by his unexpected, yet much hoped for, generous offer. I was even more ecstatic with the news that Amma was accepting me into her service. All my dreams had come true, and I was jumping for joy. I refrained from giving Nealu a hug, but I did thank him profusely.

Now that I was officially in her service, the first thing I wanted to do was buy Amma some clothes and personal items. I expressed my wish to Nealu, and he liked the idea. So the following day we headed out together to the nearby town of Oachira. One of the first things I bought was a comb so that she didn't have to use the communal one ever again. I purchased a few pieces of floral fabric to be stitched into skirts, also a few yards of white fabric for short-sleeved shirts. Guessing her size, I also bought some bras and panties plus a variety of toiletries. Excitedly I also bought a few yards of shiny fabric, which I planned to stitch into a Krishna skirt myself. Much to my surprise, Nealu then pointed to a collection of white saris, suggested I choose a couple for myself, and asked if there was anything else I needed. A softer side of Nealu was beginning to seep through his disciplined exterior. My heart filled with the warm love of a little sister.

My next assignment was to take over the set-up of the temple and the care of Amma's bhava clothes and ornaments. Her cousins weren't upset in the slightest by my enthusiasm. They seemed content just to spend time in the temple when Amma got ready. Her sisters, however, were another story. From their perspective, Amma was Sudhamani, their sister, and they were used to sharing everything, down to underwear. So naturally, it didn't go over too well when I tried to implement rules such as: "You cannot touch Amma's things." I became rather obsessed with keeping her clothes clean, ironed, and neatly in place, and I was infuriated if I entered her room and found things missing.

One day I made the grave mistake of confronting one of her sisters.

"That's *Amma's* bra!" I angrily exclaimed, pointing at the dirty strap poking out of the neckline of her blouse.

I couldn't understand what she said, but I didn't really need to. Her tone got the point across. All I could hear was her shrill voice screaming: "Blah, blah, waaah ... madama (white woman) sniff, shriek, vlaavlaa, vija! Kaakaaa madama!"

In her opinion I was nothing but a troublemaker "madama" who had no right preventing them from wearing their sister's clothes. This was a point, however, upon which I strongly begged to differ.

During the early years, Amma only bathed on her Krishna and Devi days, which were Tuesday, Thursday, and Sunday. She would then go to either of two homes in the village, where the women fought over who got to bathe her. I was amazed at the affection these women held for her and imagined that they didn't even know why they felt the way they did. I curiously observed that Amma behaved like a simple village girl as she sat among these women on the floor in her petticoat. Over laughter and cheerful conversation, the neighbor women lavishly coated Amma's hair with coconut oil and massaged her scalp. After the oil had soaked in, they proceeded to the outdoor bathing space. I chose to stay inside to give them some privacy. Within a couple of minutes I heard laughter.

I couldn't resist.

I peeked inside the enclosure but spontaneously jumped backwards and let out a tiny squeal of embarrassment. Amma was stark naked, covered in soap lather, not at all self-conscious as the women scrubbed her body.

The startled look on my face made them laugh even harder.

After the bath, the women dressed Amma in a fresh set of clothes that they had washed and saved from a previous visit. One of the women then ran to the kitchen to prepare tea and snacks while the other stood behind Amma towel-drying her hair. On one such day Amma jumped out of her chair and, to my astonishment, sat in my lap and gave me a big hug. She said something in Malayalam that the villager translated into broken English.

"Gayatri will work and work and work, then die in Amma."

I was stunned by this statement and interpreted "dying in Amma" to mean become spiritually one with her. I felt elated to know that according to Amma's words I would achieve my goal of becoming one with God. At least that is how I understood the translation at the time.

For all I know Amma could have said, "Gayatri will work herself to death for me."

I was speechless.

After a few moments, I noticed once again that Amma was gazing at my anklets. This time I thought, *Why don't I just give them to her.* I'd already handed over my silver collection, which was being made into a crown for Krishna, so why not these too. Acting on impulse, I reached down to unhook them.

As I did so, I noticed that Amma was removing the ones she was wearing.

I rose to my feet, bowed before her, and with deep emotion tied them around her ankles.

Much to my surprise, before I could move back to my seat, Amma tied her anklets on me.

At the time, I viewed it as a marriage of my soul to hers.

Back then, when possible, Amma spent most of her time outdoors. Many nights we slept in the open beneath a blanket of stars. I loved lying there in the soft sand gazing up at the moon and a myriad of twinkling stars. After I lay down, Amma had this peculiar habit of lying diagonally across the two mats with her legs on top of me. Even though I treasured these moments and was delighted by her playful ways, sometimes the sleeping position turned into torture. Her legs were sturdy, and they became heavy after a while. But

I dared not move lest I disturb her sleep. Often I lay there for hours in sweet agony, not praying for devotion but, *Please, please, please roll over*—especially if I needed to get up and pee.

Among the many people who regularly attended these evenings was a group of young men from Haripad, a small town some twenty minutes away. Because Amma's father opposed their visiting at other times, they had to make the most out of these evenings to spend time with Amma. After Devi Bhava, I sat inside the temple while they all talked, laughed, and joked until the wee hours of the morning. I caught Amma several times yawning and rubbing her eyes, but she never said that she needed to sleep. Some nights she would get up, go to her room, and lie on the bed. The men then scurried to the back of the house and huddled around her window to continue their tales. They were nice enough fellows and seemed very fond of Amma. But after a couple of weeks and many sleepless nights, I began to view their behavior as inconsiderate. I used to think, *Okay, come chat and laugh for an hour or so, but when you see her yawning, can't you take the hint and show some respect?* Knowing Amma would never say anything, I decided it was time for an intervention.

Because I desired to understand Amma's needs and what she was saying, I quickly picked up a few words of Malayalam such as comb, skirt, bath, water, sleep, and eat. Amma's elder sister spoke a little English, so with her assistance I learned my first sentence in Malayalam. I told her what I wanted to say, then listened carefully to her translation, wrote the words down phonetically, and repeated them over and over until I had them memorized. I was armed and ready with my verbal ammunition for these poor unsuspecting chaps. The following evening after about an hour of them peering through the window and much small talk, I stood up and said, *"Kure divasangalaayittu amma urangiyittilla; dayavaayi ningal onnu poku"*. This meant, "Amma hasn't slept in many days, so please leave." Amma leapt off her bed and began laughing hysterically when she heard me blurt out my first sentence in Malayalam. I was not at all confident with my pronunciation, but everyone seemed to have understood. The men at the window were stunned and didn't quite know what to think. But seeing Amma laugh, they joined in—until, that is, they realized I was dead serious. Suddenly they were staring at each other. The expressions on their faces switched from amusement to bewilderment and annoyance. I wasn't privy to the rest of the conversation that evening. But I do know that they left after ten minutes and were much more courteous in the future. Amma didn't seem to mind my stepping in. She used this incident as a humorous conversation piece for quite some time.

My dream of living in Amma's presence and being her personal attendant had come true. However, along with that glory came a lot more work than I had ever imagined. I soon realized there were many basic duties I needed to perform every day. For example, getting water onto the property was a major ordeal, and it took many years before we got a direct water line from the county. As water only flowed from the community pipe a few hours each day, Nealu had a small concrete storage tank built at the front of the house. In the middle of the night, Amma's sister and I would haul fresh water for cooking the following day's meals, then two buckets each, over and over until the tank was full. This was an arduous task.

The tank water was used mainly for bathing. Thanks to the fact that the kakkoos (toilet) was perched over the swamp, we didn't have to haul any water for flushing. After you walked the plank and took care of your business, an all-natural, instant form of recycling took place. Hearing the splash, tiny fish zeroed in like torpedoes and, amidst violent thrashing, feasted like frenzied piranhas.

Due to the shortage of water, laundry had to be done elsewhere. Once a week I'd tie a huge pile of Amma's, Nealu's, and my dirty clothes into a sheet, throw the load over my shoulder, and head to a house we called Akkara Veedu (house across the river). I enjoyed this task immensely even though it meant walking two miles each way. The mother at Akkara Veedu and her daughters had been friends of Amma's family for years. Amma frequently visited their home and would sometimes stay overnight, so these people knew me well. They were poor, and their home was simple, but it was set on a few acres of land amidst lush foliage and tall trees. The place had an amazingly serene feel to it. In front of the house, nestled behind tall bushes and a neatly swept courtyard, were shrines with tiny clay oil lamps flickering in the breeze. Local beliefs held that snake gods inhabited this land. So in order to live in harmony alongside the snake gods, the family had built these shrines and set out daily offerings.

Whenever I arrived, the mother came running out to greet me with a warm hug and an enormous toothless smile. She would exclaim, "Gayatri mol (daughter)." The woman was barely five feet tall with a petite frame tortured by years of hard labor. Her skin was prematurely aged and crinkly, yet it was soft, and her big brown eyes were set deeply in her gaunt face. As swiftly as she came out to greet me, she would scurry off to the kitchen to make me a cup of tea in typical Indian hospitality. While the tea was brewing, I took the clothes to the washing area situated at the far end of the property by a pond, and I sorted them into three separate piles. The washing stone was a large chunk of granite propped up at one end about eighteen inches off the ground. Tucking the hem of my skirt up at the waist, I carefully waded into the pond so as not to stir up any silt, and I collected water to soak the clothes. After I finished slowly sipping on my tea, I would handwash everything with the aid of a scrubbing brush and occasional pounding on the rock. The daughters all worked very hard running the household and making rope for their livelihood, yet they insisted on helping me rinse and hang the clothes. By the end, I was exhausted, filthy, soaking wet, and covered in soap, but I always felt great satisfaction watching the clean clothes flapping and dancing in the gentle breeze. After I bathed, it was off to the kitchen, where I sat cross-legged on the floor and consumed a wonderful home-cooked meal of rice and curry. It was from close contact with women like these that I learned a lot about the cuisine, culture, and generosity of the Indian people.

By the time I had finished my lunch, the clothes were usually dry. So I would take them off the line one by one, neatly fold them, tie up the bundle, and head home. Often I had to rush because I needed to be back in time for my cherished sunset duties. Before daylight faded, I always swept inside the temple and the verandah with a specially designated brush. Then with a thigh-high broom made from the inner stem of coconut branches, I swept the sand around the temple. I particularly enjoyed seeing the clean, semi-circular strokes in the sand. The process was a form of meditation for me. After washing my hands, I'd sprinkle holy water in and around the temple and light the oil lamps. Dusk was notably serene in the village. With the setting of the sun, peace would enter my heart. From neighboring homes, the fragrance of incense wafted through the air carrying faint whispers of, "It's time to pray." Crows finally ceased their incessant and pesky cawing and were settling down for the night. Women dropped their chores—even if only for a short while—and sat before an oil lamp. With not-so-melodious voices but hearts full of emotion, they sang simple songs of praise to their God. At dusk the sea breeze softened, giving gentle kisses as it passed by, and it seemed as though all of nature would slip into prayerful silence.

SEVEN

AN ASHRAM IS BORN

Several weeks had passed since we arrived at Amma's, and the whole time Nealu had been camped out in a tiny room at the front of her house in the midst of her family's daily activities and racket. Even though they were hospitable and gracious, especially because he suffered from extreme migraines, this wasn't an ideal living situation. Nealu desperately needed peace and quiet. So he asked Amma if he could build a small hut on the far side of the property. Amma told him she had to run it by her father because the land was in his name. Much to our surprise, the father readily agreed. Dimensions were decided upon, money exchanged, local laborers hired, and—under the supervision of Amma's father—construction commenced.

Within a few days something didn't seem right. The concrete foundation was huge, and there were poles creating a dividing wall, as if there were going to be two structures. With Chandru's assistance, the matter was brought to Amma's attention, and before our eyes she flew into a rage and stormed toward the house.

We scurried behind her not quite sure what was going on, but we refrained from entering the house. We waited outside while she engaged in a heated argument with her father. Neither of them seemed to care much about restraint, so the volume continued to escalate as each tried to emphasize an opposing point of view. The only words I could make out were sayippu (white man), panam (money), and kallan (thief).

Turning to Chandru, I asked, "What are they saying?" I was quickly hushed.

My frustration from having to rely on a translator was mounting, and this incident only intensified my desire to master the Malayalam language as soon as possible.

Wearing an air of victory and a smile on her face, Amma exited the house and said "va" (come). We crossed the sandy compound, and, while we stood before the early stages of the hut, she revealed the truth. Nealu and I were in shock when we learned that her father had enlarged the plans to include a shop so he that could sell items to visitors on Bhava nights. His little business venture came to a screeching halt, and Nealu was stuck with a hut much larger than originally agreed upon.

Amma's father was short and stocky with dyed moustache, huge belly, and legs as bowed as though he were riding a horse. He came across as arrogant, aggressive, and money-obsessed. He was rarely found in a prayerful pose. Quite the opposite of Amma's mother, who was devoutly religious, soft spoken (most of the time), humble, and pious. Her father also had this disgusting habit of strutting around with his dhoti folded above the knees and no underwear. How do I know this you may wonder? One day, it so happened I was facing his direction when he bent over, and let's just say I was reminded of the rear end of a bull. I wasn't the only one to have been graced with such a sight, and it was a common joke among many of us.

On one such day Amma screamed, "Dad, go put on some underwear," as she fell to the ground in fits of laughter. Her mother, turning red in the face, slapped him across the arm then mumbled and grumbled something as she stormed into the house. But nobody could convince him to change his ways. The only solution was to quickly turn your head whenever you got the slightest hint he was about to bend over.

However, like everyone, he did have some good qualities. Thankfully a sense of humor was one.

Within a week or so the hut was complete, and Nealu, breathing a sigh of relief, moved into his new digs. Unfortunately his dream of being able to rest undisturbed was short-lived.

Viewing the hut as a haven from the harsh regulations of Amma's father, Balu and a gentle-natured lad named Sreekumar took a gamble and began sleeping there after Bhava nights. For whatever reason, the old man never uttered a word. Once they realized their risk had paid off, they began staying several days in a row. Amma spent hours on end in the hut with these young fellows—talking, laughing, and practicing bhajans (devotional songs) while Nealu lay in the corner in blissful agony. At mealtime, it became a ritual for her to make little balls out of her rice and curry and hand-feed one to each of us "children." I was never that enthused about the custom, but I participated. I wanted to feel included.

Eventually, a couple more of these spiritual sons (as they were called) arrived, and the duration of visits increased. Meals were still being prepared by Amma's mother and sister. It was obvious that the work of feeding these extra mouths was starting to wear on them. I tried to help the best I could by hauling water and chopping vegetables, but it wasn't long before civil war broke out. After many spicy verbal exchanges between Amma and her mother and sister, which resulted in them shedding tears and having tantrums, it was announced that they would no longer cook for us. We had to fend for ourselves. Amma responded by declaring she wouldn't set foot in their house again and was moving to Nealu's hut.

Little did we know at the time, but this was the unofficial beginning of an ashram that would become a multi-million-dollar international organization.

The hut was approximately ten feet by twenty feet. Considering that Nealu had more space than originally planned, a small portion of the hut had been converted into a kitchen. Its simplicity fondly reminded me of the kitchen I'd had in Tiruvannamalai, complete with kerosene stove on the floor, a couple of shelves suspended by rope, and a small washing area that drained outside.

Holy Hell

Nealu, making room for me and Amma, moved to the farthest corner and slept lengthwise, while we positioned ourselves in the opposite corner facing him. Modesty wasn't an issue. There was no such thing as pajamas—you simply slept in the same clothes you wore all day. My main concern was that I had Nealu's face just one yard from my feet. To spare myself any embarrassment, I swiftly learned how to sleep keeping my feet elegantly crossed, with my sari around my ankles.

At that stage I didn't know much about Indian cooking, nor were there any cookbooks lying around. I had to pick up kitchen skills and fast. Whenever we went to Akkara Veedu (the house across the river), I spent much time observing the women and their different preparations. I learned which spices went with which vegetables, how coriander was compatible with all spices, but that you never mix cumin with aniseed. I watched how they transformed freshly grated coconut into a smooth paste by grinding it over and over on a slab of granite with a weighty rolling pin. Many dishes I learned simply by eating them, and if an ingredient or technique weren't apparent, I'd ask and take it from there. Most of my cooking skills were learned through observation and much trial and error, but it wasn't long before I mastered the art. To help out, Balu and Sreekumar sometimes showed up with a large bundle of freshly cooked tapioca root and coconut chutney carefully wrapped in a wilted banana leaf. Other times, it was a steel, multi-tiered carrier (called a tiffin-box) full of rice and several different dishes. I often wondered if their families were sending the food, or if they were sneaking off with it; either way it was much appreciated and ever so tasty.

Now that Amma had declared independence from her family, her next step was to stake claim on the money collected on Bhava nights. Up until then, each evening her mother came into the temple at the end and rushed off with the collection bowl. Her parents were using this money, along with the earnings from her father's modest fishing business, to support the family. Amma decided that this business model had gone on long enough. She instructed me to take charge of the money instead.

The mere thought of this sent chills through my body, for I knew the family would object and sparks would fly. The following evening, as Krishna

Bhava was drawing to a close, I anxiously waited inside the temple to carry out my secret mission. Just as I left the temple, her mother spotted me taking off with the bowl. In a fit of indignation, she tried to yank it from my hands. No way was I going to let the money out of my grip. I took Amma's instructions to heart.

Accepting defeat, she ran to Amma and started wailing and complaining as though I had just assaulted her. With tears streaming down her face, she pointed at me and went on and on, madama this, madama that. Naturally, I felt terrible, but I was merely obeying orders. This little loss of income to her family was only temporary because within a short period, Amma began supporting them and making up for it many times over.

By now Madhu had also become smitten by Amma and returned for a second visit. He donated money for the construction of two additional huts, then temporarily moved into one of them. However, he never became a permanent fixture at the ashram and pretty much came and went as he pleased. No longer was Nealu the sole white man, for a French chap who went by the name Ganga had also fallen in love with Amma and had given up his life in Tiruvannamalai. He was tall and well-built, with a proud, lion-like, male energy about him, and he possessed a curious combination of keen intellect and emotional vulnerability.

The first Indian men to move in were Balu, his younger brother Venu, and Sreekumar. Venu was the natural yogi of the bunch. He had a quirky sense of humor, and he wasn't as caught up in the mother/son relationship with Amma as the others. He was quite content sitting in his hut meditating, practicing yoga, or studying Sanskrit. Whenever I was sent to fetch him, he was either upside down doing a headstand, or seated in lotus position with his stomach sucked in doing pranayama (breathing exercises). Balu and Venu's mother died when they were very young, and they were raised by their auntie, who cared for them as her own. Their father had re-married and gone on to have more children, but they had very little to do with him and his new family. This lack of family ties and no sister to marry off, enabled them to settle right into ashram life.

Holy Hell

Another young chap who visited regularly was Ramakrishna. He was well groomed and good-looking like the others, with his seventies-style side burns, little moustache, intense eyes, and pigeon toes. He mainly visited on weekends because he worked full-time at a bank in his hometown some five hours away. The exertion of travel could explain why he always seemed so moody and sat around sulking until he got Amma's undivided attention. As much as he wanted to quit his job and come running to Amma's side, he was torn—he was the eldest son, and duty-bound to help pay for his sister's wedding. Finally, unable to bear the separation, he came up with a solution and transferred to a bank some twenty minutes from the ashram.

Next up was Rao and his buddy Pai.

These six young men became part of Amma's inner circle, her senior disciples, her head swamis.

Plus a whole lot more.

Back then there was a peaceful, relaxed, and carefree atmosphere at the ashram, even though it hadn't officially been declared one yet. There were no timetables to follow and no set regimen of meditation, although meditation was a part of our daily practice by choice.

One evening Amma was sitting in the hut with Balu and Chandru, so I decided to join in the fun because I didn't get to spend a lot of time with her during the day. At first, Amma ignored me as she often did and continued her conversation. All of a sudden, she turned to me and with an annoyed look on her face said, "What are you doing sitting here? At sunset a spiritual aspirant should either be meditating or chanting the Lord's name. Now go away at once and don't let me catch you sitting around like this ever again."

This was the first time I had been chastised by her, and it came as quite a shock. I did what I was told but not without feeling hurt and confused. As I left the hut, I thought, *Why am I being singled out? Shouldn't the men have to meditate too? Was she being mean?* I sat behind the temple, hugged my knees to my chest, plopped my head on them and had a good little cry. After a short while, I surrendered and came to the following conclusion. Even though it doesn't seem fair, she is my guru, so it *has* to be for my highest good. Searching for even more reasons to justify what just happened, I foolishly thought, *Perhaps they need more attention to encourage them on their spiritual path. Perhaps I'm more spiritually advanced and ready to be disciplined.* Thus began the first of many, many years of perhaps… perhaps… perhaps….

I wanted to be just like an Indian woman. I mimicked women's mannerisms—the way they dressed and tied their hair—but there was a lot more to it than that. Many characteristics of this free-spirited and feisty Western woman needed to be tamed. Such a drastic change was going to take quite some time and effort, as numerous parts of me were determined not to go down without a fight. Adapting to difficult physical conditions—sleeping on the floor, no running water, poor sanitation, eating with my hands—was a piece of cake compared to the personality changes I had to undergo. I was often told by Amma not to talk so loud, which seemed rather ironic when India was the noisiest and most inconsiderate country I'd ever been in. There was no such thing as personal space, and I frequently had people shouting to one another within inches of my eardrums. One day, I was rushing to bring Amma something to drink and wanted to get it to her as fast as I could, so I ran. She reprimanded me and told me not to run, saying, "Each step you make should be an offering to the Lord."

Fair enough, I thought.

Another day I was caught laughing and giggling with a couple of women and told, "Women shouldn't be heard laughing like that. There are men in the next room, and they might mistake it for sexual flirtation."

Bloody hell, what next? Don't run, don't talk, don't laugh, and don't fart. Don't breathe will be the next rule. The reins were being tightened, and this wild bronco was fighting like hell.

Another sacrifice I had to make was swimming in the ocean. Recreational swimming was not part of the local culture, but on occasion the ocean was included as part of a religious ritual.

Holy Hell

One day, at the conclusion of several days of reading of the Vishnu Bhagavatam, an ancient epic in honor of Lord Krishna, we all went in a small procession to the ocean. Once we arrived at the seashore, people cautiously began wading into the water fully clothed. I wasn't sure if it signified a blessing or purification, but I didn't really care. Here was my chance. Without hesitation I ran into the water and started jumping and diving over the waves in pure ecstasy. When I surfaced I could have sworn I heard Amma calling out to me from the shore. I quickly turned around and saw her frantically waving her arms around, signaling me to come in. At first I panicked and thought, *Oh my God, is there a shark?* But upon further observation I noticed that the entire congregation of villagers was staring at me, fixated. People were laughing hysterically, having an absolute riot watching this madama frolic in the ocean. It turns out, in my eagerness to dive into the water, I failed to notice that no women were going in.

Ooooops.

Obeying Amma's orders, I bade farewell to the cool, salty water and dragged my legs—now tangled in ankle-length clothing—through the waves back to shore. *Oh well, maybe it was a big no-no, but at least I got wet,* I thought. Even though I was fully clothed, the soaking wet underskirt, blouse, and sheer white sari began clinging to my body, leaving nothing much to the imagination. Adding more fuel to the fire, the nipples on my then cute and perky little breasts were standing upright saying "hi" to everyone.

With a mortified look Amma asked, "No bra?"

There I stood, dripping wet, sheepishly looking at her, shaking my head. I hadn't worn a bra in years, even though I now finally had something to put in one. I was a late bloomer. In high school I used to stuff my bra with cotton wool, for I was embarrassed by my flat chest and needed to keep up with my blossoming classmates. But this was about to change, almost the very next day. The poor little things were harnessed inside a stiff cotton India-made bra with cups that resembled ice cream cones.

Exasperated and humiliated by my shapely display, Amma yanked a shawl off one of the older women and covered me. Even though the Arabian Sea was only a few hundred yards from the ashram, I never swam in it again.

All I wanted in life was to know God. I believed through devotion and surrender as Amma's personal attendant, I could achieve such a goal. To maintain my position, I needed to fit the mold perfectly. Therefore, I was willing to do anything and make any kind of sacrifice.

It was a slow death for this wild white woman named Gail. But she eventually surrendered and became one with the new persona named Gayatri. She calmed down and became far more reserved and disciplined. She morphed into the perfect white Indian woman who could speak the language and wobble her head in true Indian fashion.

Yet deep down I never forgot and was proud of the fact that I bore the stamp: "Made in Australia."

I already knew many customs, such as never to serve food or give anything with your left hand, for that hand has only one designated purpose—to wash your bottom. I knew that if I touch my hair or a broom, I have to rinse my hands, as those things are considered impure. During her menstrual cycle a woman is disastrously impure. It is forbidden for a woman to enter a temple or participate in any religious ceremony during this time. Many homes have designated huts for women to stay in until they are "pure" again.

Considering there was a temple on the property where Amma manifested her Bhavas, no menstruating women were allowed, myself included. On the other hand, I was told Amma didn't have a menstrual cycle.

She was a divine being, ever pure and free from "the curse."

I had been forewarned of this little custom and told I could stay at the neighbor's house once my dreaded flow arrived. With a rough idea of the due date, I kept a bag packed, ready to flee the premises immediately. Unfortunately, my first menstrual attack arrived in the middle of the night while I was sitting in front of the temple during Devi Bhava. I began to feel some cramps, so I made a quick dash to the bathroom just to discover, sure enough, I was impure! I didn't dare cross the property to retrieve my bag,

Holy Hell

so I waited for someone to come to my rescue. I was hoping one of Amma's sisters or her mother would come by, but unfortunately the first person wound up being Nealu.

"Umm, I have a problem," I bashfully said. "I need to disappear for a few days. Can you bring me the little bag that's hanging in the hut?"

Without any verbal acknowledgement, he understood my dilemma and came back a few minutes later with my bag. Making sure not to make contact with myself and risk the transference of impurities, he placed the bag on the ground before me. We were told that even the slightest indirect contact with the menses would harm Amma, and that was the last thing we wanted to happen.

I spent the next four days camped out on the floor of the neighbor's house, sleeping, reading, eating and sleeping. It was a crowded household with three grown sons, their wives, and little children, along with the grandparents. On the afternoon of the fourth day, it felt safe to return, so I asked for a clean set of clothes to be brought to the house and hung in the bathroom. The family then fetched some fresh water so I could take a bath and purify myself. I took the belief so to heart that I washed my bag, my toothbrush, my soap and even sprinkled water on the book I was reading. Trust me, I would have washed that, too, if it were possible.

I don't think the family approved of my being there, for the following month I was transferred elsewhere. The next two cycles I found myself on the uneven, rocky floor of a poor family's hut some five minutes from the ashram. Amma occasionally bathed at this house, so she made prior arrangements with them to accommodate me during this time. I always shrunk with embarrassment to have to stand outside, announce my arrival, and then say "I'm out," the common term for menstruation in Kerala. The womenfolk then dashed into the hut to move out of the way any food items, clothing, or straw mats that I might accidentally touch and contaminate.

On the brighter side, this family was very loving. In contrast to the previous experience, I didn't feel like a nuisance. The family's hut consisted of two rooms and a kitchen. In the daytime I lay on the floor of one of the bedrooms on my designated menses mat. In the evening I moved to the kitchen and slept next to a pile of firewood riddled with cockroaches.

I don't know the exact reason, but the following month a special hut was erected just for me on the edge of the ashram, right by the swampy water. Calling it a hut is a stretch. Kennel is the right word—only seven-feet long and four-feet wide. No floor had been installed, so I slept on a straw mat in the damp sand. This was okay in the daytime. Unfortunately, living in the sand were an infinite number of tiny insects driven crazy at night by the flame of my kerosene lamp. This made eating dinner, a plate full of rice gruel and coconut chutney, absolutely miserable. I was constantly picking the tiny bugs out of my porridge after they dive-bombed to their death like kamikaze pilots.

Initially I thought the hut was going to be a great way to endure four days of separation from Amma. I couldn't go near her, but at least I could see her from a distance and hear her voice. But instead of feeling a sweet longing to be in her presence, I was tormented by the sound of her interactions with everyone else while I was cooped up in my dog shed, as an untouchable. The lunch ceremony pained me the most. I could hear Amma laughing and joking with everyone, calling out their names, and I pictured them all kneeling before her affectionately getting their little ball of rice. I lay there in sweet anticipation of hearing her say to someone, "Go send this to poor Gayatri." I waited and waited but never heard my name, so I thought, *Oh, Amma must be planning on delivering it herself.* After half an hour, I heard people leaving the dining hall, so I quickly peeped out just in time to see Amma crossing the compound in the opposite direction. Alas, it seemed I *was* forgotten.

How could she forget me? My mind exploded in a fit of hormonal rage. I was furious and yelled out, "Hello … don't forget you've got a dog here in the shed."

Nobody heard me though. I decided the only remedy was a mini hunger strike. *Until I get my little ball of rice, I'm not going to eat—that should teach her a lesson.* I lay down in a huff.

Holy Hell

Five minutes later, a plate of food was delivered by Amma's sister, and inside was a tiny ball of rice. I went ahead and cancelled my strike, feeling ashamed of the emotional outburst.

I only had to suffer the dog shed a couple more times. Then my kennel was torn down to make room for a laundry area. From then on I happily trekked the two miles to Akkara Veedu and stayed in their menses hut where I could rest in peace.

EIGHT

AMMA'S CHILDREN

It wasn't long before Amma and the ashram became the center of my universe and all I ever thought about or cared for. She called us her *children*—we were her sons and daughters, and she was our mother. Australia and my birth family faded into distant memory. Communication with my parents dwindled to one letter per year. Its contents merely informed them how happy I was in India with my new and improved family. I would never say I miss you, let alone allow myself to feel such an emotion, nor mention anything about returning to see them. To have emotional attachment to family was considered a spiritual flaw, and that was the last thing I wanted to be accused of. We were taught you could only become one with God if you surrendered fully to Amma, which meant stripping yourself of any previous identity and family ties. Eager and willing to conform, I wiped my slate clean and became a pure white canvas ready to be drawn upon.

Based on not much more than blind faith, I had complete trust in Amma's omnipresence and omnipotence, so without question I surrendered my mind, heart, body, and soul to her. It didn't even cross my mind that I was also handing over my power, because I wasn't aware of such a concept. Nor did it bother me to be told repeatedly how empty and worthless my life had been before meeting Amma. I believed I had boarded the express train to God, and there would be no stops until I reached my destination.

By this time Amma had developed a small following of devotees who began inviting her to spend a day or two at their homes. The exposure gained from these little trips triggered the spread of her name in Kerala.

"Gayatri, you need to pack," said Balu as he came rushing into the hut like an excited child.

"What are you talking about? Pack for what?"

"My Auntie just went into the temple and invited Amma to visit her home, and she said yes. We're leaving on the first bus in the morning. Oh, and she's hoping to keep Amma for a couple of days, so be prepared."

Balu, with his at times melancholic eyes, was quite an emotional being. He had fallen headfirst with passionate attachment into his role as Amma's son.

"I'll start packing immediately," I exclaimed.

I understood the reason for his elation and fell prey to the exact same emotion. I loved exploring new regions of Kerala and staying with different families. These trips gave me fresh insight into the culture and an opportunity to enhance my cooking skills by watching the women at work in the kitchen. I quickly ironed a couple of Amma's skirts and shirts and neatly placed them in a little travel bag along with some personal items. I kept another set of clothes ready for her to wear on the bus, but that was it—things were quite simple back then. For me, all I needed was a toothbrush, a change of clothes, my journal, and a book to read.

At five a.m. we strolled out of the ashram, took the boat across the river, and walked into town to catch the first bus out. As we boarded, I noticed many people who had been at the ashram the night before. But they paid no heed to Amma. As far as they were concerned, now that her Krishna and Goddess bhavas were over, she was just an ordinary human being. Judgmental locals raised their sleepy heads, gave us an inquisitive and critical once-over, closed their eyes, then nodded back to sleep. A good portion of the community strongly disapproved of this young woman who surrounded herself with foreigners and with good-looking men very close to her own age.

A new day had dawned, and the rays of sunshine were kindly sharing this new terrain with me. Amma was sleeping beside me with her head resting on my shoulder, and I was excitedly peering through the window, absorbing the ever-changing scenery. The bus twisted and turned its way through narrow streets lined with houses, followed by wide expanses of rice fields. Nestled amid a variety of tall trees was the occasional coconut palm, unlike the coconut jungles in the coastal regions. Suddenly, the air rushing through the window became cool, and I inhaled the earthy scent of lush vegetation and fresh water. After a couple more bends in the road, the landscape opened up, and we were driving alongside a wide river filled with muddy brown water. Men with thin cotton towels covering their loins and women with sarongs draped around them were bathing at its edge.

Breaching the serenity of the morning came the sharp sound of wet and soapy fabric being lashed against nearby rocks. Kerala was an amazingly lush, green, and beautiful state, but the price tag for such magnificence was the constant, unbearable, and utterly exhausting humidity.

Balu and Venu's auntie was standing up now, waving her arms around trying to catch my attention. I understood it was time to get off, so I gently rubbed Amma's arm, and she opened her eyes, stood up, and followed the woman off the bus. The auntie's smile was as wide as the river we had just passed. She hooked her arm through Amma's and escorted us the half mile to her home. In a frantic fit of excitement, she ordered Balu and Venu to run ahead and warn her daughter we were coming. Not many people had telephones back then, so their only option was to wait, hope, and wonder. When we arrived at their home, the daughter was standing by the front door holding a steel pitcher full of water.

As we drew closer, Balu began instructing his cousin. "Kneel down, pour the water over Amma's feet, rub them, and now touch some of the water to your eyes." He handed her a couple of flower petals, which she nervously sprinkled on Amma's toes. I sensed she didn't possess the same level of bubbly reverence and devotion as Balu, but was obviously delighted to welcome Amma to her home.

Holy Hell

Once inside, Amma was ushered to the room, which had been prepared in anticipation of her arrival. Against the wall by the window was a single bed on top of which lay a thick straw mat covered by a blanket folded in half and a pillow encased in a pretty floral cover. The lingering fragrance of freshly extinguished incense filled the room, and the flame of an oil lamp cast a tender glow as it fidgeted in the breeze.

Whether she had slept or not, Amma always liked to spend some time with the family members whenever she first arrived. So the auntie sat on the end of the bed, lifted Amma's legs, placed them in her lap, and began lovingly massaging them. After spending a polite amount of time, the daughter excused herself and gracefully exited. Within a few minutes, except for the whirling blades of the ceiling fan, the room became quiet and Amma nodded off to sleep. I tippy-toed out of the room and went in search of the kitchen to see what was cooking.

All I had to do was follow the scent of burning firewood, fried onions, and freshly popped mustard seeds. Upon stepping inside the smoky chambers, the daughter immediately offered me a loving smile along with a cup of tea. I took a seat and while sipping on my sweet brew, studied the group of women in a flurry of chopping and grinding. One woman was sitting side-saddle on a small plank of wood with short legs, scraping coconut on the tongue shaped piece of jagged metal that was attached to the front. Two older women sat cross-legged on the floor, scraping the skin off root vegetables—no peeling or wasting in this country. The daughter was standing by the fire making a Kerala style pancake called appam. I watched how she poured a ladle of the rice and coconut batter into a small wok, and then twirled it to make a thin, crispy crust and a thicker, spongy soft center.

My Malayalam was rather limited at that stage, but my ears were constantly on the alert picking up the language. Once I figured out the root of a word—for example, bathe is "kuli"—I learned the various tenses through observation. If a person had a dry towel draped over his shoulder, I knew he was going for bath, and this situation required future tense. If he walked by with wet hair, I understood that I had to use the past tense. When a word I didn't understand emerged in a conversation, I memorized it and later on asked someone who spoke English what it meant. After breakfast I took out my pen and paper and practiced the Malayalam alphabet. Over and over I scribbled the curly and squiggly figures of sixteen vowels and thirty-seven consonants. There were soft and hard versions for several letters, three different forms of "s," four different forms of "n," and an endless variety of joint consonants. It was fun. It felt like being back in primary school learning my A B Cs.

Later, when we started to do a lot of road travel, I developed my skills by gazing out the window. I would read all the signs hanging in front of stores. First, I'd try to pronounce the Malayalam words, then I would check them against the English translations below. Through continuous trial and error, combined with my knowledge of the spoken language, eventually and slowly I was able to read Malayalam. It took many years, but I succeeded in conversing fluently, even to the point of making sharp and witty remarks. In time, I even dreamed in Malayalam.

At dusk it was routine to sing bhajans—devotional songs. People would appear out of nowhere and congregate to listen. Huddled outside the two open windows was a small crowd pushing and shoving to catch a glimpse of this woman called Amma, the source of these wondrous melodies, and the white woman by her side. The singing was an incredible magnet attracting numerous people, many of whom later became devotees.

This was how Amma's popularity began.

But in Amma's village not everyone accepted the claims of her alleged divinity. There was much animosity and disdain toward her and her family. Many villagers felt that her family was exploiting innocent people in an attempt to make a quick rupee. On occasion, when crossing the river with Amma, I would hear young men mockingly say, "Oh look, there goes Krishna." To them she was just an ordinary girl attracting people with an extraordinary web of charisma and talented theatrics. Amma chose to ignore their snickering remarks. She never uttered a word. But she avoided walking through the main street whenever we went to Akkara Veedu. Instead, we took a long and winding route through rice fields, detouring the center of town where we would become the center of negative attention. Her father, on the other hand, couldn't keep his mouth shut. He was full of hot air and was always getting into arguments with the locals. His choice of words was rather offensive. His rhetoric added more fuel to the growing resentment, which eventually ignited into uncontrollable rage and hatred.

Rumor spread that a gang had been formed and that they were planning to come one night during Krishna Bhava to create havoc. We didn't know if this was true, but the idea was definitely unnerving. A week or so later, as Krishna Bhava was drawing to a close, I noticed a group of local men come through the side of the property. Instantly I could tell they were not devotees, as the look on their faces was anxious and intense. They were not dressed in the customary white or cream-colored clothing that men wear out of respect to a temple. Instead, they arrogantly strutted onto the property in multi-colored, checkered dhotis and loud colored shirts. I sensed trouble as I stood among the eighty or so people gathered outside that night. Through the corner of my eye I watched to see where they were going. My heart began to pound rapidly. They moved in close with the crowd, pretending to be watching. But their eyes were filled with anger and a shifty, sinister glint.

I noticed one of the men holding something behind his back. I was petrified they'd try to hurt Amma when she stepped out of the temple to dance, so I needed to see exactly what he was carrying. As nonchalantly as possible, I walked away from the crowd, hoping not to attract any attention from the gang. Once behind them, I quickly turned around, and saw in the man's hand a heavy linked piece of chain. Without a second thought I lunged forward. With all my might I yanked the weapon from his unsuspecting hands and flung it as far away as I could. My action was the equivalent of pulling the pin out of a hand grenade, for within seconds violence erupted. I raced away from the men toward the temple; their loud and aggressive voices were piercing the night air. The moment I crossed the temple threshold, I slammed the door shut and bolted it. Someone bolted it from the outside as well.

Mid-chorus, the singing came to a halt, and the harmonium ended with notes of discord as a tambourine crashed to the floor. Outside a massive brawl was ensuing, and inside the temple Amma was yelling and pounding on the door to be let out. A couple of devotees wrapped their arms around Amma in an attempt to control her. She was kicking and screaming, but there was no way we were going to let her out. For her sake we took charge that evening.

I later learned I wasn't the only one who had noticed the gang's arrival. Amma's father, along with a few relatives and supportive local men, had seen them too, and they were just itching for a fight. Amid the sound of fists thumping and hands slapping, men and women were shouting and screaming at each other. It was a dreadful feeling to be trapped inside the temple, not knowing what was happening outside, or if anyone was being seriously injured. With shock and adrenaline coursing through our veins, it seemed as though the brawl would never end. But ten minutes later it was over. The fighting had subsided. But a new commotion was escalating—the emotional and traumatized voices of those who had participated in or witnessed the brawl.

In a flash Amma was standing on the verandah surrounded by tear-strewn faces of disheveled devotees and relatives all trying simultaneously to share their versions of the event. I couldn't quite make out what they were saying, but my overall impression was one of triumph.

Amma's elder sister came pushing through the crowd to tell her rendition. Her face was flushed and dripping with sweat, her blouse torn, and at her waist she clutched the many folds of her sari that had come undone during the fight. Amma's grandmother then took center stage and began dramatically re-enacting her role in the brawl as she showed off her swollen eye. Only a few devotees had engaged in the fighting. As for the ashram residents, their main concern was to keep Amma safe inside the temple. The brawl boiled down to a family feud with a bunch of disgruntled locals. The troublemakers were long gone now, and nobody seemed seriously hurt, but everyone was seriously shaken.

Despite this incident the gatherings continued as usual, and Amma continued to gather followers and fame.

Holy Hell

A couple of weeks later we visited the home of a young lad who, although his parents were devotees, was himself caught in a plight—his sister had to be married off before he could join the ashram. The family lived one hour south of the ashram. After spending the weekend with them, we were to head back in the afternoon. This was a Bhava day. Considering that bhajans always started at five p.m., I presumed that shortly after lunch we would be on our way. But such was not going to be the case. Two o'clock went by. Then it was nearing three thirty. I couldn't take my eyes off the clock. Finally I could no longer entertain the marvelous virtue of patience. I turned to Amma and said, "It's getting late. Should I ask the family to call a taxi?"

Hearing those dreaded words, the young lad—whose head was tucked in Amma's lap—began sobbing uncontrollably. Without uttering a word Amma glared at me and placed a finger over her lips as if to say, "Be quiet."

Affectionately stroking the lad's head, she tried to soothe his aching heart by saying, "My darling son, don't cry. Mother isn't going far."

Crap, I thought to myself. *He'll be coming in the taxi with us; can't he do his crying there?*

My "to do" list continued to harass me by repeating itself over and over. Before too many people arrived, I needed to sweep the temple inside and out along with the surrounding sand. The huge brass lamp and water pot had to be cleaned and polished. Her Bhava clothes had to be ironed and, at the very least, her Krishna crown polished and set in place before the singing commenced. I began to wonder if Amma wasn't aware of the many duties awaiting me. Or was it that she didn't care? Neither of these possibilities sat well with me.

In an attempt to be a good disciple and master the fine art of surrender, I tried to remain calm and trust everything would work out just fine. But I couldn't sit still—not when I had already experienced Amma's annoyance if things weren't ready, or if they weren't exactly as she liked them to be.

Impatiently I left the room and went in search of some moral support from my spiritual brothers. I thought if one of them said something to Amma, then maybe she'd be more willing to oblige. I soon realized I was on my own and was not going to get much backing on this little venture. In their minds, as long as we were back shortly before five p.m., everything was just hunky-dory.

Instead Balu offered the following advice: "Amma will give the word when she's ready. You shouldn't question her ways but try to surrender instead."

Well, that was helpful. It's easy to preach about surrender when the problem doesn't concern you, I thought to myself.

Thankfully, shortly afterwards Amma came out of the room and with a glowing smile announced, "Children, call a taxi. It's time for mother to leave."

The father of the household ran to the phone while the women huddled around Amma for their departure hugs. With her head shawl neatly in place—this had become her signature look when in public—Amma gave each of the family members a hug and a sniff on the cheek (Kerala's version of a kiss). I breathed a tiny sigh of relief, knowing we would soon be on our way. But I still felt anxious because of the one-hour drive and the wide river between me and the temple.

Within ten minutes the vehicle arrived. Amma finished her goodbyes, and we piled in. Standard practice was two rows of us seated one on top of the other on the back seat. Amma sat in my lap, and three in the front squeezed up against the driver. In India one could get away with traveling in such a manner.

At four forty-five our cross-river boat skidded into the squishy mud on the temple side of the river. Without hesitation I jumped out first and briskly walked until I was out of Amma's sight. Then I ran to the hut and threw my bag into the corner.

A startled Nealu, who had stayed behind as usual, sat up and innocently asked, "Why are you so late? I was beginning to worry."

With sweat running down my face and tears of exasperation welling in my eyes I replied, "Not now," without even looking at him.

Holy Hell

I dashed out of the hut across to the temple, not noticing the few people already seated on the verandah. Rushing inside, I picked up the brush and started sweeping, but after a few strokes tossed the thing against the wall and stormed out. Aware that an emotional outburst was imminent, I ran behind the house and made a beeline for the kakkoos. I dashed up the plank, tossed the rice sack door out of the way, felt thankful nobody was squatting inside, then leaned against the wall and started crying. Suddenly from the other end of the plank, I heard the kind and concerned voice of Sreekumar.

"Gayatri, are you all right? What's wrong?"

In between sobs and sniffs I managed to reassure him that I was fine. Eventually I came out from behind the curtain feeling rather embarrassed. Wiping the tears from my eyes, I thanked him for his concern and told him I had to hurry back to the temple.

"I don't think you should go in there right now," he warned.

"What do you mean?" I pressed for an explanation as I continued walking.

Apprehensively he replied, "Amma saw you toss the brush then storm out of the temple, and she is furious. She told me she doesn't need anybody's help. Now she is in there cleaning."

I froze in my tracks. My heart felt as if it had just tripled in weight. "Do you think if I say I'm sorry she will let me take over?"

With a worried look on his face he said, "I strongly doubt it. She seems pretty determined right now. But you should at least try."

I sheepishly stepped into the temple. But before I could utter a word, her eyes doubled in size. "Get out of here," she snapped.

I departed at once like a tail-tucked dog.

In a desperate attempt to remedy the situation, I decided to iron the clothes and do some of the other work, hoping that would be okay. She didn't subject me to any further punishment. Shortly after five p.m. the singing began as usual.

The following day, however, I was informed that if I couldn't perform my service with wholehearted devotion and care, she would find someone else who could.

NINE

DAYS OF BLISS

My life in the early years of the ashram was simple, sweet, and laden with spiritually charged blissful moments. This was especially true during my most cherished time of day—the evening bhajans. Through the emotion and devotion evoked by the music and lyrics, my mind would unwind and gracefully fall into the lap of my heart. With my mind subdued, I was able to connect with the Divine (God, Higher Self, whatever name you prefer), and a warm sense of peace and solace would permeate my being. The songs that were written and sung in those days were passionate, raw, and powerful entreaties to God. The lyrics were full of meaning, and the music brought forth strong emotion—unlike the bhajans of later years, which were more like pop songs with catchy tunes and shallow lyrics. The fairest comparison I can draw is this: what does classical music have in common with disco? Answer—not much.

Many nights during bhajans Amma entered what appeared to be a state of ecstasy. Occasionally she would get up from in front of the temple and stagger off to the coconut grove. There she would continue laughing, crying, and calling out to Krishna or the Divine Mother. Her face emitted the purest divine rapture. Sometimes it took several hours for her to come down from such a state. Meanwhile we, the handful of residents, sat a small distance away keeping a watchful eye until she returned. I was told that sometimes she would try to hurt herself or crawl into the swampy waters. I never witnessed such an event.

One evening her father overheard her and became annoyed, thinking she was suffering from hysteria. Storming across the property, he began shouting, "Sudhamani. Hey, Sudhamani, snap out of it. Stop that. Have you gone crazy?" Suddenly, and much to our horror, he smacked her on top of the head saying, "Maybe *this* will bring you back to your senses."

I was mortified but didn't know what to do. It was her father after all. But before he could inflict any more hostility, a couple of the fellows jumped up and tried to reason with him.

"Acchan (father), she's not suffering from mental illness. She is in a state of divine bliss. Just let her be," they pleaded.

This interpretation was pretty hard for him to comprehend, considering that she was his daughter and that he didn't possess much of a spiritual streak. Perhaps upon realizing he was outnumbered, or that we were more concerned with his aggression than Amma's state, he relented and headed back to the house muttering something.

We were distressed and annoyed by her father's behavior, so the following day the matter was brought to Amma's attention. In a cool and understanding tone she replied, "As a father, he was only acting out of love and concern, so there's no need for any of you to feel anger toward him."

In my mind I tacked on another sentence. *It's not his fault he's so ignorant.*

In those days my heart was quite in tune with Amma. No matter where I was or what I was doing, my mind was constantly dwelling upon her. I could be in the middle of cooking a large cauldron of rice and suddenly the feeling would bubble up from my heart that Amma was thirsty. Following my instincts, I'd rush from the kitchen with a drink in hand and track her down. Often, just as I arrived, I would hear her say, "I'm thirsty." Moments like those made my heart sing.

Sometimes, though, I would get caught in a kind of booby trap and not know what to do. For example, after abandoning the huge pot of rice that was cooking over a wood fire, Amma might ask me to sit and rub her legs. Naturally my immediate reaction was to obey. But as I massaged, gradually my thoughts drifted to the kitchen. *Has the flame died? Has the rice overcooked?* I knew that if the batch got ruined, I couldn't very well pass the buck and say, "But you asked me to rub your legs." On the other hand, if I seemed distracted and didn't massage her with full attention, she'd get angry, give me a kick or a slap (whichever was more convenient), and tell me to go away. I can't tell you how many times I got caught in such situations. There was no winning—whichever way I turned, I'd be in trouble. I consoled myself by writing off these incidents as tests from the guru. But I never quite understood what these so-called tests were supposed to prove.

Looking back, I now see there was a third option.

I picture myself standing before her, quite self-assured, then calmly and diplomatically saying, "Amma, you have asked me to rub your legs. But I need to draw your attention to the fact that I am in the middle of cooking lunch for the ashram. How would you suggest I handle this predicament you have placed me in?" Oh, that sounds so wonderful. But that wasn't the case for this twenty-one-year-old. She feared, "Obey or else."

On another note, if that *had been* me back then, I doubt Amma would have accepted me as her personal attendant. She needed someone innocent, naïve, and trustworthy, with one hundred percent blind faith.

That was me.

Over the course of my twenty years at the ashram, but primarily in the earlier days, I was blessed with many unforgettable spiritual experiences. There was one incident in particular where I entered what you could call an "out of body" state. I don't recall why, but that evening during the bhajans, instead of sitting on the temple verandah, I sat alone, some distance away amid a hedge of bushes. Serenely I was singing along. Then out of the blue my mind became increasingly one-pointed. My heartbeat began to race. It was as though my entire awareness was being sucked into a tiny point of existence between my eyebrows. My singing came to a gentle halt, and I began to weep. My body was sitting tall, gently swaying to and fro with the music. Before I knew it, I was sobbing uncontrollably. Then to my astonishment the tears stopped. I began laughing hysterically. Then, as swiftly as a snap of the fingers, not only was I laughing but I was witnessing the laughter. Somehow my identification with the person who was both laughing and crying separated. I became a witness to the event. In that moment I was given a sneak peek into a magnificent state of bliss.

That evening I lay in the sand for at least an hour after the singing concluded, unable to talk, immersed in a quiet space of deep peace, physically drained.

In those precious early years there were no crowds—apart from Bhava evenings—so we were free to roam around, sit under a tree and read, or meditate in the temple undisturbed. Only on Fridays would a couple of local women show up and spend the entire day sitting in front of the temple. They sat somberly, fasting and observing silence, with only the occasional movement on their lips as they whispered the Lord's name. The mere sight of these women brought God to the forefront of my mind. I admired their patience and determination, and I was curious as to the significance of their penance, and why Friday was their chosen day.

I learned that Friday is the day dedicated to the Divine Mother. During their observances these women were praying for the health and longevity of their husbands. In rural India women were expected to serve, honor, and obey their husbands.

I understood how such a custom could come into being. However, from a Western woman's perspective I had trouble accepting such expectations. Serve your husband? Sure, why not, as long as you are loved and respected. Honor? Rather dubious about that one. Obey? HELL NO! The mere thought formed knots in my stomach.

By nature I possessed a rebellious streak. I recall that at age ten I once took a stand against my music teacher at school. One day this lady announced to everyone in my class that if we didn't attend band practice we could no longer be on the basketball team. All the girls in my class took heed of the threat and reluctantly grabbed their fifes that afternoon. Not me. I wasn't going to be bossed around in such a manner.

The following day during music class my teacher ordered, "Gail, stand up. Why weren't you at band practice yesterday?"

"Because it's not fair that we can only be on the basketball team if we go to band practice," I defiantly replied.

"Well, you are no longer on the team."

"Fine," I said, standing firm in my decision but quite sad at the same time.

I have always had trouble with figures who misuse their authority. Yet here I was. Instead of embracing my nature, I was trying to morph into someone else—into a role of subservience and obedience.

I understood the willingness of these Indian women to perform such vows, and from a practical standpoint it made total sense. Traditionally men were the breadwinners, so of course the women wanted them around as long as possible. Many families in the village were poor and survived day-to-day, so losing a husband would most certainly result in dire hardship. Their austerity and sincerity inspired me. Even though I didn't have a husband who needed preserving, I chose to observe the ritual. The intention behind my vow varied from week to week. Sometimes it was to increase my devotion. Or it was to decrease my attachment to food and sleep so that I could meditate longer. Other times it was to remove any trait of my personality that I felt inhibited my total surrender to Amma.

I was never able to sit in the same position for long. Frankly, an hour here or an hour there was all I could ever physically or mentally cope with. I must confess, by nature I was the restless type. I gravitated toward work. If I ever had to choose between meditating and a chore, the chore usually won. I didn't believe in shirking my duties. I considered them part of my spiritual practice.

Holy Hell

Looking back I see that, with me, Amma hit the jackpot. Of course, my dream of finding and serving a guru had come true. But I was more than naïve. I was hardworking (workaholic), dedicated (obsessed), determined (stubborn), and physically strong. Just imagine all those qualities teamed with a nice dose of low self-esteem—voila, the perfect "disciple" is born!

Finding the right balance between meditating and work was always a struggle, but many times I didn't feel as though I had a choice. There was much I was asked to do, and by nature I wanted to do it right. I kept the kitchen supply room neat and clean, with everything stocked accordingly. Then there was chopping and drying the firewood, which I stacked neatly outside in its shed. Usually, I'd retire from the kitchen exhausted, hot and sweaty, with eyes stinging from the smoke, and still have a huge pile of laundry waiting.

I was okay with doing a great deal of the work, but sometimes it got the better of me. For example, I had to clean up the mess in the hut after Amma had spent hours talking, singing, laughing, snacking, and lying around with all of her "sons." Afterwards I saw others sitting around meditating with serene looks on their faces. Then I'd wonder if service truly was my path, or if I was fooling myself. I was confused

The only reassurance I ever got was indirect—when Amma chastised me if something wasn't done correctly.

Finally, at my wits' end, I decided to ask Amma about my dilemma. I saw her sitting outside with Nealu, so I decided to seize the moment. It was rare that I asked any personal questions, so with slight apprehension I began: "Amma, I often find myself working or cleaning when I feel I could be meditating. Sometimes I think I will just leave the mess for someone else, but I am unable to walk away saying 'it's not my job.' I feel as though I'm always sacrificing my time. Is this sincerity, or am I crazy?"

With a sweet smile on her face she replied, "Daughter, you're not crazy. Out of your sincerity, you want to keep the ashram neat and clean."

I began to relax and feel relieved that finally I had my answer. But in the very same breath she said, "You're leading such a useless life. Do you ever cry for devotion?" Saying this, she got up and walked away.

Feeling ever so dejected, I turned to Nealu, screwed my face up, and squealed, "Huh?"

He graced me with a sympathetic smile, shrugged his shoulders and raised his hands, as if to say, "Beats me."

That was the end of our little discussion, and I wound up more confused and tormented than ever. It was impossible to know what she was implying when she contradicted herself like that. I remember analyzing and trying to decipher some hidden meaning in her words. I concluded that she couldn't simply praise me, for that would have boosted my ego. I needed to be humble. So maybe she was trying to tell me that without focus on God my work was useless.

I could have come up with many more explanations. But I decided to stop there. My head was already hurting.

Around the same time I made another attempt to gain insight. I sought Amma's advice as to what image to meditate upon.

"My feet," was her instant response. "Try to visualize them residing in your heart."

It's customary for devotees to worship the feet of their guru. It is believed that the feet transmit grace, and that meditating upon them helps the devotee absorb the vibration of their guru—someone they believe has realized oneness with God. I was ecstatic because I had a photo of Amma's feet wearing *my* anklets. I believed any restlessness I'd experienced in the past would vanish now that I had the perfect image to focus upon. I placed the photo in a frame, found a pretty piece of fabric to set it on, and then grabbed my meditation rug. Inside the temple I sat erect and glanced at the photo for a while before closing my eyes. I tried to hold the image of her feet in my heart, but they soon vanished into thin air. Not willing to give up, I repeated the process over and over but found the image wouldn't stick. I also noticed that my concentration preferred to hover around my third eye.

One day Amma saw me sitting in front of the temple with a discouraged look on my face.

"Gayatri, what's wrong?" she asked with a hint of humor.

Holding the picture up, I said, "You asked me to meditate on these. But as soon as I close my eyes they take off."

Amma's quick and clever response was, "Well then, you need to chase after them, catch hold and hang on tight, so they won't run away again."

Alas, easier said than done—they outran me every time.

I finally gave up on the feet and tried a variety of different images. I used Amma in Krishna Bhava, one of her meditating, then a generic image of Krishna, and one of Durga. Nothing seemed to work. I began to suspect I would never find the perfect photo, so decided to try a new technique.

What I found worked best was to simply repeat my mantra as I concentrated on my third eye. Eventually my mind became still. The mantra naturally ceased as I journeyed deeper inside. For the most part the problem was solved.

From then on I rarely asked Amma any personal questions. I began relying on my inner guidance, or what I naively called back then my "inner Amma." When I was in a clear space, every question I asked was answered promptly, void of any painful or confusing contradiction.

Another highlight for me in those days was Krishna Bhava. Even though I knew it was Amma underneath the crown, glitter, and jewels, there was a softness and sweetness to the evenings. It was a time of consolation, a time when I could forget her occasional harsh ways and the physical strain of my workload. After an hour or two of basking in the loving and lighthearted atmosphere, I felt renewed. Many evenings I had the opportunity to stand next to Amma and hold the plate of sacred ash, bananas, and pitcher of holy water.

One night I noticed something unusual. A newcomer entered the temple, and Amma's face lit up as though she'd known him for a very long time. I got the sense he was an ardent devotee of Lord Krishna, and it crossed my mind—if Amma was indeed manifesting Krishna, then maybe she'd been witnessing his devotion for years.

I began to think how lucky I was to be standing so close to the same divine being who blessed the world with the Bhagavad Gita, one of the most important and sacred scriptures of the Hindu faith. The Gita contains the discourse Krishna delivered to Arjuna before the start of the Kurukshetra war. I found myself thinking how wonderful it would be if, in a similar way, Amma were to give me some words of wisdom. The thought gradually became so intense that my heart began to pound in anticipation.

Suddenly Amma turned and looked at me. *Oh my God, she's heard my prayer. I feel it. She's going to impart a profound teaching.*

She gestured for me to bring my head close, as if she wanted to whisper something in my ear. My heart raced as I leaned forward. I closed my eyes to concentrate fully on her sacred words.

She softly whispered, "We're almost out of bananas."

On evenings when I wasn't serving, I loved to sit in the temple and watch Amma interact with the devotees for a while, then close my eyes and meditate. When Nealu came to sing, there was an immediate and tangible shift in the atmosphere, and my mind would soar. Despite his constant physical suffering, Nealu possessed incredible spiritual depth and intense longing and love for God. When he sang, this passion was palpable.

One evening the temple was crowded. I was unable to find room to sit, so I stood in the corner praying to Amma for a space to appear. I believed that this tactic had worked on previous occasions, that within a few minutes someone would stand up—miraculously, I thought—and leave the temple. If this happened, I believed it was not mere coincidence. It was Amma hearing my prayer and subtly coercing the person to get up. This night I waited and waited, continually looking at her and praying.

After half an hour and no appearance of anywhere to sit, I began to feel upset. My inner conversation went something like this. *Don't you know how special these evenings are for me? Why won't you grant my wish? Is my devotion not pure enough? Are you punishing me for some reason?*

Feeling rather distressed, I left the temple and sat outside in the dark to wallow in my dejection. After a short while I realized that brooding wasn't going to get me anywhere. So I crossed my legs, sat up straight, and began to meditate. I don't know if it was from my intense yearning or from the devotion floating through the air, but within minutes these words arose from my heart:

> Oh, how my heart yearns and pains to soar through the sky on the bird of your name.
> To be absorbed in each repeat of your name and never return to this land of duality.
> To be carried off like a dust particle by your cool and soothing breeze.
> Alas, I am anchored and weighed down by so many unfulfilled desires.
> I pray, give me the strength and determination to break the chains, and let my wings spread and soar off into the eternal sky.

Another magical and blissful memory from the early years was a late-night return journey from a devotee's home in the village. Many homes were too far to walk to, so we would rent a canoe. A local boy who frequented the ashram was our designated pole driver for the thirty-minute ride upstream. Amma and I climbed into the back of the canoe, followed by Balu and Sreekumar each carefully holding one side of a harmonium, then Venu hugging his set of tablas. The canoe gracefully pushed off from the shore into the quiet of the night. The only sounds were the tapping of the pole as it hit the side of the boat and the swish of the water as it moved aside for us. In the distance I could see the swaying lanterns from several shrimp nets that intermittently lined the river and only came alive at night. The nets were attached to the end of large poles, and they dipped into the water where the light from the lantern lured the unsuspecting creatures. The nets stayed underwater for ten minutes. Then with the aid of men pulling down on a heavy rock, the nets were lifted out of the river into the air. I could hear the faint voices of the men bouncing off the river as they discussed the fortune or misfortune of their catch.

Nature was also playing her part in adding more grace and magic to the evening. The moon was shining brightly, and its reflection was gleefully dancing beside us like a ballerina in a luminous tutu. As we glided through the water, a cool and gentle breeze caressed our faces.

Just when I was feeling enraptured by the enchantment of the evening and thinking it couldn't get any better, Amma burst into song. "Srishtiyum niye, srishtaavum niye, shaktiyum niye, satyavum niye, Devi…" (Thou art Creation, the Creator, Energy and Truth…O Goddess…!) I felt joyful and blessed to be part of this divine serenade, and didn't want that evening to end.

TEN

THE OPERATION

It was a mellow afternoon in late August, 1981, and Amma was relaxing at Akkara Veedu for the weekend. She was lying on the narrow porch with her head resting in the lap of the elderly mother of the household and her feet in the lap of the lady's daughter, Chitra. Amma was dressed in a brightly colored ankle-length skirt and an old Devi bhava blouse with faded brocade at the end of the short sleeve. Her hair was loose, and her wavy locks casually draped over the woman's lap. With keen enthusiasm, the old woman gently scratched Amma's scalp, then pinched at the roots and dragged her fingers along a few strands of hair. The typical purpose of this grooming technique was to remove lice eggs, which were then popped between their fingernails. This was a favorite pastime among the village women, and the lucky recipient always had a serene almost sleepy look on her face.

I'd just returned from the bathroom and could no longer contain my anxiety about something that was causing me grave concern. I stood in the sand before them and blurted out, "Things are not where they should be."

Naturally, my statement wasn't taken seriously. They all started to laugh at this silly madama, making me think I had mispronounced something.

Maintaining a solemn face I said, "I think I have a problem." This time I pointed to my lower abdomen.

Amma sat up. In a concerned voice she asked, "What do you mean?"

This was a perplexing situation and hard to explain because I didn't know what was wrong.

With a worried look on her face, Amma yelled for one of the boys to come translate. *Oh God.* I was mortified, but knew this was necessary if any sense was to be made out of what I was trying to say.

Squirming in my skin I explained, "Whenever I squat it feels like things inside have dropped down."

"How long has this been going on?" Amma asked.

Flushed with embarrassment, I replied, "My abdomen has been hard for a while, but this new thing has only been for a couple of weeks."

I let out a long and heavy sigh, relieved to finally have this out in the open. She told me to come near. She placed her hand on my belly and pushed. When she felt my swollen and rock-hard abdomen, her face turned grave.

"You need to see a doctor right away."

Until that point I'd been suffering from denial. Kind of hoping I was just imagining things or that it would go away by itself.

But I knew now the problem was serious.

The following evening Amma arranged with a devotee from Quilon to take me to see her gynecologist. The very next day, I was lying on the doctor's examination table being pushed and prodded by a pair of hands inside rubber gloves.

After a brief examination the doctor announced, "You have a prolapsed uterus."

"But how does something like that happen?"

"It usually occurs in older women after having too many babies. In your case, being a Western woman, it's probably from too much sex. I'll just push everything back in place."

Before I had time to react, or even to take in her preposterous accusation, with one quick jerk of her hand she pushed everything upwards. I let out a scream of agonizing pain and almost fainted on the table. It felt as if I'd just been stabbed in the belly.

"You can get up now, everything is fine," she commanded in a cold and dry tone.

I was shaking and winded from the ordeal, but managed to get dressed. I left the room with tremendous haste and disbelief. I was used to Indian men generalizing about Western women's supposed promiscuity. But I was livid that a woman, a medical professional, had made such an ignorant statement.

When I stepped into the waiting room, the lady who'd accompanied me jumped up and asked, "So, what did the doctor say?"

Still fuming and with tears in my eyes, I merely said, "She says I have a prolapsed uterus. But I think I need a second opinion."

A few days later I was at a different doctor's office. After a few gentle pushes on my tummy, I was given a different diagnosis. With the utmost courtesy and confidence, she said, "You have an ovarian cyst and need surgery as soon a possible."

I gasped and froze in horror.

Even though I was relieved to finally have a proper diagnosis, the thought of surgery terrified me. In shock, I sat across the desk from her and set a date. The operation was to be performed in three weeks time at the Quilon Government Hospital.

Continuing in her perfect Indian English, the competent doctor explained, "Only at the time of surgery will I know the extent of damage, and what I might have to remove."

In a quivering voice I said, "Damage? What do you mean by that?"

"Well, it all depends on the size of the tumor and how far it has spread as to whether I'll have to remove one or both ovaries, and the fate of your uterus."

"Oh that's all," I exclaimed in a relieved tone. "I don't care about my reproductive organs. You can remove them all as far as I'm concerned."

Now it was the doctor's turn to look shocked. I suspect she'd never heard anyone—especially a twenty-two-year-old—talk like that before. Growing up, I never envisioned children as part of my life, and particularly not now after joining the ashram.

Suddenly my face lit up. I realized that a hysterectomy would mean the end of my dreaded monthly periods. No more stomach cramps or being thrown into quarantine ever again.

With a naughty smile on my face I asked, "At the time of surgery, do you think you could just remove everything no matter what?"

Probably thinking I was crazy, she shook her head and replied, "My dear child, that would be unethical. Let's just wait and see what God's plan is."

Later that afternoon, on the bus ride back to the ashram, the reality of my situation had a chokehold on me once more. My elation from the possibility of no more menstruation was short lived. In truth, I was scared to death about having surgery. I was also worried about how Amma was going to react. *I hope she doesn't become too upset when I break the news.*

An hour later, I was sitting before her with tears in my eyes explaining what the doctor had said. At first she seemed distraught. She even shed a tear. Then her expression turned firm. "Daughter, where is your faith?" she said. "Thousands of people have operations every day. Why should you be so afraid?"

This was not quite the response I expected. However, I believed she cared and was merely trying to make me strong enough to accept my fate.

During my waking hours a jolting current of anxiety flowed through my body. Nights were filled with terrifying dreams—lying on an operation table, surrounded by strangers, and being hacked open.

In addition to fear of the surgery, other matters weighed heavily on my mind. In government hospitals in India the care was minimal. Patients were required to bring a relative or close friend to look after them. The doctor said I might have to stay in the hospital for a week. So I worried about who'd look after me. Services such as emptying the bedpan, giving sponge baths, and providing meals were not offered. Nor were medicine and supplies. Those needed to be purchased from outside pharmacies.

When I expressed my concern to Amma, she said, "Don't worry. I'll send my mother with you."

I almost had a heart attack on the spot.

Amma's mother wasn't well herself. She tended to lie around sleeping most of the time.

I dared not say anything. But I sure had a few thoughts on the matter. *What! How on earth can she be expected to do all that running around? Not only that, she doesn't speak English, and I'm hardly fluent in Malayalam.* Under normal circumstances, I managed okay. But I didn't want to be lying in a hospital bed after major surgery struggling to communicate.

I was overwhelmed with anxiety, and I felt doomed. Not once though did it cross my mind to go back to Australia for the surgery. That would have been a clear indication of lack of faith and devotion.

Ten days later a well educated young Indian woman named Mahati showed up out of the blue. She was on a two-week break from her doctoral studies in Madras and planned to do a bit of touring in Kerala after spending a day or two at the ashram. However, upon meeting Amma she was smitten and decided to stay put.

The two of us soon became good friends. When Mahati learned that I was going in for surgery, she offered to look after me. This was a huge relief. Mahati spoke eloquent English. And she possessed amazing self-confidence and great street smarts.

Amma's mother insisted on coming along. This touched my heart and made me feel cared for.

With each passing day the mass inside my abdomen grew. I had to leave the last two buttons on my sari blouse undone, for it no longer fit around my waist. I was constantly short of breath, anemic, and my lips were turning purple. I avoided going into town because villagers were starting to gossip that I was pregnant. That was a natural assumption because I looked five or six months along.

Eventually the dreaded day for admittance arrived, and the three of us were dropped off at the entrance of the hospital. My surgery wasn't for four days. I had to find ways to pass the time and not think too much about what lay ahead. Mahati daily went out for a bit of sightseeing. The rest of the time she had her nose buried inside a book. Amma's mother happily spent most of her days curled up on a straw mat in the corner of the room, sound asleep.

I don't recall why they had me check in so early, but I believe this was standard procedure in India. Each day there were a couple of blood tests, a brief visit from the doctor, and the occasional surprise. The most memorable was the day before the surgery, when I was taken into a room and, much to my horror, there stood two nurses aids, dressed in emerald green saris, armed with razor blades. *Oh no, how humiliating.* My face cringed, and I squirmed within my skin on the table. Everything suddenly felt very real and my heart began to pound with anxiety. I peered over to the clock on the wall, and it hit me. *This time tomorrow, I'm going to be unconscious on the operating table.* I felt like crying but knew I had to hold it together and be strong.

After a restless and almost sleepless night, my eyes opened to the momentous day of September 21, 1981. I was weak from fasting and tightly wound from the adrenaline running through my body. I stood up and dressed myself into the pre-operation outfit of loincloth, dhoti, and sari blouse worn backwards. There was no such thing as a hospital gown or cap in that place. I tied my golden locks into pigtails, then sat on the bed while Amma's mother braided them as per hospital regulations. At the appropriate hour, nurses came to escort me down the hall and across to the surgery wing. As I was leaving, Mahati grabbed my hand, gave it a squeeze, and wished me well. Amma's mother cast me a loving smile, placed her hand over her heart, and wobbled her head. Before I turned the corner at the end of the corridor, I paused and looked around to see that they were both still standing in the doorway, watching me. I gave them an awkward smile and a corny wave. I thought, *I wish Amma was here.* As I made my way through the hospital, I tried my best to ignore the gasps and impolite, loud whispers of people who repeatedly used the words "madama," "pregnant," and "abortion."

The nurses pushed on a swinging door, and we reached our destination—a waiting room outside the operating theater. They told me to sit on the wooden bench and wait, and then they vanished. I sat alone, nervously looking around at the stark, dirty walls, and twiddled my thumbs. Within a few minutes one of the nurses reappeared and stood before me holding the most gigantic syringe I'd ever seen in my life. She told me to stand up, turn around, lean forward, and hold on to the top of the bench. Then she warned, "It might hurt a bit." My face grimaced, and every muscle in my body became taught. I could only imagine what "a bit" meant. When she rammed the needle into the base of my spine, I gasped, and my heart skipped a few beats. Afterwards, I slid down onto the bench and began wrestling with the tears that were screaming to burst forth.

I transformed my emotion into a nervous laugh and said, "Look what's happened. I pray to God for devotion, and I get an operation instead."

Suddenly the door to the theater burst open, and a pair of eyes peering over a mask focused in on me and nodded. It was time. I stood up and walked through the door into a cold—and what I hoped to God was a sterile—operating room. A nurse removed my dhoti and told me to lie on the table. I nervously crawled up and lay there with legs spread wide as my ankles and wrists were strapped down. My loincloth, the only remaining piece of modesty apart from my blouse, was removed, and a nurse began stuffing me with gauze and cotton wool. I was mortified and humiliated, but mad at the same time. *For heaven's sake, how insensitive. Couldn't they wait until I was unconscious to do that?* Before I could worry too much about feeling like a hunk of meat on a butcher's block, a mask was put over my face.

"Now take a deep breath," said the anesthesiologist. "I want you to count to ten."

"One... two... it's not working," I cried out in a panic. I was petrified they would start slicing into me before I lost consciousness.

"Now just relax," reassured my doctor as she gently placed her hand on my forehead. "Please just count to ten. I promise you won't feel a thing."

Surrendering to my fate I tried again. "One... two... three... four...."

Several hours later, delirious, I opened one eye and caught a glimpse of a bag of red liquid suspended above me. Shifting my gaze around the room, I saw several faces staring back at me. I recognized none of them. I was drifting in and out of consciousness. It was like looking through a foggy window while half asleep. Some time later I abruptly regained consciousness, forced awake by the irrepressible sensation of nausea. I tried my best to fight off the urge to vomit, for I feared the consequence of such convulsions on my freshly stitched abdomen. A nurse insisted it had to come out—it was the anesthesia—and suddenly I was throwing up a bright green liquid. Afterward I began to recognize everyone in the room. I saw Amma's brother-in-law sitting on the bed holding my legs firmly in place. Another was the lady devotee from Quilon.

With an amused smile, she said, "You've been putting up quite a fight. You've been singing western songs and trying to dance."

I managed to move my lips into a faint smile as I wondered what song it could've possibly been. In fact, I still wonder today. Glancing out the window, I noticed it was becoming dark, and the eerie reality of what had transpired earlier in the day set in. I was weak and terribly scared but had to take a peek at my belly. I gently lifted the sheet and gazed down to see my middle section no longer swollen. It was flat and wrapped in gauze.

Feebly I turned to Mahati and asked, "Do you know what they took out? Did the doctor say anything?"

With restraint she replied, "All I know is the doctor removed a massive eight-and-a-half-kilo tumor and performed a hysterectomy." Eight and a half kilos is nearly nineteen pounds.

"So does that mean she took everything?"

"Don't worry about any of that now, just rest. You can ask her tomorrow."

Now that I was awake and seemingly fine, the visitors began to take leave to go back to their respective homes and families.

"Wait," I protested. "Did Amma say anything? Is there any message from her?"

They looked at each other, and the woman coyly replied, "Not yet, but I am sure you will hear from her soon."

Once again, I was told to stop worrying and rest. Mahati left along with the others, informing me she was going to pick up some dinner for herself and Amma's mother. Then the room fell quiet. I never heard her return, nor was I disturbed by any noise or light. I drifted off to deep sleep. But some time later in the wee hours of the night I awoke—this time not to nausea but to excruciating pain. I began to moan.

Hearing me stir, Mahati sat up and came to my side. "Are you all right?"

"No, my belly really hurts. Can you call a nurse and get some pain medicine?"

She hurriedly left the room in search of assistance. After a few minutes the door re-opened. I eagerly watched to see who entered. Alas, she returned with nothing but a grave look on her face.

"I couldn't find anybody but a night watchman, and he says the whole place is locked up, and you'll have to wait until the morning."

"What!" I exclaimed in dire distress. "You mean to say there's not even a night nurse?"

"No, I searched everywhere, and there's not a soul in sight."

I bit my lip, turned my head to face the wall, and whispered, "Okay," as I silently began to weep. *How am I going to get through the night?* For what felt like hours, I lay there wide-awake gazing out the window fully aware of the searing and burning pain from the incision and the throbbing gashes inside my hollow abdomen. Amma's mother sat on the bed for a while rubbing my legs, trying to offer whatever moral support she could. In a desperate attempt to isolate myself from the pain, I began to fantasize, when a car drove by, that it was Amma coming to visit. Each time though, the wheels continued to turn. No engine stopped, nor did any car doors open outside the building—they all kept driving. I felt dreadfully alone as I lay there in my hospital bed throughout the remainder of the dark and starless night.

After what felt like an eternity, dawn broke. Along with the first magical rays of sunlight, the hospital and its staff came back to life. Amma's mother was awake sitting propped against the wall with her legs stretched out, shaking her head in disbelief that I had spent the entire night without pain medication. Mahati scurried out of the door once more, but this time successfully returned with assistance. After the nurse administered the shot of pain medication into my rear end, I glared at her with the most disdainful look of displeasure. I explained I never, ever wanted to go through such a horrendous night ever again. The poor nurse of course was not to blame. But in the true Indian spirit of womanly humility, she didn't utter a word. She just nodded her head and left. A little later that morning, I felt someone gently nudging me on the shoulder. I opened my eyes to see the doctor entering my room.

With a professional smile on her face she said, "Good morning, Gayatri. How are you feeling?"

I was slightly incoherent and groggy from the recently administered medications. I mustered a feeble smile, but before I was able to answer her question, she began.

"You'll be pleased to know the operation was a success, but I had to perform a full hysterectomy. One of your ovaries was inside the tumor, and your uterus was severely affected. As a safety precaution I thought it best to remove your second ovary as well."

"Safety precaution?" I squeaked.

"I can't say for sure until we receive the biopsy results, but things didn't look good."

Seeing the worried look on my face, she rephrased it. "Let me just say this. You're fortunate we performed the surgery when we did. I have a feeling you'll be all right. We probably caught it just in the nick of time."

Subconsciously ignoring her implications I asked, "Was it really eight and a half kilos?"

"Yes, and you made it into the newspaper. Oh, and by the way, to dispel any scandal I did a quick walk around the wards with the basin containing your mass. I announced for anyone wanting to see your aborted baby to come take a look."

"Oh, that's gross. I can't believe you did that, but thank you."

Suddenly, I vaguely recollected the image of a bag of red liquid dangling above me after the surgery. "Doctor, was I given a blood transfusion?"

"Yes, we had no choice. You lost a lot of blood during the surgery. I'll be back the same time tomorrow to check on you. You're a very brave girl." Saying this, she turned on her heels and left the room, but not before I got her to write a prescription for pain medication.

The trauma and fear of surgery was behind me, but it seemed the road to recovery was going to be an uncertain one. I cringed whenever I remembered a stranger's blood was flowing through my veins, and worried some of their personality traits or negative tendencies might rub off on me. *Would I become less spiritual? Would my longing for God decline?* Little did I know, but lurking within the anonymous blood was something far more life-threatening, something that would land me back in the hospital within a couple of months.

Later that afternoon I received word that Amma was going to pay me a visit the following day. It would have been three days since my surgery and almost a week since I'd seen her. My mind was still haunted by anguish from that sleepless night, and my heart was filled with mixed emotion. Although I was excited and looking forward to seeing her, I was sad she hadn't come sooner. Daily a few devotees from Quilon came trickling in. Even though I recognized their faces, I didn't really know any of them. As much as I appreciated their concern, it was exhausting to sit up and engage in conversation. I knew though I had to be polite and courteous. I was representing Amma now, and my conduct would reflect back on her.

The following morning, as usual, a nurse came to administer my daily injection, and hook me up to the intravenous glucose drip. That day, she instructed it was time to get out of bed and take my first steps. She pulled the sheet down and suggested I swivel my legs around off the bed. Mahati and Amma's mother each held one of my arms as my feet touched the floor. For a second, my head spun. But once that effect subsided, I placed my weight on the floor and slowly stood upright. The first thing I did was shuffle across the room to the mirror, then gasped with fright when I saw the reflection staring back at me. I was ghostly white and ghastly emaciated because I hadn't eaten in almost five days. With the aid of my helpers, I took my first steps out of the room, down the hallway, and back.

A little later, at roughly ten a.m., the door flung open, and Amma entered the room followed by a mini entourage. She asked them all to wait by the door and came to my side. Seeing her standing before me at long last, I became emotional and started to weep. She stroked my forehead, wiped the tears off my cheeks, and told me not to cry. Then very gently she rolled the sheet down to my waist, lifted it slightly, and looked at my bandaged abdomen. Holding one hand over her heart, she turned to the couple of devotees in the room and expressed how much it pained to see her children suffer. I was touched, and any anguish I'd been carrying melted away. She told me to sit up, and she sat on the bed beside me. A couple of Amma's Indian "sons" were also in the room. After giving me a nod of recognition, they asked Amma if they could eat the breakfast they'd just purchased.

"Of course, my children. You must be starving," she unhesitatingly replied.

I didn't expect Nealu to visit due to his poor health, but I noted the absence of Ganga, my tall and self-assured French brother. He did, however, show up a couple of days later by himself. He confided that he and Venu had wanted to come the day after my operation, but Amma had strongly objected. Her explanation was if they showed such kindness and sympathy to me while I was in hospital, we might develop some emotional attachment. So out of either obedience or fear, Venu refrained from visiting me, while Ganga obviously paid no heed to such narrow-minded nonsense. He felt it unfair, and simply unethical, not to visit me. In this instance he chose to obey his own moral compass.

During Amma's visit the time passed rather quickly. Before I knew it, Balu was standing beside my bed asking, "Amma, can we go now?"

I may have just had major surgery, but without engaging any other part of my body, I gave the heartless fellow a thump on the back, just as I would have done to my little brother were I still living at home.

Amma laughed and seemed humored by our sibling rivalry, so I chuckled along with her—chuckled, that is, until she rose from the bed and agreed it *was* time to leave.

She turned to me and said, "Daughter, I want you to come back to the ashram in one week's time."

She gave me a kiss on the forehead. Then as swiftly as a magician's puff of smoke, Amma and her entourage vanished.

ELEVEN

THE RECUPERATION

I was informed by my doctor that the stitches would be removed in a couple of days. Barring any unforeseen complications, I should be discharged in a week. She went on to say it would be best if I took two months' rest before doing any strenuous work.

With genuine curiosity and concern she asked, "What are conditions like at the ashram? Do you have anyone to look after you? Do you have a proper bed to sleep on?"

When the reality of her questions sunk in, my mind and heart collided like a gigantic wave on a sea wall. There was no bed waiting for me, only a straw mat on the floor. There was no running water, and conditions were far from sanitary. How would I bathe? Even if someone kept a bucket of water ready, I wasn't able to bend or lift anything. Apart from Amma's sister, who went to college, and her mother, there were no other women around. Were Amma, Nealu, Ganga, or the other Indian fellows going to wait on me? I strongly doubted it. Nor would I want them to. It was clear that Amma wanted me to return to the ashram, but how on earth could I obey her under such conditions? At lightning speed, my mind reviewed the various scenarios and NO was the only word that screamed back at me.

I had my answer. With disguised hesitation I replied, "I'll be staying with a family who live near the ashram for the first couple of weeks."

"Well, I am glad to hear that. Make sure they feed you lots of fruits and veggies."

Before I had gone in for surgery, the women at Akkara Veedu suggested I stay with them for part of my recovery. I declined, saying I couldn't bear to be away from Amma that long—a fact that still rung true. I was going to miss Amma. But I needed to make this sacrifice in order to heal properly and not burden anyone at the ashram.

After the doctor left, my mind sank into a quagmire of worry. I realized the tricky nature of my predicament. If I obeyed Amma, I risked injuring myself, making a poor recovery, and possibly getting an infection. If I chose to take care of myself, I risked the consequences of disobedience—which I knew from experience could be rather unpleasant.

My mind was made up. I was going to stay at Akkara Veedu—it was the most practical solution. There were several women in the home, a spare bed, plenty of clean, fresh water in their well, plus Amma visited there often. I thought surely she would understand and perhaps even agree it was a brilliant idea. Nevertheless, I was nervous about breaking the news to her.

The afternoon fell quiet, Mahati had gone out, and Amma's mother and I were gently dozing. After a short while, I felt the presence of a visitor and opened my eyes to see the smiling face of Pai, one of Amma's spiritual sons. Rubbing my eyes and sitting up slightly, I asked, "What brings you here?"

"I'm on official business," he replied with a cheesy grin. Raising a cloth bag that was in his hand he asked, "Guess what I have in here?"

His mere presence had me confused enough. "I don't know. Why don't you stop teasing and just tell me."

"It's a piece of your tumor. I'm taking it to the Trivandrum Medical College for biopsy. Do you want to see it?"

"No," I shrieked. "I don't want to see it." But immediately I had second thoughts. As creepy as the idea was, I did wonder what the thing looked like. "Okay, just a quick peek."

From inside the bag, he lifted a huge glass jar and walked toward me.

"Yuck, that's disgusting." My stomach churned, and I found it hard to believe the ugly, discolored chunk, sitting pickled in liquid, was from inside me.

"Thanks, Pai. You can put it away now." My curiosity was satisfied. Shaking my head, I exclaimed, "I can't believe the hospital doesn't take care of that. You have to personally deliver the tumor?"

"This is not Australia," he humorously reminded me.

As uncomfortable as it was to see him walking around with this rather personal foreign object, I was touched he was willing to go to such lengths on my behalf.

A few days later Amma made another brief visit accompanied by a family of devotees. When I told Amma I'd be discharged in two days, the family offered to pick me up in their car because they were headed to the ashram anyhow. I was just about to thank them when they excitedly announced.

"Yes, we're taking Amma to Kanyakumari for the weekend. We're going on a family outing."

My heart sank. I felt left out, hearing that she was going without me. I loved that place and had visited it a couple of times already with Amma and a small group of followers. It's a popular pilgrim site and tourist attraction located on the southernmost tip of India. It has an ancient Goddess temple overlooking the rocky coastline, and it is one of the few places in the world where you can witness the sunrise and sunset from the same beach.

Before Amma took off, I knew I needed to express my thoughts about where I would spend the first part of my recuperation. Apprehensively, in a cross between a question and a statement, I said, "Amma, I'm thinking about staying at Akkara Veedu for the first part of my recovery."

She cast me a blank look and said nothing—not necessarily a good sign. I had a suspicion she disagreed, so I dropped the subject. I didn't want to push the matter and have her officially disapprove and have to officially disobey.

Eleven days after my surgery, I was free to go. I couldn't wait to get out of the place and away from the stench of disinfectant.

As promised, the family arrived, and the three of us were driven in the direction of the ashram. My trip, however, was two miles shorter, for I alighted at Akkara Veedu. Mahati jumped out of the car and grabbed my luggage, while Amma's mother hurried ahead to announce my arrival. I slowly and carefully walked down the neatly swept sandy path to their home. Two of the daughters came rushing to greet me. The mother, who had been at the far end of the property making rope, came scurrying as well. My heart was overjoyed to receive such a warm welcome. At the same time, I started to choke with emotion. I was so grateful to Mahati and Amma's mother for sacrificing two weeks of their time to take care of me. I didn't know when I would see Mahati again. So I took her by the hand, thanked her profusely, and then we gently hugged. Our emotional parting of ways was cut short when the impatient family honked the car horn. Amma's mother gave me a loving smile and told me to be well. I watched as the two women walked along the tree-lined path and sat back in the car, which then sped off.

My eyes filled with tears. Once more I was battling with the pain of separation from Amma. I managed to console myself with the hope that in a couple of weeks I would be strong enough to return home.

Once the car was out of sight, the girls looked at me and with startled eyes exclaimed, "Gayatri akka (elder sister), oh my God, you've become so thin! We need to fix that."

They helped me up the two-foot slab into the main house with its loosely nailed-together horizontal plank walls, crumbly cement floor, and thatched roof. My bed was by the entrance in a narrow hallway, and I was instructed to lie down and rest. Within half an hour, they brought me milk and a boiled plantain, after which followed a never-ending stream of food and loving care.

An hour or so later, Amma popped in on her way to Kanyakumari. Even though her visit was brief, I was happy. As she was leaving and hurriedly giving the women folk a goodbye sniff, I got a bright idea. Looking at Amma with a hopeful smile I asked, "On your return in two days, can you pick me up so I can attend Krishna Bhava?"

With her arms still wrapped around the elderly mother, mid sniff, she turned, gravely looked at me, and replied, "Daughter, I don't think you're strong enough yet to get in and out of the canoe and cross the river. That could be dangerous. And besides, you need to rest."

"I'll be fine. I don't know if I can bear to be so close yet so far away during Krishna Bhava," I pleaded.

Giving me a half-hearted smile, she replied, "We'll see." Then the family whisked her away.

I felt certain that Amma wouldn't be able to refuse my heartfelt plea. So by three o'clock that Sunday afternoon, I was ready. Chitra had given me a bath, and I was dressed in a fresh set of clothes anxiously waiting for Amma to arrive. I was okay until four o'clock. But when five o'clock rolled around and still no sign, I began to worry. *Why hasn't she come? Maybe their car broke down?*

Finally, by six o'clock, I had to accept the fact they'd driven right by. I was heartbroken. My hurt feelings teamed with my stubborn and rebellious nature. The combination made me all the more determined to cross that darn river. The family tried to dissuade me by saying such things as, "Maybe Amma felt it more important you rest." After several futile attempts, they realized nothing was going to change my mind. So Chitra went in search of a taxi. Upon return, she dashed into the house, got changed, and then jumped into the cab with me. Ten minutes later we were standing at the dimly lit river's edge scratching our heads, trying to figure out the safest way for me to step into the unstable canoe. Chitra hopped in first then held her hands out. I was tremendously weak, but my desire to be with Amma was so great that, with her help, I managed to get in and back out on the other side safely. I took a deep breath, let out a long sigh, and grinned at Chitra as we gingerly made our way down the path toward the ashram.

As I drew closer, my heart began to pound. I smiled with anxious anticipation of seeing Amma and her reaction. *Would she be happy to see me? Would she laugh and shower me with love and affection? Or would she say I'd been foolish and scold me for my lack of surrender?* Deep down I felt that this journey was foolish, but the call of my heart knew neither risk nor reason.

As we walked across the grounds to the temple, people stared at me with astonished looks. I couldn't tell if they thought I looked like a super-skinny ghost, or if they were thinking, w*hat on earth is she doing here?*

For a brief moment I stood in the sand gazing at Amma, allowing my heart to soak up her smiling and shimmering image. When I'd mustered enough courage, I turned to Chitra and with a nervous smile said, "Wish me luck."

We walked toward the temple. She helped me step onto the verandah, then I stealthily slid through the doorway and stood in the corner leaning against the wall. After staring at the floor for a few seconds, I slowly raised my eyes toward Amma. Right at that moment she turned and smiled at me with such sweetness that my heart melted. With a mischievous twinkle in her eyes, she held her hands up gesturing, "What are you doing here, crazy one?"

I felt so relieved by her response that after smiling at her for a moment, I lowered my eyes and began to cry. Through my tears I saw her signaling me to come near. She embraced me with a long, warm hug and looked deep into my eyes as she sprinkled a handful of flower petals on my head. With a tender look she told me to go and rest in the hut.

A couple of hours later, upon hearing the opening bells of Devi Bhava, with slight apprehension I made my way toward the temple once more. Even though I had received much affection during Krishna Bhava, I feared her disposition could be more serious this time.

Sure enough, after giving me a brief hug, with a stern look on her face she said, "It was very unwise of you to disregard my words. How could you take such a risk? Now go and rest."

With an aching heart I made my way back to the hut, lay down, and plummeted into pain and sorrow. Chitra came in behind me. Seeing my face, she immediately understood what had happened. She didn't utter a word, but her expression told me she had anticipated as much. Slowly it began to sink into my consciousness that this visit hadn't been such a wise move after all. Another thought crossed my mind—maybe she's angry about my staying across the river.

At the end of the program, she came into the hut and I got my answer.

"Didn't I tell you to stay here for your recuperation? You wouldn't listen, chose to stay at Akkara Veedu, and now you come here against my wishes. You know what? Considering you want to stay there so badly, I think you should just remain there."

I swallowed hard and meekly asked, "But for how long?"

"Until you're better," she replied, looking the other way.

"But that could be two months. I was only planning to stay there a couple of weeks until I felt a little stronger. I didn't want to burden anyone here." Seeking the tiniest fragment of consolation, I pleaded, "Can I at least come once a week for Krishna Bhava?"

Her eyes were gaining intensity, so I knew that was my last shot to try and change her mind. "If Amma wants you to visit, she will let you know," were her emphatic and final words. Case closed.

I became numb and speechless and felt like I was being punished. With tears in my eyes, I nodded as if to say, "Understood."

Seeing how upset I was, she softened slightly and said, "Don't be sad. Amma will come on the weekend to visit. Now go. People are waiting for you outside."

She walked me to the doorway, gave me a kiss on the cheek, then smiled at Chitra and the family who were taking me back in their car. Like a zombie I turned and followed them out of the ashram. All the bubbly excitement, love, and devotion from a few hours before had left me for dead.

After reaching the house, I lay on my bed lamenting and replaying the woeful events of the evening. I was emotionally and physically exhausted. Within a couple of minutes "my story" began losing potency, and I drifted off to sleep.

The following morning my eyes opened to what looked like a glorious day. Through the gaps in the wooden planks, I could see the sun glistening on the dewy leaves and hear the birds chirping. A cool breeze was squeezing its way inside. I began to smile. But before I could engage in any more wondrous emotion, the memory of the night before started glaring me in the face like a mean gangster. Once more, my heart fell heavy. I carefully rolled over to face the wall. Suddenly I was in no rush to get out of bed. I thought, if I have to pee really bad, then maybe. Other than that, nothing doing.

I was overwhelmed with the sting of Amma's words. My mind was tormented and confused. I couldn't understand why she had to be so harsh. *I was only trying to take care of myself, is that such a crime?*

I surmised though, in her eyes, she saw it as lack of faith. *Maybe everything would've worked out just fine had I obeyed and stayed at the ashram. If I did possess one hundred percent faith, then I wouldn't be lying here now in such anguish.* Silently, I began to weep and became lost in thought over the complexities of the path of devotion, a path I was so eager to traverse. It seemed I'd already deviated and fallen into a gigantic ditch. I pictured myself sitting at the bottom of a dingy, dank pit, looking up, wondering how on earth I was going to crawl out. *How could I remedy this situation? Would Amma ever forgive me for disobeying her?* I felt sick in the stomach with worry.

There was a gentle push on my door. As it creaked its way open, the room filled with light from the new day.

"Gayatri mol (daughter), are you not getting up?" enquired the mother of the house.

Discreetly wiping the tears off my cheeks, I rolled over to render a smile. I could tell from the loving look on her face that she'd been briefed on recent events.

"Why don't you go clean your teeth and wash your face so you can have some breakfast," she suggested.

"Okay," I replied, still wallowing in dejection. I let out a sigh and shoved my wounded feelings aside.

Hours and days trickled by. Finally it was time to head back to Quilon for a check-up. Chitra accompanied me on the one-hour bus ride, ensuring that I got a seat and that nobody bumped me along the way. Shortly thereafter, I was seated once again in front of my doctor.

"How are you feeling?" she smiled from across her desk.

"I'm still a little weak and don't have much appetite, but I think I'm fine."

Her gaze shifted upwards, and I caught her staring at my thinning scalp.

"Oh, and for some reason I'm losing a lot of hair. This morning I had a pile filling both palms. Is it perhaps from one of the medicines I'm taking?"

"Yes, I was about to go over that with you." She leaned gravely into her desk. "You might recall after the surgery I expressed concern. Well, as a precaution I put you on an anti-cancer drug, and one of the side effects is loss of hair."

Oh great, just a minor detail.

"How long do I have to keep taking it?" I asked, fearing I'd be bald in a week if the hair loss continued at the same rate.

"I do have some good news," she smiled. "Your biopsy report shows you do not have cancer. It was only a borderline malignancy. That being the case, a total of ten days should be sufficient, so just three more days. Oh, and don't worry. Your hair will grow back," she reassured me.

Incorrectly.

She went on to explain that a portion of the tumor was bone-hard and had probably begun forming when I was twelve years old. She took a quick look at the scar on my belly, remarked how well it seemed to be healing, and then asked me to return in a week's time.

On the bus ride back, my health concerns hopped into the back seat. Snuggling up against me was the nagging worry of how to regain Amma's favor.

Later that afternoon, as promised, Amma came to stay for a couple of days. Seeing me was not the sole purpose of her visit, but I was happy nonetheless.

She often used Akkara Veedu as a rendezvous point to meet with young men who were not yet ready or able to join the ashram. She would spend hours on end locked inside the family's shrine room alone with them. The family welcomed everyone with bright smiles, warm hearts, and good food. Sunday afternoon gradually rolled around, which meant it was time for Amma to leave.

She'd been rather sweet during her stay, so I took it as a sign she was no longer angry and maybe, just maybe, I could come for Krishna Bhava. Excitedly, I asked Chitra to give me a bath. With tiny butterflies fluttering around in my stomach, I waited on the verandah.

Amma came out of the house to say goodbye. So I quickly stood up and with a nervous smile asked, "Can I come too?"

Amma's face turned as dark as a thundercloud, "Did I not make myself clear? No, you cannot come. You are to stay here."

I obeyed this time.

A few weeks went by, and thanks to all the rest and good nutrition, my health improved. Correspondingly so did my torment.

I felt I'd learned my lesson and most certainly suffered enough. So I decided to make another trip across the river. I didn't consider it disobedience, rather a willingness to prove how eager I was to return. I needed to make sure she wasn't just testing me. I had read many classic stories portraying the suffering and sacrifice that disciples endured to win their guru's favor. I was merely trying to follow their example. This time, accompanied by the mother, we walked the two miles to the ashram to attend the Krishna and Devi Bhava. When the program was over, I went to the hut to plead for permission to return.

Amma was lying down, so I kneeled by her side and asked, "I'm feeling okay now and really want to come back. So please, can I?"

As icy as an arctic wind she replied, "Daughter, you will have to live with the consequences of your choice a little longer."

I couldn't believe my ears. "But haven't I learned my lesson? Haven't I suffered enough?"

"In order to realize divine truth, one must have absolute surrender and obedience to the guru. Amma feels you haven't fully learned your lesson, otherwise you wouldn't be here protesting."

I could feel my mind, body, and vocal cords constricting as I listened in shock.

"Now go back to *your* Akkara Veedu without any more arguing and wait till Amma gives you permission to return."

Adding a touch of finality, she rolled over, ordering Balu to switch the light off and shut the door.

I peeled myself off the floor and, like a lump of lead, stepped out of the hut. With dramatic synchronicity, the moment my foot touched the sand, a huge thunderclap struck, and the power went out. Within seconds rain began pelting the land, thrashing upon the thatched roof like a percussion instrument. Rather than run for shelter, I stood paralyzed in the downpour feeling like a child who'd just been rejected by its family. Amma's words rang in my ears as the salty tears streaming down my face mingled with the rain. I staggered toward the temple where my chaperone was waiting, my way illuminated by occasional flashes of lightning. Through the dim light, she must have seen the distraught look on my face. Tactfully she said nothing except, "Let's wait for the storm to pass."

A while later, under the shelter of her umbrella, we journeyed together in silence back across the river to Akkara Veedu.

The entire next day I lay in bed sulking, unable to shake the feelings of abandonment. Maybe I'd made a mistake, but that had been five weeks ago. The lesson seemed way out of proportion. Summoning an urgent call from my soul, I prayed for insight. Suddenly, an extraordinary sensation of peace flowed into my heart. Closing my eyes, I fell deep within myself, beneath the clamoring of my mind, to a place of profound quiet.

All right.

I said this within my heart.

I understand and will do my best to surrender completely.

The next weekend, Amma paid another visit, and I was determined not to utter a word. If she wanted me to come back, then *she* needed to say so.

As soon as Amma entered the house, she rushed up, gave me a warm hug, and to my utter astonishment said, "Amma is very happy. My darling daughter Gayatri is coming home."

Go figure.

Finally I was back at the ashram after having survived major surgery in a government hospital, barely dodging the cancer bullet, and six weeks of mental torture. I was eager to do Amma's laundry and even the cooking, but I felt it best to heed the doctor's advice and wait a couple more weeks before doing anything too strenuous. Meanwhile I lapped up the opportunity to read, relax, and spend time near Amma, because I knew before long, I'd be working round the clock again. I was delighted with this turn of events and tickled pink to see the fellows chop wood, haul water, and come flying out of the kitchen coughing, spluttering, and wiping the burning smoke from their eyes.

Alas, my little bout of entertainment was short-lived. I quickly realized that Amma didn't share my sentiments. It was breaking her heart to see the men do so much physical work. She was constantly sympathizing and cajoling. She even lent a hand with winnowing and cleaning the rice. One day it broke *my* heart to hear her ask, "Is Gayatri not better yet?"

The problem was this. Indian men are accustomed to being revered and waited on hand and foot by their mothers and sisters. Amma had been raised most certainly with the same family values—hence her concern. The laundry was done, the meals served, the plates taken away and washed, and only after the men had finished eating would the women of the family even consider sitting down for their own meal. End result: the ingrained superiority complex of Indian men.

Even though I knew it wasn't part of the culture for men to do such menial tasks, I couldn't see what the big deal was. In my mind, we were living in an ashram, and we were supposed to be spiritual aspirants. So why should they be able to use "upbringing" or "tradition" as an excuse? Lord knows, I wasn't able to play my "madama" card too often. This was a part of the culture I tried to accept but had a real hard time swallowing.

A couple of weeks later Amma was invited to a devotee's home in Quilon. We headed there after Devi Bhava on the early morning bus. Once we arrived at the house, I felt much weaker than usual. I assumed this was from lack of sleep.

By evening I was somewhat better. I decided to sit behind Amma to fan her as we sang. About halfway through the second song, from the tiny exertion of waving the fan, I was overcome with exhaustion. I paused for a second. Just when I was thinking I might collapse at any given moment, Amma turned around and glanced at me. Suddenly (for some crazy reason), I got the notion this was a test. I saw it as a challenge to overcome my physical weakness and prove my devotion. With renewed courage and perseverance, I succeeded in fanning her until the singing concluded over an hour later.

Even if this experience had been just a projection on my part, I learned that when we align the power of our mind behind the desires of our heart, we can accomplish anything.

The following day I was extremely tired as I squatted on the bathroom floor hand-washing Amma's clothes. My arms were so weak I could barely move the scrubbing brush to and fro. My legs no longer had the strength to support me. So I knelt in the soap suds on the cold, hard marble floor.

Suddenly my body started to shake. I felt I was going to be sick. I had no choice but to quit and lie down.

After resting for a couple of hours, I went to the bathroom and was mortified when I saw the trickle of dark amber urine flowing from me. This was a hue I was way too familiar with. That's when it hit me —nausea, no appetite, exhaustion, "Oh no," I cried.

It must be hepatitis again.

Having gone through this when I first arrived in India, I knew exactly what to do. I took matters into my own hands. After seeking Amma's permission, I hopped in the family's car and asked the driver to take me to the nearest lab. I asked for a cup then handed over the urine sample requesting they test for bilirubin—a test I knew would reveal if I had hepatitis or not.

A couple of hours later I went to pick up the results. Sure enough, my suspicions were validated. On the slip of paper in my shaking hands I saw the dreaded word "positive."

Immediately I got on the phone with my doctor. She advised I check into the hospital right away. She was concerned that this trouble could be complications from the surgery.

"Can I call you back? I need to get Amma's permission first."

"Fine, do whatever you need to. But I expect to see you first thing in the morning."

Once back at the house, I tracked Amma down and informed her of the news. Naturally she told me to follow the doctor's advice. This was the answer I was anticipating, but I'd been in enough trouble recently that I wanted to observe the correct protocol.

The following morning I was back in the hospital with a syringe in my arm drawing blood for a battery of tests. Then, much to my amusement, I heard the familiar, squeaky wheels of the glucose drip stand rolling my way. Sure enough, the rig was parked by my bed. A needle was jabbed into the large vein on the top of my bony hand, and the magical liquid was on its way.

This time, my stay in the hospital was brief. After three days, I was discharged. They couldn't find anything wrong.

"All your tests came back negative," exclaimed my doctor as she stood before me with a perplexed look on her face. "I'm going to sign your discharge papers. But you need to call me right away if you have any more symptoms. You understand?"

I nodded. I was elated to hear I could go home. Yet I was slightly dubious, for I was certain I had hepatitis—seemingly, though, the disease was no longer in my body.

I left the hospital carrying my overnight bag and slowly made my way to the street to catch a bus to the terminal. I stood back and waited for everyone else to board. I was light-headed, in no shape to be knocked around. Then, with a firm grip on the railing, I climbed onto the bus with my wobbly legs, and I stood in the aisle. At the main station I alighted and strolled through the crowded chaos in search of my bus. Finally in the distance I saw my lucky number, so I headed swiftly in its direction with the hope of securing a seat. I looked at the metal sign dangling in front of the red and yellow bus and read out loud "Vallikavu." This brought a smile to my face, for I felt proud to be able to read Malayalam. But I felt more proud because the sign meant that I was heading home. Hopefully, this time, to stay.

There were plenty of empty seats, so I made my way down the aisle and took a window seat on the left side. Shortly afterwards the driver turned the ignition, the bus began to vibrate from the roar of the engine, and we were on our way. Some ten minutes out of Quilon town we were approaching my favorite place and the reason for sitting where I was. The bus drove onto a bridge suspended high above a mile-wide estuary. To my left, in full view, was the sparkly blue ocean. Its cool and salty air came charging through the windows, making my heart overflow with serenity. As I gazed out toward the beautiful expanse, I was filled with longing for infinite peace and wisdom. Simultaneously nearly every head on the bus turned and faced the ocean too. This response always made me smile, for I believed it meant that all human beings, aware or not, sought eternal peace.

As my destination drew nearer, I began to worry about what I was going to tell Amma and everyone about my supposed bout of hepatitis. Would they think I had imagined everything? Even though nothing showed up in the blood tests, I felt certain at some point the illness was there.

Twelve years needed to pass before I'd gain any insight into the matter. In 1993, while on tour in the United States, I had comprehensive blood work done. When I saw the results of the liver panel, my eyes almost popped out of my head. There it was in plain English: hepatitis "A" antibody—positive.

This I already knew from my early travels in north India.

But what came as a complete surprise were the following words: hepatitis "B" antibody—positive.

Finally I had proof of its existence at some point in time—most likely contracted from the blood transfusion. But how it disappeared so rapidly, I will never know. Was it only a mild case of the illness? Perhaps I have a strong immune system? Did the hospital make a mistake?

Or was it a miracle? At the time I wanted to believe so.

But who's to say when the interpretation of such events rests entirely upon the disposition of one's faith?

TWELVE

OUR MOTHER, OUR GURU

Within two years what began as a one-hut ashram had transformed into a cluster of nine huts. The family home was now ashram headquarters. Amma ceased being referred to as Sudhamani, a fisherman's daughter, and was officially entitled Mata Amritanandamayi (The Mother of Immortal Bliss), a name chosen for her by one of her "sons." Donations—money, gold jewelry, and food—began trickling in. An adjacent piece of land was purchased, and a new home was constructed for Amma's family. Due to Amma's increasing popularity and the number of visitors frequenting the ashram, it soon became hard for her to move around or maintain any sense of privacy. She couldn't head across to the bathroom or sit outside and clean her teeth without people gathering.

In the morning it was customary to see her sitting in the bare sand with her wavy locks dangling over her shoulders, dressed in a petticoat with sarong wrapped around and tied at the neck. Her tooth-cleaning ritual began by dipping the index finger of her right hand repeatedly into a black substance called oomikadi (charcoal of rice husks) and rubbing her teeth with it. Within minutes she'd be surrounded by a tiny audience of ashram residents. Naturally she became engaged in conversation. While Amma was smiling and laughing with black gunk all over her teeth, I'd dash to fetch a tumbler of water and an eight-inch piece of the inner stem of a coconut palm leaf, which she used as a tongue cleaner.

If any devotees were around, they too would seize the opportunity to be in her presence, and this was causing us a great deal of distress. It was hard to say anything because Amma didn't seem to mind. But we felt she shouldn't have to deal with visitors the moment she got up. In fact, we felt it no longer practical for her to continue living in the hut, not to mention sharing the common bathrooms.

Despite her repeated protests, Nealu took it upon himself—which he couldn't have done if she were truly against it—to finance the construction of a two-story dwelling for her. Ganga, the highly intelligent and slightly stubborn Frenchman, drew up the plans and spent months coordinating and supervising the construction. He had to keep a constant eye on the workers, who often had a mind of their own. Occasionally he put his foot down with Nealu, who didn't always see eye-to-eye with Ganga's vision. Downstairs became the ashram meditation hall, and upstairs was a simple room with attached bathroom and tiny balcony.

It took a while for Amma to move in. For the first couple of years, she often gave up her space to accommodate special guests during festivities.

Although she encouraged us to look upon her as our mother, she slowly began enforcing the guru aspect. She began insisting we prostrate before her and show reverence at all times, especially in public. She carefully reiterated it was not for her sake, but for us to gain humility and the sublimation of our egos. No longer could we follow our individual routines of meditation and spiritual practice. We were to function as a group on a rigid timetable. By four-thirty a.m.—on days not following the Krishna and Devi Bhavas—we were to be bathed and ready to meditate for two hours before chanting the Lalita Sahasranama (thousand names of the Divine Mother). To top it off, classes were starting up. She was bringing in a retired professor of philosophy to teach Hindu scriptures, and also a pundit to teach Sanskrit.

This new regimen caused me considerable aggravation. *How on earth can I tend to my duties and also follow this new schedule?* I wondered. Most of my daylight hours were spent in the kitchen. In the evenings, I'd meditate for at least an hour, sing bhajans, and then after dinner sit quietly writing my reflections down in a journal. What I wrote varied from my feelings and aspirations, to perhaps an incident with Amma, or some quotable words she had said during the day.

Despite my resistance I didn't really have much choice. I had to give the new routine a whirl.

The early morning meditation was always a mighty struggle, and not just because of my restless nature. Amma hardly ever went to bed at a reasonable hour, which meant neither did I. If she did, then without a doubt she'd awaken at some godforsaken hour saying she was hungry or thirsty or something. Other nights she had trouble sleeping and would complain of restlessness. She would want her legs or tummy massaged. I had to be ready to jump into action whatever time of day or night it was. I frequently struggled with exhaustion—a price I was willing to pay for the honor of being her attendant.

Initially, to ensure everybody was obeying orders, Amma would sneak down her staircase, peep through the window of the meditation hall, and do a head count. After a while though things got lax, and Venu frequently failed to show up. He much preferred to perform his little regimen of yoga and meditation in his hut. One fine morning while I was seated cross-legged, jostling between a state of meditation and sleep, I was disrupted by the roar of Amma's laughter. My eyes sprang open to see Venu being dragged into the meditation hall with his ear lobe tightly pinched between Amma's fingertips.

Jokingly, yet meaning every word, she reprimanded, "You can meditate all you want at other times in your room. But if you want to progress spiritually, you need to learn obedience."

Some of us preferred sitting on the verandah where it was cooler, but Amma insisted we stay inside to avoid being distracted. Despite this a young chap, even though he'd been reprimanded a couple of times already, continued to sit outside. One day Amma caught him there and ran, grabbed a big stick, began jokingly whipping him around the legs a few times, and then shoved him inside.

Making a public spectacle of him, she said, "When I close my eyes, he opens his. When I open mine, he closes his. When I'm before him, he pretends to be afraid. Yet when I'm not around, he continues to disobey my orders. What faith does he have? Does he think just because I'm not around, I'm not aware of what he's doing?"

Hearing the ruckus, Amma's grandmother, who religiously sat every morning in front of the temple making garlands from hibiscus petals, hobbled over to find out what was going on. Upon seeing Amma with a big stick in her hand, she let out a mighty laugh.

Amma turned to her and asked, "Have you never beaten your children with a stick? Well likewise, I have to beat mine. I've got twenty-five of them now and am going to have a heart attack soon."

The old woman's eyes glistened with delight, and her lips curled up around her toothless gums. The sight of this made us all break out into hysterical laughter.

Amma took a seat on her specially reserved carpet, and her mood turned serious. As recorded in my journal:

> Spiritual practices are the only true wealth in this world. One way or another, you must attain concentration of the mind. If you're restless or falling asleep, get up, walk around, and chant your mantra. After some time, sit down and focus once more. Gradually you should develop the patience and discipline to sit for at least one hour without moving. Even if your concentration is weak on a given day, this practice will help you go deeper within.

Thankfully, not all my struggles in meditation culminated in frustration. From my continued efforts to gain concentration, I found that my mind gradually became more focused. A couple of months after the new timetable had been implemented, I underwent a powerful experience. During the evening bhajans, Amma began singing a song that always stirred my heart with deep emotion. Suddenly I was overcome with a powerful yearning to know God. An intoxicating ecstasy welled up from within. My body started swaying from side to side, and my hands spontaneously began to hold themselves in unfamiliar positions. For a split second, I felt self-conscious and wished I could bathe in the bliss without being seen by others. At that precise moment, there was a power failure, and the ashram was plunged into darkness. The only remaining light was the flickering orange glow from the oil lamp inside the temple.

Power blackouts were not uncommon. But having my prayer answered so dramatically sent me soaring even higher. I began sobbing while the singing continued to fuel my devotional fire. A few minutes later I was briefly distracted when I caught a glimpse of Amma's mother. She was coming from the house carrying a kerosene lantern. I closed my eyes again. I could feel the light drawing nearer but was unable to control my sobbing.

Amma's mother put her hand on my shoulder, held the light up to my face, and asked, "Gayatri, what's wrong?"

Instantly I was catapulted off of my heavenly cloud and began freefalling until I landed with a thump back on planet Earth.

The following day, as I reflected on this experience, I wondered if it had resulted from my increasing efforts at meditation. In a moment of insight, I saw the mind as a well, and I saw meditation as a gradual drilling process through which the mind deepens. If the well of the mind is shallow, it will be filled with ground water. But if we persevere, eventually our mind will be filled with the crystalline spring-waters of truth, love, and wisdom.

Despite my struggles with meditation, this experience served as a great source of inspiration for me to continue my inner quest.

As I needed to start cooking for the ashram by six-thirty a.m., Amma pardoned me from chanting the thousand names after the meditation. Instead she made me promise I would recite them at some point later in the day.

Even though the cooking was completed around noon, afterwards I needed to clean the storeroom, ensure that all the grains and spices were stocked, then chop and sort firewood. To make matters worse, I also had to attend the classes. When that pesky bell rang, I was supposed to drop whatever I was doing and head to the study hall. If it happened to be laundry day, I became especially irritated, for not only was I hot, sweaty, and covered in soot, but my sari and underskirt would be sopping wet and covered in soap. At times I felt like Cinderella as I plopped down on the cement floor and sat cross-legged on my meditation rug.

We each had a slanted wooden desk approximately two feet wide and eighteen inches deep, just large enough to fit over our crossed legs and hold a textbook and note pad. As I dragged the desk over my lap, I'd look around and see everyone else as fresh as daisies, with serene looks plastered on their faces, ever so eager to partake in the knowledge. Despite the discomfort from the damp and musty clothing sticking to my body and my frustration that the class was disrupting my day so terribly, I often found myself enjoying the lessons.

Later in the day, once all my chores were complete, I'd grab my meditation rug and sit among the coconut trees to chant the thousand names—as promised.

I wasn't always grateful for Amma's strict regulations. Sometimes I felt she was cruel and unfair. Before my evening meditation and the devotional singing, I liked to take a quick rinse and change into a fresh set of clothes. It felt great to wash away the sweat and grime from the day, plus I found it easier to concentrate—fresh body, fresh mind, so to speak. One afternoon, as I was crossing in front of the temple with a bath towel flung over my shoulder, I was stopped dead in my tracks.

"How many baths do you need in a day?" Amma snapped. "Any little time you get should be spent in meditation. Look at her, instead of meditating, she's bathing a hundred times a day."

I didn't say anything, but felt hurt and angry. During the hot months of the year, which were about nine in all, my body was often covered in prickly heat rash. It seemed cruel to be denied a splash of cool water in the evening, but what could I do? Her words were final, and surrender was the only option. Once my initial reaction subsided, I tried to accept her harsh words as being what she called them: Grace. I tried to view them as the result of my prayers and yearning to know God. I wrote in my journal:

> Mother's Grace is her scoldings. With each scolding, we progress if we can take heed, or at least fear her words. The other day, I was filled with sorrow at my pitiful state of no detachment, meditation, or remembrance of my goal. I was feeling stagnant. When will I progress? Within two days it started. From Amma's hand, a spoon came flying across the room at me along with the following words: "Go back to Australia, get married, or stay in a lodge. You should be chopped into pieces and hung out in the sun to dry." This is the way Mother pushes us along. First comes our desire for progress, then she beats us with the stick of discipline.

Alongside my deep love for Amma was a considerable amount of fear. One morning, just a few months after my arrival, I and a couple of others were seated on the bench in the dining room waiting for breakfast to be served. Amma's sister came from the kitchen carrying a steel container full of rice gruel and placed it on the table. Using the ladle, we began pouring the bland white porridge into our steel plates as she served coconut chutney. When I looked down, I saw the tiniest blob of chutney, maybe the size of half a teaspoon sitting in my saucer. I became annoyed and thought, *How on earth can I eat this tasteless slop without any condiments?* From early childhood, I was rather quick-witted, and the fact that I was now in an ashram where a foreign language was spoken didn't seem to hold me back. Suddenly I remembered the song "Oru Tulli Sneham" which means "A Drop of Love," converted it into "Oru Tulli Chutney," and sang it out loud.

In my excitement, I forgot Amma was in the room and began to laugh at my own clever lyrics. Hearing her voice, but not understanding what she was saying, I turned around expecting to see her enamored with my wit. Instead she was charging at me with eyes engorged and arms stretched out in front as though she was going to throttle me. This all happened very quickly. Before I knew it, instead of attacking me, she turned and slammed her head into the concrete wall. Simultaneously we all leapt off the bench and gasped in horror. Balu rushed to her side and began rubbing the lump that was forming on her forehead. He hurled me a look of disgust. I didn't dare go near her, and my stomach was writhing with remorse.

In a fit of annoyance, she shoved Balu's hand away, turned to me, and said, "A spiritual aspirant should have self-control and not be so attached to food. Only if one gives up the taste of the tongue can they enjoy the taste of the heart."

As it turned out, the family was grinding more chutney. But now it was too late. Everyone had lost interest in eating. I was distraught. If only I had been more patient, I thought, this whole incident could have been avoided.

At the same time, I found it hard to believe that my clever lyrics had warranted such a violent reaction.

Understanding that I was upset, Amma tried to console me by saying, "Mother is not angry. It is only because of love that she can't refrain from correcting her children."

My faith was steadfast. So was my commitment to doing whatever it took to be her attendant.

Little did I know this commitment would eventually include carrying, and helping Amma conceal, many of her dark little secrets.

Before meeting Amma, I was told she was "pure," meaning free of her monthly menstruation. This purity was proof of her divinity. I believed this and had no reason to think otherwise, until one day in 1982.

I don't remember the exact date, but I do remember the exact moment. Amma was going to the bathroom when I noticed a large blood stain on her petticoat.

Thinking she was hurt, I gasped and with tears welling in my eyes exclaimed, "Blood, Amma, blood."

Pointing to her bottom, she calmly replied, "Back."

"Back?" I repeated.

With a cheeky grin, once again she insisted, "Back," meaning it was hemorrhoids or something.

I could tell this was not the case, so insistently replied, "No, it's front."

She finally gave in and admitted it was "front," acknowledging it was menstruation.

For a moment I was in shock. But I let it go. This discovery did not affect my faith. It made me feel trusted and special. She had her menstruation every month from that day onward, and I did my best to help her conceal the fact. I always knew it was a secret. Not once did it ever cross my mind that it was a lie. I was so wound up in my devotion and in holding onto my dream position that the full implications of the deception were lost on me.

I either blocked out or completely forgot the truth. Her biography clearly stated that she was "pure." Amma obviously knew this claim to be incorrect. She allowed it to be published anyhow.

THIRTEEN

DISHONORABLE DISCHARGE

We, Amma's band of youths, were a fine mixture of talented musicians, speakers, writers, and spiritually eager souls, but initially we were rather immature and rough around the edges. Apart from Nealu, who'd led an extraordinarily orthodox life with his previous guru, none of us had much exposure to traditional ashram behavior. This made cultivating the proper attitude toward Amma difficult, especially when most of us looked upon her as our mother. By 1983 there were two more female residents— "inmates," as we were called (ironically)—living at the ashram. One was an Australian woman who called herself Saumya, and the other was a young Indian woman I will call Vidya. To help chisel us into shape, Amma announced a new set of ashram rules on October 27, 1983. There was to be no more talking between boys and girls. (Even though we were all in our twenties, she refrained from calling us men and women.) Also, she appointed Nealu to enforce proper guru/disciple etiquette.

This appointment stirred up a bit of resentment among the young Indian men. They felt Nealu was too personally invested. They knew he judged them. He considered their free and familiar ways with Amma disrespectful.

With proud defiance they resisted his rules and advice, feeling he didn't understand where they were coming from.

I was caught somewhere in the middle. I could understand their point of view, but I liked and looked up to Nealu—most of the time. Ganga tried his best to tolerate Nealu's "holier than thou" attitude. But if there was ever a dispute, Ganga always took the side of the Indian men.

Chandru had completed his scriptural studies at Chinmaya Mission and returned from Bombay cockier than ever in his new yellow robes. He had been officially initiated into brahmacharya, a period of religious education and strict celibacy—the equivalent of becoming a monk in Western tradition. Chandru thrived in this newfound role of teacher. He sat quite comfortably before us on his elevated platform. I had to give him credit for achieving success in his classes because they were far more structured and intellectually satisfying than those of the old philosophy professor.

Chandru only lived part-time at the ashram, for he was under contract with Chinmaya Mission to teach at their various centers. Nevertheless, he played a major role in spreading Amma's name throughout Kerala and Bombay. His proselytizing attracted thousands of people to her.

Unfortunately, Chandru's new status went to his head. He began misusing his position to gather his own flock—predominantly of women. A few years later we were shocked to discover that he was spreading not only Amma's name but the legs of many of these women as well.

Because Amma was the center of our little universe, our single-pointed adoration generated a bit of competition for her attention and affection. Balu in particular had a very rough time adjusting to the arrival of some of his spiritual brothers and watching Amma shower them also with her love. One day she spent several hours alone with Sreekumar trying to soothe his aching heart, for he was being forced by his family to leave the ashram and take a job in Bombay. Having to share her in this way really upset Balu, and he began obsessively pacing back and forth with a dark, somewhat disturbed pouty face. Later that afternoon when he didn't show up for lunch, Amma grew concerned.

In a flustered state she exited the dining hall shouting, "All of you, spread out and look for Balu."

We searched high and low, and Amma ran around calling out his name. But there was no response. He was nowhere to be found. Amma feared he had run away. Just as she was ordering his younger brother Venu to head across the river, someone came running up puffing and panting.

"Amma, I've found him. He's on your roof with the door bolted from the outside."

Without wasting a second Amma made a dash for her building and went flying up the staircase.

She banged on the door, shouting, "Balu. Balu, my son, open the door."

Through the air vent I could see him lying flat on his back on the scorching hot cement under the blazing sun, stripped down to his underwear. He lay there stiff as a board, completely ignoring her.

Choked with emotion and with tears in her eyes she pleaded, "My darling son, why do you punish Amma like this? Get out of the hot sun and come to me."

Seeing how upset she was, Ganga climbed onto the roof from one of the window ledges and unlocked the door. Amma rushed to Balu's side and sat him up.

"Gayatri, go fetch some water. He's delirious."

I ran downstairs and hurried back with the glass, which Amma held to his lips. He took a few sips.

"Help me stand him up," she said to one of the men. Then she tied his dhoti back around his waist. With the helpless fellow's arm draped around her shoulders, Amma escorted him down to her room and told everyone else to leave.

"Gayatri, quickly, bring my food," she ordered in a worried-sick voice.

She proceeded to make balls out of her rice and curry and hand-feed him, all the while reassuring him of her undying love. I remember sitting nearby, watching in utter disbelief as she doted on him. Secretly I was thinking, *Big baby! How pathetic.*

At the time I viewed his out-of-control behavior with naivete. I see now that he was in the early stages of mastering the art of manipulation—his dark and indirect way of asserting his role as alpha-male with Amma. I had no idea that I, too, would eventually become subject to his obsessive and manipulative nature.

Incidents like this drove Nealu absolutely crazy. They led to the downward gaze he occasionally cast upon some of these young men. His condemnation arose not from jealousy nor from a desperate need to feel loved—like some of us—but from his own, more mature understanding. It pained him to see Amma go through such ordeals, which were triggered by what he considered childish behavior.

Over the years I observed that Amma responded to each of us in accord with our disposition toward her. Nealu wanted a guru, so she treated him like a disciple and rarely showed any concern or compassion when he suffered from his relentless migraine headaches or back pain. The rest of us wanted a mother, so for the most part she enabled and took delight in the role.

As Amma drew more followers and fame, she began applying a little pressure on the Indian men. One of her frequently used disciplinary tactics was to stop eating, or at least threaten to stop. One day she was having her lunch when one of the fellows in the room started joking. Sitting off to the side, I could see Amma's mood changing with each humorous word he spoke. My head was turning left, then right, keenly observing the mounting tension on Amma's face and the innocent oblivion on the joker's. Knots were forming in my stomach. All I could think was, *Oh, oh, I see a tornado coming.*

Suddenly Amma's steel plate went spinning across the floor like a Frisbee.

Flicking the rice and curry off her fingers, she stood up and declared, "I will not eat for the rest of the day. Devotees will misinterpret this playful and close relationship you boys have with me. In order for them to grow, they need to witness your reverence and devotion. You must be more reserved in my presence. Otherwise in public you won't be able to control yourself. Instead of sitting quietly to my side repeating your mantra, you're making jokes."

The two of us sat patiently in the room while Amma lay down on her bed in protest, facing the wall. There was an uncomfortable silence and I felt bad for the fellow. I was a seasoned veteran to such behavior, but this was a first for him, and he was in shock. I hadn't witnessed Amma react in such a manner with any of the men, so I was clueless as to how "act two" would play out.

After five minutes, she rolled over.

"Gayatri, go fetch some more rice."

When I returned, she was sitting on the floor gently caressing the fellow's head, which lay in her lap. "My darling son, Amma could tell you were feeling bad. Amma didn't want to inflict any more suffering." Instantly the wings of my sympathy spread and took flight out the window. I handed Amma the rice, discreetly rolled my eyes, and sat down.

I felt relieved. Rather than just single me out, Amma was putting some pressure on the Indian men.

But my relief was short-lived. Now that she was tightening the screws on them, she accordingly bumped it up a few notches with me.

I never imagined that things could get any tougher than they already were. But Amma had no difficulty finding new ways to torment me—not certainly through trivial hunger strikes or brief bouts of "the silent treatment." Until that point her disciplinary measures for me had always been hitting, kicking, slapping, and verbal abuse ("scolding" as I naively called it). But now she was getting ready to use the greatest weapon in her vast artillery. Aiming straight at my heart, she was about to pull the trigger and deny me my greatest joy—that of serving her.

In May of 1984 a young man along with his teenage sister arrived at the ashram after traveling a couple hundred miles from the neighboring state, Tamil Nadu. It was a quiet weekday with no visitors, so he was fortunate to find Amma sitting outside by the temple. Throwing his bag onto the ground in a fit of emotion, he dropped to his knees, then spread out in full prostration. With his face buried in the sand, he sobbed loudly, "Amma, Amma, Amma."

She got up from where she was seated, went over to him, and touched him on the shoulder. Lovingly, she asked him to stand.

With tears in his eyes, he implored, "Amma, I seek your blessings. I will not leave until you have cured my sister. She suffers from seizures and mental illness. My parents are aged, so they can no longer cope. I cannot work because I must care for my sister. So we have become poor, and we suffer immensely. We have seen many doctors, and they cannot find a cure. She is your child, so you must rid her of this illness."

Amma seemed genuinely concerned and full of compassion as she wiped the tears from the lad's eyes. I, too, felt sympathy for their sad state, and my heart went out to the poor brother.

The sister though was downright spooky. I shuddered when I caught her staring at me with her intense eyes. She was terribly unsettled and flinched each time Amma tried to touch her.

Turning to me, Amma ordered, "Gayatri, I want you to give her one of the new rooms behind the kitchen." I nodded in obedience. But her next command struck me with panic. Looking at me, Saumya, and Vidya, Amma said, "I want the three of you to take turns in caring for the girl." I froze on the spot, speechless. I was not at all enthusiastic about this order. But I tried my best to conceal the fact.

For the first two days the girl seemed relatively normal. My main discomfort was from her dizzying body odor. On the morning of the third day, however, things began to intensify.

By mid-afternoon her body was thrashing wildly—seizures accompanied by vomiting. Her condition continued for several days. At times she became violent and tried to hurt everyone nearby.

Even though I was genuinely busy most of the day, I began taking on extra chores—an excuse to get out of caring for this girl. My aversion to her rancid body odor and to bathing her kept increasing, and the sight and smell of her vomit made my stomach curdle. I was swiftly losing sympathy.

Once again it was my turn. I reluctantly headed to the room. As always I took a peek inside before daring to enter. As I stealthily pried open the shutter, the sour stench of percolating vomit crept up and punched me in the face. The girl squatted in the corner of the room like a caged animal. Her eyes were wide open, eerily glaring at me through the hair strewn across her face.

Holding my sari over my nose, I stood frozen in horror at the devilish sight. Not only was the room splattered in vomit—one of my saris had somehow found its way into the room and was lying in a puddle of the muck.

I snapped.

For the love of God, I didn't sign up for this, I thought. *What's she still doing here? Any fool can see she's not going to get better. Having faith doesn't guarantee a cure.*

Fearing that the girl might pounce on me if I went in, I cracked the door open, poked a long stick inside, dragged my sari out, then quickly shut the door. I fled the scene carrying the stick with my filthy sari dangling from the end. I cringed at the thought of hand-washing the garment, but I couldn't throw it away. I had only a few saris to my name.

Suddenly I got a bright idea. I'll give it to the local washer man. Problem solved. Or so I thought.

Later that evening when I went to Amma's room, I was surprised to see she wasn't there. I assumed she'd gone to the kitchen to check on things, something she often did late at night.

As I crossed the compound, I heard her voice. It was not coming from the kitchen but sounded as though she was in the girl's room. Instantly my heart sank. I got the sickly feeling that I was in big trouble.

When I came around the corner, there was a small audience huddled in front of the room. This meant without a doubt that Amma was inside. Standing on my tiptoes, I managed to catch a glimpse through the window. The girl was thrashing her limbs, and Amma, along with Saumya, was trying to pacify her. They got struck a few times in the process. It pained me to witness this. I felt that this mess was entirely my fault for having left the girl alone.

After some time the girl calmed down. Having laid her down to rest, Amma came out of the room. When Amma caught sight of me standing amid the crowd, she briskly turned her head away, allowing just enough time to cast me a look of disgust.

In an annoyed tone Amma complained to everyone gathered around, "When I came here, this poor girl was all alone, lying in the dirt and vomit. Gayatri was supposed to be taking care of her. I can't imagine how Gayatri could be so callous to abandon her like that. What pains me even more is that Gayatri refused to touch her soiled sari and gave it to the washer man."

I was already accustomed to getting criticized in public, but I was not at all prepared for her next statement.

Looking me square in the eyes with absolute disdain, Amma declared, "I do not want to be served by someone who is unable to serve others. From today onward, until you have learned your lesson, I no longer require your services. I know quite well how to take care of myself, thank you very much."

Saying this, she stormed off. Moments later the thundering slam of her front door reverberated across the ashram.

Everyone began dispersing. I was graced with a few sympathetic smiles, several looks of concern, and a few glances laced with judgment—something like, "How could you!"

I watched Saumya strut off joyfully. She was normally quite hard to read. But this evening there was no mistaking the sheer delight spread across her face.

The only person who remained standing beside me was my buddy Vidya. Her large, dark brown eyes sympathetically gazed up at me, and I sensed her sharing my distress. Even though at times she was cantankerous, and she frequently went out of her way to push my buttons, deep down we had a strong sisterly bond.

"Gayatri akka (elder sister), you poor thing. What are you going to do?"

All I could do was shrug my shoulders and sigh. This had come as a terrible blow. Never before had I heard such painful words. In an instant my entire world had blown into smithereens, and now it lay at my feet like a pile of shattered glass.

In an attempt to pick up the pieces and console myself, I turned to Vidya and said, "After Amma's had a good night's sleep and a chance to cool down, I'm sure everything will be all right. She's probably just trying to emphasize how unacceptable my behavior was."

"Well, Saumya didn't help matters," Vidya replied with a snicker.

"What do you mean?"

"Well, how do you think Amma knew you gave your sari to the washer man?"

"I don't know. I just assumed she *knew* because she's Amma. You mean to say it was Saumya who told her?"

"Yes. When she saw how angry Amma was with you, she jumped right in and complained a whole bunch, including how she saw you heading off with your sari at the end of a pole."

"Bitch."

Accepting my fate on that gloomy night, I began searching for somewhere to sleep and something to sleep on. My bedding—a straw mat, thin blanket, and pillow—were trapped on the balcony of Amma's room. Despondent, I headed to the dining hall and unlocked the steel cupboard where everything I owned was stored on one shelf. I grabbed a couple of saris and bundled them up to form a makeshift pillow. On the floor a few straw mats were strewn here and there, so I stacked them one on top of the other and shoved them into the corner. I lay facing the wall, curled into a ball. I yanked the sari over my face and gently cried myself to sleep.

The following day, after I had finished my kitchen chores, I decided to head to Amma's room and test the waters. At that point I still believed that this blow-up was merely a temporary demotion, a threat on her part. Like a dog with its tail between its legs I stood in her doorway. With my eyes I asked for permission to enter.

Upon seeing me, she ran to the balcony, picked up my bundle of bedding, and hurled it at me.

"Take your belongings and get out of my sight," she screamed. "Did I not make myself clear? I don't need you. Go find somewhere else to stay, and learn a little humility." She then slammed the door in my face.

My mind went blank, and my heart capsized as the truth began to sink in.

Oh my God, I think she is serious.

I scooped up my bedding and made a slow death-march down the stairs. I relocated to one of the newly constructed huts behind the kitchen where I lay motionless in disbelief, staring at the woven palm-leaf roof.

For the last four-and-a-half years my entire life has revolved around serving Amma. What am I supposed to do now? I understand that what I did was wrong. I should have shown more compassion to the girl. But am I such a terrible person that I have to be thrown out like this?

Through the dull and aching pain in my heart, I began searching for possible bright sides to this sudden turn of events. The only consolation I could find was the fact that at least I would get a good night's sleep. I was beginning to feel exhausted from the years of relentless labor, lack of sleep, and poor nutrition. The diet for us residents was strictly vegetarian. Breakfast and dinner was white rice gruel with either mango pickles, coconut chutney, or—if you were lucky—some mung beans. Lunch was rice with watered-down curry and a tiny serving of vegetables. Milk and yoghurt were considered too expensive, so were never served. Basically, we subsisted on devotion and a protein-free diet.

So in some ways, this exile was a blessing.

A week or so later, despite the brother's earnest prayers and Amma's seeming compassion, the sick girl showed no sign of improvement, let alone a cure. So they left.

My punishment continued.

Daily I managed to receive updates ranging anywhere from "Amma's still really angry with you" to "She's not sure if she ever wants you to serve her again." On and on it went, the perpetual public criticism and harshness from Amma and my relentless struggle to accept the treatment as being for my highest good. Although my body was finally getting some rest, inside I was suffering immensely. I was absolutely heartbroken. After I had finished the kitchen chores and made my way back to my isolation hut, tears would well in my eyes when I saw Amma's clothes dancing in the breeze—laundered by someone else. Not allowed to polish the Krishna or Devi crown or to iron the silk saris—the banishment crushed my spirits. I couldn't wait to hear Amma laugh at one of my corny jokes again. I needed to see her brilliant white teeth and dazzling eyes smile at me once more. Despite how physically hard it had been to serve Amma, that effort was nothing compared to the hardship I now endured. My mind was constantly agitated, and I had permanent knots in my stomach. It was torture.

No one else could fully comprehend my pain. The few who were sympathetic dared not show much concern for fear they were going against Amma's wishes. Nealu tried a few times to offer some philosophical words of advice, but his stoic delivery acted like a mosquito repellant. Vidya checked in daily to see how I was doing. But it was hard for anyone to lift my spirits when my entire life revolved around Amma. I tried to be strong and muster every ounce of faith and devotion, but it was hard not to take this rejection personally.

All in all, this crisis was very isolating. I didn't know how much longer I could continue in such despair. Something had to change. I wanted Amma to love me again, to treat me nice.

That was when I remembered a quote I had recently read by Sri Ramakrishna Paramahamsa:

"As a dog never leaves his master's home, whether he is fed or not, whether his master beats him or is kind, in the same way one must be completely resigned to the guru. He, who can take refuge at His feet and stay resigned under all conditions and circumstances till the last, will indeed obtain Divine Grace."

This saying had become my life's motto. It reflects the state of absolute surrender I aspired for. Thinking to myself, *I wonder if a shift in my attitude will turn things around? What if I stop resisting the treatment and try to accept it?*

This concept might be difficult to comprehend in Western society, with a culture emphasizing individual freedom. Nonetheless, surrender of one's will to a master is common among Eastern religions and is believed to lead the individual to "absolute" freedom. Hinduism in particular is saturated with tales of extreme tests and cruel treatment inflicted by gurus upon their disciples in order to measure their faith, strength, and commitment. The story goes that if these tests are passed, the guru, through divine power and grace, then bestows the disciple with illumination. Supposedly a genuine guru can do no wrong. All his or her actions, no matter how strange or extreme, are performed only for the highest good of the disciples.

Over the ages this belief system has been exploited by many charlatan gurus who have subjected their disciples to tests and demands of absolute obedience, yet have not possessed the power to bestow any such form of grace in return. I simply believed that Amma possessed divine wisdom, and that through serving her, I too would be granted the vision of God.

Hence my willingness to accept whatever treatment she threw my way, no matter how harsh or cruel it seemed.

One night almost two months later Amma called for me. I stood before her listless and clueless as to what she was about to say.

"Move your things out of your room. Sreekumar is sick and needs to stay there."

Where am I supposed to sleep now? I silently wondered.

"You may sleep back upstairs in my room."

In an instant my exile was over.

I had trouble rejoicing, however, as the news was too fresh and my pain too raw. I felt I had learned my lesson, though. I didn't want to go through that again.

My duties returned one by one. Within a couple of weeks I was fully reinstated. There never really was an official ending or discussion about the dishonorable discharge. Nevertheless, I felt extremely grateful and relieved it was over. Everything was back to normal.

For a while anyhow.

FOURTEEN

SOMETHING'S COOKING

Since arriving in India, I always felt an advantage over my European and American comrades because I didn't have to worry about visas or leaving the country. Being an Australian citizen and member of the British Commonwealth, I could stay indefinitely. However, in July of 1984 the Indian Government began talking about making a drastic change to this rule, and Australians were also going to require visas. For months I anxiously awaited news from the local authorities as to my fate. Were they going to force me to leave India? If so, for how long? I also began to wonder if my recent removal from Amma's service was preparation for a journey overseas. Had Amma, through her divine wisdom, foreseen this terrible change of events? Was it part of a weaning process?

The thought of being sent back to Australia made me sick in the stomach because I feared getting caught in the jaws of materialistic Western culture. Thanks to the ashram's negative imprinting, I was convinced that married life was meaningless and full of suffering. To be born a woman was a curse, due to all the weak emotions supposedly inherited. Not only that, I had come to believe it was impossible to lead a spiritual life in the West amid all its temptations. Once again I was seated on the hair-raising roller-coaster ride named anxiety.

By this point in time, Amma was attracting large crowds in her home state of Kerala and gaining popularity in other regions of India as well. We figured it was just a matter of time before Amma would send some of us to the Western world to spread her name. The only thing we didn't know was who, or when. This worry lurked constantly in the back of our minds and none of us, including myself, felt safe. Even though we believed Amma would eventually travel abroad, we had no clue how such an event would come to pass. Where would the funds come from to sponsor such an event? We were already struggling with the ever-increasing mouths to feed and often had no money to buy supplies or pay the electric bill. So the prospect that Amma, along with a mini entourage, would travel to America, Australia, and Europe seemed really far-fetched.

This was all about to change, and much sooner than we could have ever imagined.

Ganga, being a French citizen, was only allowed to stay in India for six months at a time. So he drew the first lucky number. He could have flown to Singapore or Sri Lanka to renew his visa, but Amma insisted he return to Europe.

It was around this time that Amma decided to establish seniority within her ashram. Balu was the first to be officially initiated into Amma's clan and receive the yellow robes of brahmacharya.

Because Ganga was about to travel abroad, Amma made sure to initiate him as well. Many tears were shed, for he was reluctant to leave her side. But from 1984 onward he worked full-time in Europe laying the foundation for her mission. During his first years in Paris he was determined not to charge any money for his talks. He had no savings of his own and dedicated all his time to her service. He lived on twenty-five dollars a week, which was what people were donating to him without being solicited.

When Amma heard that, she was shocked. She advised him to charge for his talks and workshops and to use the proceeds to support himself. She added that one had to adapt to local culture and habits.

He followed her advice. He eventually became highly appreciated for his unique blend of talks that included, of course, what was requested of him by Amma and her devotees. They also included his own experience and enquiry along the Path of Knowledge from his many years of spiritual practice before meeting Amma.

During these years of service he developed a wide network in Europe. Even people who were not Amma devotees would come and listen to him. After seven years of that, in agreement with Amma, he decided that it was time to settle down and let people come to him. A British devotee donated her wealth to purchase a farmhouse in France close to the Swiss and German border. Ganga was multilingual. Thus not only English and French, but also Germans and Swiss could come to the new center, which he called "Maison Amrita."

One day as I was reflecting upon his plight, imagining how I would feel if I were being sent off, the following words of inspiration arose from my heart.

> Only what we are ready to hear, Mother will say.
> Only what we are ready to receive, Mother will give.
> Only what we are capable of doing, Mother will ask us to do.
> We must have faith in Mother and not look so much at her words,
> but try to find her voice in our heart.
> It is that voice which is more reliable, for it bypasses our mind.

A few months later the visa problem was back. There was an article in the newspaper regarding Commonwealth citizens. Upon seeing this Amma said, "Last week I had the feeling you will have to leave the country."

I was in shock. "When will I have to leave?"

"I think so," was her ambiguous reply.

"How soon?" I asked once again.

"Not too soon."

Her response left me feeling anxious but also a little frustrated with the fact that she wouldn't give a straight answer. *Why does Amma have to tease like this? If she knows the future, then why doesn't she just say what it is!*

Despite the eventual need for a visa and the agonizing months of worry it generated, I never had to leave the country. I was only sent away a couple of evenings to give speeches in nearby towns, where numerous Hindus were being converted to Christianity. The local organizers thought if people could see a white woman speaking in Malayalam about the glories of Amma and Hinduism, they might be able to suppress the Christian influence.

Even though Amma's prediction bore no fruit, her miscall didn't shake my faith. I merely accepted it as part of the "testing" and "working on us" theory we all believed in. If she made a prediction which came true—it proved she was divine. If it didn't—well, she was just testing us. What a foolproof system!

Where possible, Amma kept an eagle eye on, and tried to be fully involved in all of the ashram operations. She frequently scrutinized the meals I prepared for the residents, wanting certain flavors and a conservative use of ingredients. She also performed random raids on the storeroom to ensure nothing was being wasted. Therefore, the kitchen was an arena where I constantly got into trouble. For example, I wrote these notes in my journal:

> June 12, 1985
> Last week when I was cooking sambar (lentil and vegetable curry), Mother opened the pot and saw a lot of vegetables. Actually, water still had to be added. Mother gave me a stern look and told that I'd get it when I came upstairs. There was only ten minutes to class. I had to eat some kanji (rice gruel) and give Mother some kanji water. I thought, Oh my God! I am not ready to hear her harsh words like the ones she gave me two days before. She'll probably refuse the drink anyhow, the way she usually does when she is angry. So out of fear, I avoided going upstairs.

Holy Hell

After lunch Mother was saying, "Look at her devotion! Because of her fear of me, I didn't get anything to drink this morning. I told her she would get it when she came upstairs, so she avoided me."

I said, "Mother, your face was just like a Goddess of Wrath, so naturally I was afraid."

Mother replied, "Even if you knew I would kill you, your faith should be such that you would do your duty."

It was an average, quiet day in 1985, and lunchtime in fact. My kitchen duties were complete, and I was sitting by the temple contemplating what to do for the rest of the afternoon.

Out of the blue, Rao came shouting, "Amma's calling. She's in the dining hall."

I had no clue as to why, but from the smug grin he was juggling on his face I got the feeling I was in trouble. Once I reached the doorway, I saw everyone seated cross-legged with their partially eaten plates of food before them, as though someone had hit the pause button. Tension was definitely in the air. My heart sank, for I knew without a doubt, I was going to get it. I just didn't know what for. No sooner had I stepped into the dining hall, than Amma began whipping me with a few pliable and stinging sticks of a broom made from coconut branch stems. One strike landed right over my ear.

"There's too much salt in the food," she screamed. "Are you trying to destroy my sons? Whatever they gain in meditation will be lost because of you. Only one who has delivered children can understand my pain." (She had never given birth, to my knowledge. This was merely her way to express the depth of her bond.) She went on to explain, "Just as salt spoils milk, it will also spoil spiritual aspirants. The ojas (Sanskrit for 'fluid of life') which builds up from meditation will be destroyed through too much salt."

I was taken aback. I had tasted the food and felt certain it was not over-salted—not according to my taste buds, anyhow. In my mind I began arguing with her. *According to your rules, I'm not supposed to use too many vegetables, or coconuts, or lentils, or chili, or oil, and now salt? How on earth am I supposed to make the food edible?* It felt as though the only ingredient I could add without ever getting into trouble was water. Nutrition was never a concern of Amma's (although she ate fish twice a day). But I knew better than to question or try to defend my stance. Remaining silent with as blank a face as possible was the only option if you didn't want to aggravate her further.

> Notes from an ashram meeting:
> Vitamins, vitamins, vitamins! All you boys think of is food. What are you lacking here? You fat slobs! Vitamin B? Vitamin C? Yesterday you were all eating for your existence, now it's for taste. Spiritual aspirants gain vigor and strength from sadhana (spiritual practice), not from vitamins. A true aspirant does not even think of taste, let alone vitamins. He naturally loses interest in the tongue. Now I get it. You're all here for the food and not for spiritual practice. Until now, I hadn't understood this. If any of you believe in my words, why all this talk? None of you come and say, Amma, I'm not having good meditation and keep falling asleep. It's only: the food is no good. I want to go to Haripad to visit my home. Children, you are at the right age now. Sadhana is more than enough. You don't need these vitamins. You all think it is to save money.

For the first few years, I primarily cooked for the ashram residents. But as Amma's popularity grew, devotees began arriving earlier in the day. Often they showed up around lunchtime, just after I had finished cooking—so I would have to start all over again. This was frustrating. Our resources were limited, and I was apprehensive over the risk of cooking too much and wasting a lot of precious food. Up until late 1985 everyone who came to the ashram was fed for free, and we relied solely on donations in the form of food items and money.

Eventually Amma felt that this honor system was no longer practical. She instructed that a separate dining hall be built. After that, devotees were required to purchase their meals. In this way, Amma altered the traditional ashram model and set the foundation for the business-minded and money-driven orientation of her organization.

Due to my increased responsibilities and constant travel with Amma, I began to find it impossible to continue as ashram cook. The duty was handed over to a couple of Indian householder women. Where possible, though, I tried to maintain supervision and responsibility.

Considering that I viewed my service to Amma as my spiritual practice, I strove to maintain the utmost concentration whenever I was tending to her needs. However, being a mere mortal, I was bound to slip up every now and then. One day, mid morning, Amma was freshly bathed, seated on her bed in her petticoat, and I was standing to her side towel-drying her hair. Vidya was in the room. She had wanted to ask Amma a question for a very long time. Due to Amma's busy schedule, chances to talk were becoming rare, so I saw this as a window of opportunity for her. Turning my head for a split second, I looked at Vidya and gestured that she seize the moment.

Instantly Amma ripped the towel out of my hands shouting, "Move away. Don't touch me. Whenever I ask you to do something, straight away your mind goes off to something else."

Darn, I've done it again, I thought to myself, standing frozen not daring to touch her. Without moving I snuck a sideways glance at Vidya and caught the tension on her face. She bounced her eyeballs a couple of times, acknowledging that she was aware of the pickle we were in. I never really knew how each scenario would play out, but I assumed that within moments the two of us would be kicked out of the room. Much to my surprise, Amma nonchalantly ordered me to comb her hair. Believing the episode had passed, I felt the muscles in my chest begin to relax. But I remained ever so focused on what I was doing. Amma gestured for me to hand her the two piles of letters that were sitting on her bedside cabinet. One stack was from devotees, and the other was from her resident children. She spread them like a deck of cards all over her bed, selected a couple, then lay down to read. As she finished each one, she tossed the open letter aside, grabbed a couple more, and was eventually surrounded by a sea of white paper. After a short while she closed her eyes and, with a crunch, rolled over on top of them.

Witnessing this endearing action, we snuck a grin to each other but remained motionless on the floor like mannequins in a store window. Patiently we waited for Amma to get up, get dressed, and head out for the day. After a while, the lunch bell rang, but we paid no heed. Neither of us budged out of fear of getting into trouble again. The only movement we dared make was to inhale and exhale. My legs were starting to go numb, but I chose not to change their position lest a bone crack and disturb her.

After ten minutes Amma sat up. In an annoyed tone she said, "Why didn't you go for lunch? You must go when the bell rings."

It was becoming increasingly hard to know the right thing to do—or even if there were such a thing. At times my heart felt like a ping-pong ball smacked back and forth by her unpredictable and ever-changing temperament. Based on such moods, the names she called me ranged anywhere from Gayatri mol (daughter), Gayatri mummy (mother), madama (white woman), panna patti (rotten dog/bitch), to a nerve-shattering "GAYATRI!"

Serving and living with Amma was like walking a tight rope. I could never really relax, and I had to watch every step. Amma must have sensed the toll it was starting to take on me, so she decided I needed a little pep talk. These are her words, which I faithfully recorded in my journal:

> The one who serves a guru has no other God than guru. People will always be watching you, as you are closely associated with Mother. Your humility, actions of reverence, and character will benefit people. Through you, they can gain devotion. It is obvious you haven't learned anything yet from my removing you for some time. Your removal was not out of anger either. Instead of your going up, I saw you going down.

So I thought, why should I be the cause for anybody's occurring sin? Let her do some meditation and contemplation.

If we think of our own comfort—e.g., missed food, not getting sleep—those thoughts will drain our energy, and we will become more tired. Whereas, if we live to serve others, our energy will become charged. Every thought, every action, should be offered to the guru. The one who is with Mother should gain liberation to show that service alone is enough. I have full faith that through service one can attain God Realization, no doubt at all. You must achieve it.

In the old days, you were innocent and able to know all that I wanted without even asking. But for some reason, through your sakhi bhava (friendly, familiar behavior) and loss of reasoning, you started to go downhill and felt me as always scolding you. But it is told in the Bhagavad Gita that only if we are scolded and chastised will our ego die. Who has the most love, the one who strokes or squeezes the boil? I am full of love for you, even if I don't show it outside. Inside I am always kissing and praying for you. Often, I would be crying for you. Don't you remember me telling that I could never dispense with your body even if you die? And that from the minute you arrived in the ashram I gave you full responsibility? The money was taken from Acchan (father), and its charge handed to you. Every place you have responsibility. Nobody else in the whole ashram have I given such trust to. Could you not have consoled yourself with these thoughts?

Your being with me will cause some to love and respect you, and others will become jealous and criticize you. Whatever they say or do, accept it with folded hands. Remember, it is only through their ignorance, so don't become more ignorant than them. Accept both as one. Offer all to Amma. See all as her will. Some will come to you asking questions, prying about what is going on. Keep it all inside. Don't say anything, even to the closest. Just say, Mother has asked me to serve her. Please don't ask anything from me. Ask her yourself if you want to know anything.

Daughter, I am not blaming you. I know that anyone would fall into sakhi bhava through constantly being with me. But you must try. Read books on those who served saints.

I went to work immediately. I diligently began studying various books, taking notes, and trying to figure out where I was going so wrong.

FIFTEEN

THE PLOT THICKENS

In January of 1986, Amma's parents were moved once again. Their old house had another story added and was converted for use as guest accommodations. The parents never seemed to mind the inconvenience and were actually quite obliging. I can't say for sure, but the fact that each new home they were given was an upgrade from the previous one might have had something to do with it.

The ashram was bursting at the seams. Every time a new room was built, it usually meant that five more people were coming to stay. Money and gold continued to pour in. More and more land was purchased, and the surrounding swamps were filled in and reclaimed. In an attempt to keep up with the ever-growing demand for accommodations, the ashram had begun construction of a massive three-story prayer hall with numerous rooms. In addition, Amma added another story to her own building, with a tiny bridge linking it to the prayer hall. Oddly enough, even after the hall's completion there still didn't seem to be sufficient lodging.

We began traveling farther and farther away from Amma's little fishing village in Kerala, doing programs at various temples. Politicians were starting to take note. At many of the venues they became the official guests of honor. This attention secured them the devotees' votes, potentially, in the next election. Their presence, in turn, fed Amma's power and celebrity. Like a wild creeper she was planting roots throughout Kerala, Madras, Bangalore, New Delhi, and Bombay, with talk of overseas next on the agenda. Ganga was already in Europe raising money and igniting interest in the hearts of many. Madhu, although I rarely saw him anymore, was following suit in his French paradise, Reunion Island. Nealu's elder brother visited India, became an ardent devotee, and expressed a desire to host and help sponsor Amma's visit to California. Around the same time an American woman named Kusuma showed up sharing the same vision. She decided to take plans a step further, and she excitedly headed home to lay the groundwork for Amma's first US and European tour. No longer was visiting the Western world a figment of our imagination, a distant dream. It was about to become reality.

I was excited but slightly nervous at the same time. I was anxious about how I would feel being back in Western Civilization after living in India for nine years. Would it weaken my resolve to stay in India? Would it stir up any latent worldly tendencies?

To help publicize and raise funds for this major event, Kusuma came up with a plan to drive across the United States with Balu, Chandru, and Nealu. A few months before Amma was to arrive in the US, the four of them hit the road like a band of wandering minstrels, singing Amma's praises and glories wherever they went.

At 11:30 a.m. on May 14, 1987, it was time to depart for our very first world tour. Amma had spent the last several days calling the residents one by one to her room, giving them some last-minute advice and attention. I stood guard in the doorway armed with a list, crossing off their names as they entered and using a wristwatch to let Amma know when their ten minutes were up.

Holy Hell

Shortly before stepping out of the ashram, Amma made the following announcement to all those huddled around her: "When I return, I want to be immersed in bliss from the amount of prema (loving devotion) you hold for me. I want you all to pine for me like the Gopis (a group of cow-herding girls famous in ancient Hindu texts for their unconditional devotion) when their beloved Krishna left them."

Gradually we made our way out the front gate and proceeded down the path to the water's edge. As we climbed into the boat, the dozens of faces that lined the riverbank simultaneously began sobbing and wailing.

Amma turned to me and asked, "What am I to do? Should I laugh? Should I cry?" Crossing her hands over her chest, she called out, "Don't be sad, my children. Amma's not going anywhere."

The boat pushed away from the shore, sending everyone into a frenzied crescendo, "Amma, Ma, Amma, Ma, Ma, Amma."

Eventually, separated by a wide expanse of water, the tear-strewn faces and heart-felt pleas faded into the distance. Coming into view on the opposite side of the river was another large crowd waiting to bid Amma farewell. A few minutes later we were seated in the car about to embark on our three-month tour. In a grand procession of twelve vehicles elaborately decorated with flower garlands, we proceeded to the Cochin Airport. There too a large crowd was gathered, and there too tears were plentiful.

After much pushing and shoving, eventually we were quietly seated in a VIP lounge, safely away from the emotional hysteria outside. Now it was time for the influential people to make their entrance. With mildly arrogant composure, politicians and high officials of the airport, government, and police department lined up to greet Amma. I kept a smile on my face, but couldn't wait to be seated in the plane and have this long drawn-out departure over and done with.

Finally after an hour or so of this stuffy meet-and-greet it was time to depart for Madras. Escorted by police, we made our way through the crowded terminal and across the tarmac to the steps of the plane. Before boarding, Amma stopped, turned around, and for the final time, raised her arms into the air. Suddenly there was a sea of white fabric flapping in the wind. On the roof of the airport men, women, and children crowded together waving frantically. Clutching onto the wire barricade beside the terminal was a cluster of bodies smashed one against the other. Everyone was desperate to catch a final glimpse of their beloved Amma.

We climbed the stairs. As I was showing our boarding passes to the flight attendant, I peeked inside and realized we were the last to board. All the passengers, predominantly Indian, were seated, waiting, and every pair of eyes was staring at us. Toward the rear of the plane I could see Saumya, Ramakrishna, Sreekumar, Rao, and the three Indian household devotees who were accompanying us.

Upon seeing "her children" Amma began shouting to them, "Look out the window, do you see all my devotees waving us goodbye?"

I cringed when I noticed several passengers glaring at Amma with rather judgmental looks on their face. This was Kerala, her home state, and people knew who she was. I imagined them thinking, "So this is the revered Mata Amritanandamayi?"

Out of fear that she would be ridiculed, along with a little embarrassment, I turned and discreetly whispered, "Amma, sshh." My extremely well-intended and spontaneous reaction, unfortunately, didn't go over too well.

After we were comfortably seated, Amma, now exercising full discretion and awareness of her surroundings, sharply pinched a chunk of my thigh between her fingernails and whispered, "Don't you dare tell me to hush ever again. Who do you think you are, telling your guru to be quiet? If the world ever heard about this, they would stone you to death."

At 5:20 p.m. we were off. The plane lifted into the air, and I breathed a sigh of relief. The long-anticipated journey had begun. The days upon days of organizing and packing were over. I could sit back and relax now. This was Amma's first time in an airplane, so I didn't know how she was going

to react. Surprisingly she was quite calm and relaxed, at least for this short first leg of the journey.

After a sleepless overnight stay in Madras, followed by three days of very short programs in Singapore, we were on the plane headed for San Francisco. As soon as the aircraft took off, Amma leaned forward, grabbed the headphones out of her seat pocket, and put them on.

Just as I was wondering if she needed help plugging them in she said, "Hey, put your ear protectors on."

Reluctantly, I obeyed.

Peering out the window and excitedly bashing me on the shoulder, she shouted, "Gayatri, look, an island."

Amused by her childlike ways, I leaned over to see what had caught her interest with such enthusiasm. I was also slightly concerned that passengers might complain if Amma didn't keep it down. But I dared not say anything, not after making that fatal mistake a few days before.

The flight to San Francisco was long. Amma became restless and couldn't seem to get warm. I gave her every stitch of warm clothing I had packed for the flight, but it wasn't enough. I borrowed a huge jumper from one of the men, which she quickly put on. She stuffed her ears with cotton wool. The effect was truly a sight to see.

Still not cozy, she asked for her hot-water bottle.

"Hot-water bottle?" I repeated in disbelief. "I brought it, but it's down below in the suitcase."

Because I was hardwired to fulfill her every wish and aimed to please, I hurried to the galley and returned with a wine bottle full of hot water. She hugged it to her chest for a couple of minutes, then not so nicely handed it back to me.

"I need to lie down," she grumbled, tossing her pillow onto the floor. Before I knew it, she was curled up in the tiny space, pinching me on the legs to get them out of her way.

"Amma, you can't lie on the floor. It's against the rules," I meekly protested.

"Shut your mouth. I'll do what I want."

There was nothing I could do, so I sat cross-legged in my seat, squirming with frustration.

Before long, the inevitable happened. "Excuse me, Ma'am. You need to get up off the floor," ordered a somewhat annoyed airline employee.

Concealing my irritation, I leaned forward and said in Malayalam, "Amma, they are asking you to get back in your seat."

She cracked one eye open. Realizing that the command was coming from someone other than me, she obeyed without protest. But as soon as the flight attendant was out of sight, she began pushing, ordering me to move. With a single bound I stood up and raised the middle armrest. Amma stretched out on the two seats. Standing in the aisle like a fool, I grumbled under my breath, "Shit, what am I supposed to do now?" I knew I couldn't remain standing there—we were not on a bus in India. Nor could I hang by the toilets for too long without being ordered back to my seat. On the other hand, if I went to the rear of the plane, where there might be an empty seat, I wouldn't know when Amma got up or needed something.

Possessing the strong belief that there is a solution to every problem, I tapped on the shoulder of Ramakrishna, who was seated in the row behind. Even though at times he was an incredibly moody bugger, I chose him over the others knowing that he was always willing to sacrifice his comfort for Amma. He opened his groggy eyes and gave me a vacant, almost annoyed look. Ignoring his "What do you want?" I explained the situation and asked him to come get me if Amma stirred. Of course, the more practical solution would have been to ask him or one of the others to go to the back of the plane. But I knew better than to ask. I knew my place.

The joys of international travel had only just begun.

Fortunately, and much to my relief, a few years later, due to lots of foreign money rolling in, Amma began traveling in business class—which meant, so did I.

Holy Hell

After fifteen arduous hours, at four p.m. on May 18th, 1987, our plane landed at the San Francisco International Airport. Shortly before landing, I went to the restroom and changed out of my white sari and into what was supposed to be a less conspicuous outfit—an Indian churidar consisting of bright turquoise baggy pants cuffed at the ankle and a pretty pink, white, and blue floral knee-length caftan top. Saumya was wearing much the same outfit, except hers had green tones. The men changed out of their dhotis into tailored shirts and trousers. Amma remained in her usual attire of long-sleeve, ankle-length white dress draped with a white shawl. She merely refrained from covering her head.

As we approached immigration, Amma told us to spread out and to stand in separate lines to avoid drawing attention and any unnecessary questioning. Not that we were doing anything wrong. We had the proper visas. It was more a case of slight nerves and intimidation. I was a little concerned about the large percentage of trinkets and treasures mixed in with the few personal items in all the suitcases. *Will they believe us when we not-so-innocently explain they are "gifts"—even though we know darn well that they are for sale?*

One by one, we approached the various immigration officers sitting staunchly inside their glass cubicles.

"Next," came the command from the cold lips of a stern-looking officer. My heart beat rapidly as I approached the cubicle along with Amma.

"One at a time," he rudely barked.

"I'm sorry, sir, but she doesn't speak English."

"Ma'am, you need to go back behind the white line. If I need you to translate, I'll call you." He belittled me with a steadfast glare.

I did as I was told. But if he could have heard the words running through my mind, I might have been deported on the spot.

Amma glanced back at me with meek helplessness on her face. She reminded me of a schoolgirl waiting in the principal's office. I watched him asking her questions and Amma seriously replying "Yes" in her finest Indian English. I had to smile.

Before long he handed her back the passport, rudely flicking his hand, gesturing, "Move out of the way." It was my turn. He asked a couple of basic questions and was as pleasant as he was able to be. I seriously wondered if he was trained to humiliate and intimidate, to be cold, rude, demeaning, and downright disrespectful to people. I stared in disbelief at the huge banner on the wall, "Welcome to the United States of America." *Oh, yeah. The warm and fuzzy greeting I just got makes me feel so welcome.* Wham, down went the stamp. He firmly slid the passport back to me without even looking and halfheartedly said, "Enjoy your stay."

Amma and I proceeded to baggage claim, where the men were standing off to the side. Saumya was busy unloading suitcases from the carousel. Seeing Amma, she pointed up as though there was something we needed to see. We turned around and looked up to see a cluster of people waving behind a huge glass window. The two yellow-robed fellows, Balu and Chandru, stood out distinctly next to Kusuma, Nealu, and a small gathering of unfamiliar faces. When Amma saw them, she put her hand on her heart and delivered an enormous smile.

All eighteen pieces of luggage were accounted for, so it was time to proceed through customs. I awkwardly tried to wheel two trolleys. Seeing me fumble, Amma laughed and insisted I give one to her. I was slightly apprehensive, for she was the guru and not supposed to carry anything. Obeying, I gently pushed one toward her. She grabbed it with a grin while looking up at her audience.

Even though the customs agents asked a lot of questions and dug thoroughly through our suitcases, they didn't give us any problems. We got the green light. Amma proceeded out into the big, free world of the United States of America and into the loving arms of her devotees.

When we arrived at Nealu's brother's house, there was a group of about twenty people waiting to meet Amma. So instead of taking rest she told us to set up the musical instruments. We sang bhajans for an hour. Amma then spent two hours greeting everyone, embracing them with her tender hugs, and answering the various questions they posed. Once up in her room, Amma met briefly with the family members, Kusuma, and Nealu. Meanwhile, Chandru entered and stretched himself across the floor in full prostration, but no words were exchanged. There was barely even a glance. The room filled with tension. But this wasn't the appropriate moment to open that can of worms.

The back story: Shortly before we left India, one of Chandru's followers had come to the ashram requesting a private audience with Amma. She called herself Chandru's assistant. During the emotional meeting she confessed that she was pregnant and that Chandru, who had already gone to the US, was the father. To avoid disgrace for the girl and her family (who knew nothing about the situation) and to dodge a scandal for Chandru and the ashram, Amma advised her to terminate the baby. She arranged an escort for the young woman. The subsequent medical procedure succeeded in being the death of the woman's secret. Sadly, it also killed her. She died shortly thereafter from septic shock.

Now at our reception in California the first one to stand up and insist that Amma take rest was Nealu, of course. His top priority was always her comfort.

Impatiently waiting in the hallway was Balu. He wanted Amma all to himself. I knew she would be okay with that, for she was always completely natural in his presence. She could be herself.

After everyone left, Balu entered. Amma told me to close the door. Then she sat on the floor to have her evening meal. His face was sad and long, for he was suffering from the pain of separation.

With loving affection Amma teasingly said, "My little baby, come to mummy." She lay his head in her lap while she ate. Once finished, she washed her hands then lay on the bed. Balu sat on the floor to her side. I was busy clearing the dishes, and my sleep-deprived brain was wondering what to do with the leftover food, when Amma sat up and asked, "What's behind that door?"

I walked across the room and opened the door, revealing a tiny walk-in closet.

"Why don't you hop in there for a while and leave us alone," she ordered.

I was okay with the idea. I understood his desire to be alone. Besides, I was utterly exhausted. Closing the door behind me, I lay on the not-so-soft, slightly musty carpeted floor, feeling grateful for a chance to rest my weary bones.

As I lay there in the dark, a naughty smile crept over my face. I realized that Amma had just discovered a way to be alone with Balu. As far as the outside world, including her other "spiritual sons," knew, I was their chaperone. *Very clever. Very clever indeed*, I thought to myself.

After half an hour or so, the door flung open. I was startled awake, with Amma standing over me telling me to get up. I quickly stepped back into the room, switched into service mode, and gulped a couple of long breaths of fresh air while I was at it.

By nine the following morning Amma was back in the living room. There she sat until one p.m. greeting the fresh set of faces that had gathered. Later that morning, after I had prepared lunch for everyone in our group, I took a break and stood in the far corner of the room to observe. My heart was moved by the serene devotional atmosphere. Hearts were brimming with love, and eyes were filled with tears. Helping to evoke such heartfelt emotion were the uplifting voices and melodies from the bhajans floating through the air. I watched one woman cheerfully approach Amma, look into her face, and smile after receiving her first kiss. But when Amma placed her hand over the woman's heart, that all changed. Immediately the woman's eyes cast downwards, her smile turned into a frown, and she burst into tears. Amma continued to gaze at her with a deep, penetrating gaze as though staring into her soul. I was amazed at how people responded to Amma's touch. I was amazed at the sadness that arose from their hearts. I interpreted their tears as the byproduct of the empty, meaningless lives that they were trying to cover up with materialism. That is what I had been told, so that is what I believed for quite some time.

Holy Hell

The morning gatherings were all held in the living room of the Oakland residence, but the evening programs took place in different regions of the Bay Area. The venues ranged from The Yoga Society, the First Unitarian Church of San Francisco, the Badarikashram in San Leandro, to a church in Sausalito. I was rather surprised by the attendance of around seventy-five people at each location. Even though such attendance was nothing like the crowds in India, I felt it was a decent audience for Amma's first visit to the United States. Within a few days it seemed as though she had already established a following. Several faces became familiar and kept re-appearing at the various venues.

One morning while I was busy in the kitchen, I saw the postman coming up the path. I ran out to greet him at the front door. He handed me a bundle of mail. I was about to give the bundle to our hosts when I noticed an Indian stamp. Excitedly, I thought it must be from the ashram. But when I took a closer look, I saw it was addressed to Chandru from a young lady in Kerala. My heart ignited with rage. I scurried off to a quiet corner to see if there were any more letters for him. Nervously shuffling through the pile, I found one more, and that too was from a young woman. Taking matters into my own shaky hands, I decided no way was I going to give them to him. I felt certain they would contain more incriminating evidence of what we already knew he had been up to. Instead I ran to Amma's bedroom and hid them under the pillow for her to look at after she had finished the morning program.

Once Amma was back in her room, I waited until she had finished her lunch before mentioning anything about the letters. I knew if they included what I suspected, Amma would throw a fit. The inevitable showdown would follow. I slid my hand under Amma's pillow and with a nervous grin on my face handed them to her.

Intently studying my expression, she asked, "What is it? What's going on?"

"I'm not sure, but these arrived for Chandru," I coyly replied.

As swift as a lightning bolt she snatched the letters from my hand, ripped them open, and tossed one at me. Without raising her eyes from the letter glued in her hand, she ordered, "It's in English. Read it."

Kusuma was present at the time, and she was as eager as I to know the contents. Like two magnets uncontrollably drawn to each other, we scooted across the carpet and fixated on the reading. The message was something like this:

> I am constantly remembering our time together in my family's shrine room. I can still feel your warm, hard, throbbing penis between my thighs. Fresh in my mind is the sting and sweet pain I felt upon your first thrust, and how you reassured me, even though I bled, that I'm still a virgin.

I couldn't believe what I was reading. I fell into absolute shock. Not only had this act taken place in the family's shrine room, but he had also fooled her into thinking that she was still a virgin. What really had my head spinning, though, was her highly descriptive and candid language. Sexuality is a topic rarely discussed in India and kept very much behind closed doors. I knew this girl. *Wow*, I thought to myself. *These* meek, mild, naïve, and innocent young Indian women are not quite who they seem. It turns out they are horny little creatures after all—human after all. Ooooh, you little vixen, I thought.

Once I recovered from the shock of her language, I settled back into my anger toward Chandru. He was totally misusing the prestige of his robes to prey on and manipulate multiple young women.

That was it for him. Amma sent him off to the doghouse. He was somewhat tolerated for the US portion of the tour, but he shipped back to India from the East Coast and then was banished from the ashram. His tiny role in the history and building of Amma's empire was over. Through him, many people, myself included, had come to hear about Amma, but he had reached the end of his road—a dead end.

Holy Hell

After one week in the Bay Area, on Monday, May 25, 1987, Devi Bhava was held for the first time outside India. A portion of the living room was converted into a makeshift temple by hanging silk saris over the windows and fireplace and by draping curtains over a long rope. We decorated the shrine with multiple candles, lamps, photos of gods and goddesses, and beautiful flower arrangements. By six p.m. the place was transformed. A rather pleasing-to-the-eye shrine was ready. But I feared it would pale, energetically, in comparison to the highly charged temple back in India.

After we sang a few bhajans before the audience, which was huddled together in eager anticipation, the curtain closed. Amma changed into her goddess garb. When the curtain re-opened and the traditional lamp filled with burning camphor was waved before her, she sat still, with eyes closed, for much longer than usual. After a minute or so, she slowly opened her eyes and threw some fifteen handfuls of flower petals into the room. I imagined she was purifying and spiritually charging the room for the event. Then, as usual, the crowd of around one hundred people came up to her one by one to receive their blessings.

Amma had totally mellowed her routine, made it more palatable for the Western audience. She no longer danced wildly and waved a sword around in the air, grinding her teeth, shrieking, or channeling the fierce aspects of a Hindu goddess. Instead she showered her Western children with love and hugs. What a change! I imagine that many of the guests weren't quite sure what to think seeing her in costume, complete with silver crown on her head. Even so, I heard several comments like, "so powerful, so beautiful, so much love."

Thus continued the evening in the suburbs of Oakland, California, until two-thirty in the morning.

Later that morning, around ten-thirty, we drove to Santa Cruz, a town one-and-a-half hours south of San Francisco. When we arrived at the house, the place was so quiet that I thought nobody was home. Upon entering the living room, though, I saw a group of twenty people seated perfectly still, silently meditating to flute music.

Once again I was amazed at the difference in nature of these California programs compared to India. In the West people seemed more introverted, more tuned into spirituality and healing of the heart. Whereas in India everything was dreadfully noisy, crowded, and chaotic. In general people in India were far more religious, more extroverted, and certainly more concerned with day-to-day survival and with improving their material lives. I really had to re-think my perception about Western Civilization being purely materialistic.

The following day, we proceeded to Carmel to stay with Nealu's "well to do" relative Ron. Even though, according to Nealu, he wasn't terribly spiritually inclined, Ron was quickly captivated by Amma's charm. In fact, he went on to become the major motivator and benefactor behind AIMS (Amrita Institute of Medical Sciences), Amma's world-class, super specialty hospital in Cochin.

From Carmel, we flew to Seattle for five days, then back to the Bay Area for one last program before heading to Garberville and Mt. Shasta in northern California.

On June 8 we were off to New Mexico for programs in Santa Fe and Taos. Upon landing in Albuquerque, we were greeted by a handful of devotees then driven to Santa Fe, where we stayed for the next few days. We had been warned about the seven-thousand-foot elevation and how that could affect our breathing. I quickly realized they weren't kidding. The landscape was dry and barren, sprawling for miles until it met snow-capped mountains gracefully seated upon the horizon. Even though it was desert-like, there was an intriguing and haunting beauty to the place.

Once in the comfort and privacy of her room, Amma identified the presence of another walk-in closet. Nonchalantly she walked up, opened the door, and peered in. I knew what that meant and where I might be headed sometime during our stay.

A couple of days later Balu was seated once again in Amma's room. Sure enough, she told me to go into the closet.

Holy Hell

This one was much nicer than the previous closet. It had plush, cushy carpet and way more leg-room. I could really spread out. Off I went, once again happy to have some alone time and, all going well, a little rest. Time passed. My eyelids sprang open when I heard what sounded like her door opening, followed by the closing of the bathroom in the hallway. Stealthily I cracked open the closet, peeped into the room, and realized I was right. Her door was wide open, Balu had gone, and Amma was in the bathroom.

I leaped out of the closet feeling a little annoyed. *Why hadn't they called me? What if someone saw me hiding in there, what would they think?*

That's when I noticed Balu's towel lying on the floor next to Amma's bed. I approached the off-white, navy pinstripe, checkered linen towel. I picked it up and went to put it outside in case he came back for it. Instead I froze in horror when I noticed the towel all clumped together with semen.

Just as I was standing like a dummy with eyes bulging, a rather frantic Balu came flying back into the room.

"It's not what you think," he snapped, yanking the object from my hand.

Does he think I'm stupid?

He continued, "It's umm... kanji vellam (sticky rice water) and bleach. Yes, that's what it is. My towel fell into kanji vellam and bleach before I came here."

He stormed out of the room.

Meanwhile Amma was in her bathroom clueless as to the discovery I had just made, completely unaware that they were busted. Even though I never heard any sexual noises coming from the room, I'd had my suspicions for a while.

A few years before, back in India, I had put the key in Amma's door and opened it to see the strangest sight. Balu was standing on Amma's bed wearing only a thigh-length shirt, and Amma was kneeling before him with her head just inches from his groin. I panicked and quickly shut the door. At the time I brushed this strange sight aside, reassuring myself he'd probably had a rash or something wrong with his genitals that he was showing her. Not a word was ever uttered about this moment. But I did note they were extra careful thereafter about locking the door.

Unfortunately, now I had proof. Worse still, they knew that I knew. I was terrified that Amma would somehow twist the facts and turn *me* into the bad guy.

That evening during bhajans, tears trickled relentlessly down my face. These were not tears of joy, bliss, or devotion, but tears of sorrow and fear of what lay ahead.

Two days later, after we arrived in Taos, the matter was finally brought out into the open. I was sitting alone outside in the garden when Sreekumar came up to me wishing to have a talk.

With dire concern on his face he said, "Amma told me you are having impure thoughts. You know, you can only serve Amma if you have one hundred percent faith. If the faith isn't there, then she will be forced to find someone else. You might even have to leave the ashram."

My worst fears were confirmed. Obviously Balu had found time to inform Amma discreetly that I had seen the towel. Now Sreekumar, the more innocent, soft-centered, and obviously gullible of the bunch, was her messenger. I wonder to this day what cock-and-bull story they conjured to have him deliver this warning with such conviction.

Amma never uttered a word to me about the incident.

I didn't want to leave the ashram and give up what I believed to be the opportunity of many lifetimes. This was my life, my family, all I knew, and all I wanted. I had myself convinced that I was on the express train to God, and I couldn't imagine being pushed off at full speed.

In that moment I made a choice. I vowed myself to silence. Mustering every ounce of justification juice, I accepted this behavior as Amma's way of "keeping it in the family." Because she is one with God (I explained to myself), she's beyond any form of human desire, longing, or attachment. She's letting these senior fellows release any pent-up sexual frustration upon her as part of the bigger picture in her mission to save the world.

As long as I didn't witness any behavior to the contrary, this theory worked wonders. I continued to live my dream as Amma's personal attendant in pursuit of divine wisdom and God's love. If I dared let this incident affect my faith or devotion, then there was something wrong with me—I wasn't a good disciple. I dared not allow my mind to ponder the hypocrisy. The rest of the ashram, upon Amma's command, was practicing strict celibacy. At least the devotees, including many married couples, were trying. Any who succumbed to their human weakness were severely chastised, some even persecuted by Amma.

A part of me harbored a bit of self-doubt. Perhaps I was mistaken about Amma and Balu?

That fantasy, however, was annihilated a few years later when I witnessed with my own eyes Amma and Balu having sex. We had just arrived on the Big Island of Hawaii, and Balu was alone with Amma in her room. I stepped onto the verandah of the house and, as I turned, I could see them through the open windows of her room. In a glimpse I saw the two of them in bed together. Amma's legs were spread. Naked from the waist down, Balu was moving on top of her. They had forgotten to close the windows, perhaps not realizing that their room overlooked the adjacent verandah.

I gasped and swiftly ducked so that they wouldn't see me. I was livid. *No way in hell am I taking the fall for this one!*

From New Mexico we continued across the United States then on to Europe. But the remainder of this first world tour is, for me, a muddled blur. I am not sure if I was too tired, too busy, or too broken-hearted to remember. Somehow I suspect that the experience was an even combination of all three.

SIXTEEN

I NEED A BREAK

Upon return from the world tour, Amma began receiving tons of publicity. The media began writing her up as a godly woman with healing powers and the ability to bestow blessings. The key to her success had been turned, doors flung wide open, and people came rushing from every corner of the globe. When in India, we were constantly traveling all over Kerala and as far away as Bombay, New Delhi, and Calcutta. The crowds were growing larger, which meant Amma had to sit for increasingly longer durations. Despite the grueling schedule, she sat tirelessly smiling, laughing, and hugging the hundreds, sometimes thousands, of people that stood in queue before her. What the world didn't get to see was the corresponding deterioration of her demeanor afterwards. Once behind the safety of closed doors, she was no longer the sweet, loving, holy mother who was so recognizable in the role she played on stage. An entirely different persona emerged.

Her moods were unpredictable, dark, angry, aggressive, and at times violent. It didn't take much, if anything at all, to set her off, and even the slightest mistake had grave consequences. In the earlier years it had been just a slap here, a kick there, and Amma would later joke about it to my fellow brothers and sisters and refer to herself as a rakshasi (demon). However, as the number of devotees increased, so did her aggression, and her rages were no longer a laughing matter. She often justified this behavior by saying she only scolded those closest to her. For years I consoled myself with the belief that I, then, must be the closest, and I clung onto that theory like someone dangling over a cliff's edge.

Although I was no longer the ashram cook, I was still responsible for the kitchen's management. Meals were now being prepared for hundreds, sometimes thousands of people, and it was impossible to predict how much to cook for lunch. On occasion this resulted in a considerable amount of leftover rice. But as nothing was to go to waste, this remainder was incorporated into the rice gruel served at night. One evening some of the leftover rice had begun to ferment, but the young lad who was serving failed to notice. He mixed several ladles into his bucket of gruel. The paying customers instantly expressed their displeasure. They were served a fresh batch, and the other had to be tossed. I knew I would be in trouble if this piece of news reached Amma's ears, and I feared that someone would inevitably jump at the opportunity to report the incident.

The motivation for snitching on me could be as simple as wanting an excuse to talk to Amma. Or there could be a bit more calculation in it— perhaps a desire to show Amma how on top of everything she or he is, to gain a couple of "brownie points," to climb a few more notches up the hierarchy ladder, even if this meant knocking someone off along the way. This time, it turned out, one of the Indian girls who was starving for a leadership role reported the matter to Rao, who had absolutely nothing to do with the kitchen. Rather than deferring the matter to me, he felt the need to impress this young lady and take action.

It was two a.m. Devi Bhava was over, and Vidya and I were waiting in Amma's room for her to return. Her rice and fish curry were nice and warm, and her cumin tea was cooling to the perfect temperature. Amma was taking longer than usual, so I became concerned that my timing was going to be off.

That's when I heard the tone of her voice escalating from within the temple. Suddenly I got this dreadful feeling I had more to worry about than the temperature of her food.

Throwing Vidya a concerned look, I asked, "Do you hear that?"

I rushed to the balcony to try and ascertain what exactly the topic of discussion was. Through the multiple air vents in the temple wall, I could see Amma talking rather animatedly to Rao.

"I've told Gayatri a hundred times to spend more time in the kitchen. All she does is eat, sleep, and behave like queen of the ashram. Just wait till I get my hands on her," Amma was saying.

I realized once again that my fears had manifested. At the same time I thought, "Bastard! Doesn't he have anything better to do?"

"Hey, Vidya. Brace yourself. Looks like we're going to get it," I woefully reported from the balcony.

"Oh God," she moaned as a worried look imprisoned her face.

With nowhere to run or hide, we waited in dread, ready to silently endure whatever treatment was going to be dished out. My heartbeat picked up speed when I saw Amma step out of the temple. She made jokes and flashed her brilliant smile at the crowd of Indian and Western devotees who were huddled outside. I held my breath as she made her way down the spiral steps, knowing that within seconds, our fate would be realized. Facing Vidya, I made a sign of the cross and cupped my hands in prayer, as though begging for God's mercy. Simultaneously we let out a nervous laugh. We had to. It was the only way to cope in such situations.

Amma entered her room, grabbed hold of the door, and slammed it shut with such thunderous might that the entire brick wall shook. Immediately she rushed over to Vidya and rammed her up against the panel of switches by the door. Then she turned and came charging at me like a raging bull. Grabbing a fist full of my hair, she flung me to the ground and spun me around over the smoothly polished linoleum floor as she kicked me a few times.

"How many times have I told you to check on the kitchen? You lazy, good for nothing bitch, just sitting around in my room like a queen."

Releasing me from her grip, she turned and charged toward Vidya again. After I stood up and regained my senses, I had to laugh. Instead of standing like a helpless rag doll and meekly accepting another pounding, Vidya had a better idea. She ran for her life up the stairs with Amma hot on her heels. I followed, thinking that once it was all over, we could make an easy exit through the upper level across the bridge to the temple building. Now Vidya was trapped in the corner of the upstairs room in the process of receiving a couple of slaps.

Running out of steam, Amma turned to me and said, "Piss off. Piss off, the both of you." Then she stormed back to her room.

We did. Without hesitation we got the hell out of there. But first I had a very important mission to complete.

I grabbed a lime from the shelf and with a sinister giggle said, "Vidya, quick, follow me."

Naturally I was upset at being knocked around by Amma, but there wasn't much I could do about that. I could, however, exact a tiny bit of revenge on Rao for being such a tittle-tat. Stepping out onto the balcony, I hurled the lime with all my might onto the roof of his building, which was just a lime's throw away from Amma's room. With a loud crash it landed on the terracotta shingles, and the two of us bolted for our lives over the bridge, locking the door to Amma's realm behind us.

Once again exiled from Amma's room, we slumped down in the corridor of the main building. I couldn't stop laughing as I imagined the bewildered look on Rao's face when the unidentified flying object landed on his roof.

Imitating his possible reaction, I cackled, "Vidya, can you just picture Rao jumping in fright at the crash on his roof?"

We laughed and laughed and laughed until all of a sudden I realized I also wanted to cry. Choosing to ignore the wave of sadness, I stood up.

Following suit, Vidya asked, "Gayatri akka, where are we going to sleep?"

Steeped in thought, I replied, "But you know what gets me? Amma tries to blame me for there being rumors about her violent nature. Did we even make a peep? Does she not realize people have ears? How many devotees you reckon heard her tonight? Sound travels you know—and so do rumors."

Letting out a sigh, I stuffed the wounded feelings into the recesses of my heart. Then, once again, I despondently headed off in search of somewhere to lay my head for the night, this time with Vidya in tow.

To throw me out of her room became Amma's favorite form of punishment. Apart from the time I was out of service for two months, these bouts usually only lasted a couple of days. Once she had cooled off, everything would be back to normal—until the next episode.

Toward the end of 1987 it became almost a daily routine for her to threaten to throw me out and replace me with Saumya or this Indian woman referred to as Dr. Leela. Neither of them were my bosom buddies—which made it sting all the more. Leela was rather an odd bird. To call her eccentric would be a gracious gesture. Some wanted to believe she possessed a type of divine madness often found in holy people, but to me she was just flat-out crazy. Even though she was a trained doctor, she had her own spin on medicine. Frankly, I considered her dangerous. She would often misdiagnose illness, prescribe the wrong medicine, and stitch together deep wounds without waiting for the anesthesia to kick in. She also had the most terrible habit of lying and conjuring up fantastical tales against me. For whatever reason, Amma bought into them, took her side, and chastised me accordingly.

One day it all became too much to bear, and when Amma threatened to kick me out yet again, I took her up on it and stormed out. Defiantly I waltzed straight out her front door, leaving a rather stunned Amma behind. *So there*, I thought. *Now you've actually got something to complain about.*

This time I had somewhere to retreat to. We were a few weeks out from our world tour, and I had claimed one of the ground-floor rooms in the new temple building to prepare and pack Amma's things. Every inch of the room was filled with piles of freshly stitched dresses, petticoats, saris, and various towels, all numbered and inventoried. There were bags of freshly ground coriander, cumin, turmeric, chili, and nutritious red rice all labeled and destined for various parts of the globe, to be met up with later. In addition, I found the space extremely useful for storing the mountains of silk saris and other offerings Amma received daily, so I decided to hang onto the room—for as long as I could, anyhow. If Amma discovered what I was doing, I knew she would make me remove everything and use the room for accommodation instead. I had chosen the room for its proximity to Amma's building—it was just a quick dash from there to her staircase. Now, unfortunately, being so close only accentuated my pain, for I could hear Amma coming and going. I could hear her voice when its volume was raised.

The following morning after a good night's sleep I was crouched in my little sanctuary feeling somewhat numb. The room was void of any natural light, due to the concrete buildings that towered over me. I couldn't help listening to the standard commotion of the ashram, which then took backstage to the piercing sound of Amma's voice. I could hear her in her room talking rather seriously. From the sick feeling in my stomach I sensed that she was talking about me. Reports later revealed:

1) I have such a big ego since we came back from America.

2) This time I was out permanently. Previously I had been accepted back after a couple of months. Because of that, I had become too sure and egotistical. Amma certainly wouldn't be taking me on the next world tour.

My life was chock-a-block of futile attempts to please and win her approval, all fueled by a desperate desire to know God and to be loved. I was sleep-deprived, malnourished, exhausted, beaten down, and extremely confused. I doubt I was even aware how confused I was. The only breather I ever got was when I was kicked out or, in this case, when I stormed out. There was zero opportunity to gain any perspective. In order to fathom what was really going on, I needed distance. Even though I now had a tiny bit of physical separation, there would be no emotional space. Imagine trying to watch a movie with your nose squished against the screen. All you are going to see is a bunch of tiny dots, and nothing will make any sense. To get the big picture, you would need to step back. Only then would everything come into focus. I was so entangled in the ashram's self-perpetuating belief system that I couldn't find a single loose end to let me unravel the ball of confusion.

Nor could anyone understand what I was going through, or why I needed time out. Wasn't it the greatest opportunity and highest blessing to serve the master? Devotees traveled great distances and stood in line for hours on end for a mere glimpse of Amma. Residents dreamed and hungered for her to smile at them for a split second. They would give anything to converse freely with her. How on earth could they possibly grasp why I was choosing to distance myself?

I was engaged in a major inner tug-of-war with Amma. She wanted absolute surrender, obedience, and reverence at all times. I wanted her to be kind and treat me better. Alas, that was never going to happen. So until I could let go and accept my fate, the battles ensued.

A few days later a preachy, know-it-all junior brahmacharin came to me with a load of advice from Amma, seasoned with a little judgment of his own. Standing at the entry to my room was this lanky, six-foot-something beanstalk of a fellow whose joints creaked whenever he moved. His sweat-moistened brown face was silky smooth, barely disturbed by the presence of facial hair even though the fellow was in his mid-twenties. Manhood struggled with all its might to stake claim on that baby face but so far had only succeeded in planting a little bum fluff on his chin. He had just been in Amma's room, and she had been talking about me, so he felt duty-bound to come have a serious chat.

> His sermon went something like this:
> Because you have no guru bhakti (devotion) and excess negative qualities, Mother has put you aside. You need to take this in a positive sense, otherwise it will be very harmful for you. If you keep too much distance, you may never be able to regain your relationship with her. You will become dry, and only adverse affects will be gained. Today itself

you should go to Mother, prostrate at her feet, and try to cultivate the proper attitude toward your guru. No matter how much meditation we do, without Mother's grace, it is fruitless. You must mend your gap with Mother.

He continued with a little story Amma had relayed to him, exemplifying her point about the importance of reverence:

A man with good qualities may come before me, but if he doesn't show reverence, he will gain no fruit. Whereas, if a scoundrel shows great humility and does not answer back, grace will flow to him without my even knowing. Therefore, only when we gain the right attitude will we be able to make any progress.

He ended his self-righteous bout with, "Don't delay. Tomorrow never comes."

As he stood up, the loud snap of his joints ricocheted around the concrete walls and low ceiling of my room. I closely traced his footsteps to the door, swiftly shutting and locking it behind him. I collapsed onto my mattress thinking, *Jerk! What do you know about my relationship with Amma?* I smothered the pillow over my face to muffle the long and painful howls I was about to release.

I wasn't ready to heed his advice. Instead, I agonized over the awareness that no one could understand what I was going through. I had few sympathizers, and even they had no clue to the extent of my pain and suffering. I was afraid to share my inner feelings, confusion, or secrets with anyone, for Amma frequently reiterated that to destroy another's faith is one of the greatest sins. She warned that if you did so, you would incur the guru's wrath and be met with some major calamity. Infusing even more terror in her followers, she stressed that not even God can save you from the wrath of a guru. Amma also explained that she personally wouldn't do anything, but there were these subtle beings around her that would jump into action to take revenge.

In fact, her official biography is riddled with tall tales of people suffering great loss and even death from threatening, ridiculing, or merely disobeying her. I believed such nonsense at the time. So dared not share with anyone what I knew.

Anybody who wanted to remain in the ashram knew better than to criticize or question Amma. Those who dared to speak out were immediately blacklisted, deemed a traitor, and looked upon as a threat to the preservation of faith among her disciples. For example, one day a young Indian lady, well-educated and highly intellectual, expressed a valid concern to some of her spiritual sisters. Amma had just published a little book called *Man and Nature* about protecting the environment. With genuine anxiety the girl asked, "How can Amma write a book about protecting the environment and yet allow the sewage from the entire ashram to flow straight into the river?" Her statement was immediately reported to Amma, and Amma ordered the snitch to keep an eye on this trouble-maker. The snitch's loyalty was then rewarded. She was often called to Amma's room, where she would confide various ashram gossip. Or she would be called to Amma's side in public, where she would whisper something into the guru's ear in front of the entire ashram.

Basically, Amma used fear tactics to manipulate, control, and protect her flock. Like many gurus, Amma also encouraged and relied heavily upon the rationalization of her behavior by her followers. This support gave her the ability to do whatever she pleased. If she made a prediction that turned out to be a dud, she was merely testing your faith. If she did or said something you couldn't understand, she was merely working on you, trying to crush your ego. If she acted cruelly, she was merely destroying your sins, eliminating some bad karma. Just about anything and everything could be rationalized in this way. If for some reason you were still left scratching your head, then the grandiose excuse to snuff out any remaining doubt was that Amma's ways are so mysterious. In this way she had a perpetual Monopoly-game get-out-of-jail-free card.

I succeeded in rationalizing most of her behavior for a few more years. The leftovers? Well, I internalized those.

Holy Hell

Like an abused child who doesn't know any alternative, I clung onto Amma for dear life. Despite the ill treatment and the fact she rarely showed any kindness or affection, deep down I believed she loved me. I mean, she had to! After all, she was my mother.

I took this belief so to heart that one day I made it official. Much to my shame today and to my true mother's horror, I put it in writing.

I wrote to my parents only once a year. This particular letter I'm sure my mother would have very happily gone without. Seated at my little desk with my back leaning against the wall, I unfolded a sky-blue Indian aerogramme and placed my pen upon the paper. With Amma-love oozing from every pore of my body, I dreamily gazed through the coconut trees, reflecting on what I would write. From a state of absolute self-absorption in my fanatical little Amma world, I wrote (among other things) the following, "Dear Mum, even though you gave birth to me some twenty-odd years ago, you are not really my mother. Amma is my REAL MOTHER."

Without any common sense, remorse, or level-headed judgment as to how hurtful my words were, I licked that sucker, sealed it, and with a serene smile plastered all over my face dropped it off for posting. I thought it strange that I never got a reply. It never dawned on me as to why.

Despite this insensitive declaration, a couple of years later when Amma was touring Australia for the first time, my mother flew to Sydney to meet me. When her eyes laid sight upon me, her immediate and uncensored reaction was, "Jesus Christ, what's happened to you?" Desperately seeking moral support and a sane figure to bear witness to her testimony, she turned to the son of our host and exclaimed, "But she used to be such a pretty girl!"

This woman, my birth mother, was no longer just a memory from my past. Her presence was very real, and I was suddenly confronted with a slue of childhood memories and longings. A life I had tried so hard to suppress and forget about, was glaring me in the face. As Gail and Gayatri crossed paths, sparks flew like two live wires touching each other, and my mind short-circuited. I stood stunned and speechless, looking at my mother and her mortified reaction to seeing me. On the one hand, I was reeling with sadness from the affirmation that I looked so terrible. Simultaneously, though, my mind was tickled with delight that she at least thought I *used* to be pretty. This was something I never considered myself as being, and I certainly never knew that she felt that way. The last time she had seen me, I was a hip and healthy eighteen-year-old. But thirteen years had passed. My hair had never fully grown back after the surgery. My skin was sallow, and my eyes were hollow and sunken with ghastly jet-black circles surrounding them. I knew I looked tired. But I had no real clue as to how terrible I actually did look. I guess there was no way I could have prepared her for my frightening appearance.

Instantly changing the subject, she turned to me and in true Aussie fashion declared, "By the way, I AM your bloody mother."

To this day, she has not forgotten that letter, and rightfully so.

These meetings with family were always painful because they made me feel torn. I felt terrible when any relatives came to visit during our Australia tour. I had no free time. I would be either on stage or else busy in the kitchen frantically preparing food for Amma and the group. In between, I would try to engage in conversation and offer tea. Then Amma would return from the morning program and give whoever had come to visit me a quick hug. Then I would have to disappear into Amma's room.

One time my Dad, who drove every year at least five hours to see me, asked, "Well, daughter, do you want to go for a drive somewhere? How about we go to the lighthouse, or up to Mt. Tamborine where we went several times when you were a kid?"

"I can't, Dad."

He never let on at the time, but years later he confessed, "I used to worry that you were a damn prisoner or something. I could never understand why they wouldn't even let you spend a few hours with your family."

A couple of years later my mother, who no longer owned a car, showed up one morning at the Gold Coast venue after dealing with various means of public transport. The poor woman, all tired and frustrated, eventually got a ride to the home where I was once again busy in the kitchen. After I had seated her on the verandah and offered her a cup of tea, she told me about her experience back at the program.

"I finally get to the hall, not knowing where on earth you are, and am standing in the doorway looking around. Nobody bothered to ask if I needed any help. All they were concerned about was getting me to take my damn shoes off."

I chuckled upon hearing this and could just picture the zealous devotees trying to get my mother to conform to this custom.

She continued in her tone of indignation, "I eventually got fed up and said, 'I am NOT here to see MUTHA. I am here to see my daughter Gayatri.'" She scoffed out loud and said, "That sure got their attention. Finally one sweet lady offered to drive me here."

It should come as no surprise that all of my family members were extremely relieved when I left the organization. But I wasn't done yet. I had a few more years of my life to give before I would get the sense to move on.

It took six weeks before I could surrender my resistance and allow the desire to serve Amma to rise from my heart once more. We were traveling through Tamil Nadu when I was met with my soft feelings of surrender. No longer could I bear the pain of separation nor the mental torment. My anger, frustration, and hurt was now replaced by sadness and longing. I missed Amma and wanted everything back to normal, no matter how hard it might be at times. That morning after leaving Madurai, Dr. Leela, who was filling in during my self-inflicted banishment, had left Amma's pillow behind and failed to prepare anything for her to drink. I was sitting at the back of the bus but had no trouble hearing Amma's public declaration of displeasure from her seat up front.

"If Leela had any devotion, she could never have forgotten these things. The one who serves the guru should get up early morning and have everything ready by the time I am awake. The servant needs no other spiritual practice, and her service is equal to one hundred years of penance if she gives up any thought for food, sleep, or bodily attachment."

Sitting a safe distance from her outburst, I gazed out the window smiling with relief that for a change someone else was on the receiving end.

No sooner had that thought crossed my mind than I heard Amma changing course in her dialogue. *Oh God, here we go.*

Continuing her tirade, "None of you are up to the mark, and you will incur sin if you don't serve me properly. I saw Gayatri failing, so I got rid of her. This second itself, I could stop breathing and survive for years. I need nothing, and especially don't need anybody to serve me. I am the servant of the servants."

In truth, there was no such thing as a safe distance from Amma. She always managed to find a way to crush and squeeze my heart. There I sat, deflated once again, blankly staring out the window with my stomach twisting and turning. *No matter what happens, you just can't help but throw me into the mix. You don't want me getting too comfortable now, do you,* I thought. From the back of the bus, I was able to observe the reaction of many of the passengers. This was something I had often wondered about when I was in the direct line of fire. *Do people believe every word Amma says? Do they think I'm a bad person? Or do they feel sympathetic? Do they understand in their limited way that it's no easy task to serve her? Do they judge me, or do some dare to secretly judge Amma?* Of course, I had no real way of knowing what was going on in everyone's mind. But the facial expressions varied from surprise, fear, detachment, and sympathy, to judgment.

Even though Dr. Leela and I weren't the best of friends, I felt sorry for her because I knew how hard it was to have everything ready on time and nothing forgotten. In order to keep up with Amma, one needed great physical stamina and organization skills. Physically Leela was frail and often suffered from various forms of allergies. One time when she was kneeling by Amma's bed, lovingly massaging her legs, she nodded off from exhaustion. Amma became infuriated and with one of her stocky legs kicked Leela so hard it cracked a rib. The woman was in bed for a few days after. But from what I could tell, she accepted the injury with humility.

This life was more than just grueling. One needed a computer brain to anticipate anything and everything Amma might need during a road trip. If something she asked for wasn't within hand's reach within a split second, the typical outcome was verbal abuse, frequently accompanied by a slap.

Holy Hell

Therefore, even the packing and placement of her travel bags was planned with the utmost precision. I needed to be able to grab whatever she asked for even if I were pinned on the floor of the car, or trapped on the back seat with her head in my lap. I had to foresee perhaps a swim along the way, a spare change of clothing, and an extra shawl in case something spilled. At my feet there were always a basket of food and snacks and a basket of drinks. There were thermoses full of hot water, hot milk, cumin tea, and buttermilk, also a jug of water for bathroom stops. My mind was constantly engaged in plotting, planning, and anticipating the unexpected. The outcome from all this was a sharp, focused, and keen mind that was constantly thinking of Amma. My service to her was my life.

That's why her frequent statement about not needing anybody to serve her was a major button-pusher. It pretty much invalidated everything I did. It invalidated me. And it was the opposite of the truth. She was extremely needy. She expected her every whim to be immediately accommodated. Like a small child she required instant gratification of her physical wants, or else she would fly into a tantrum. But I was blind to the implications of all this. Who was I to judge my guru?

My heart was ready to give serving Amma another shot. I felt hopeful that maybe, just maybe, this time things would be different. I was ready to dive back in head-first and be done with my so-called "break."

That day itself after Amma publicly denounced Leela, much to my surprise, she called me a few times during our road stops. In the evening she sent word for me to come to her room, supposedly to tell me something. But she never said a thing. It was merely her way of allowing me back into her room without officially saying so.

The following day on the bus Amma jokingly told everyone, "I never sent Gayatri away, nor did I call her back. She left on her own accord. So I thought I'd let her come back by herself, and last night she did."

Thus ends the story of my much-needed break.

SEVENTEEN

MY GURU, MY GIRLFRIEND

Thankfully, Amma didn't always behave like a tyrant. Many times over the years she expressed what seemed to be profound love for and trust in me. Her actions were often endearing and childlike, and they made my heart swoon with love. She definitely possessed charm and a magnetic charisma. Because I was constantly by her side, devotees gave me the nickname "Amma's Shadow." This was the precise notion Amma wanted to portray, for it worked wonders in protecting her unblemished image. As far as the devotees knew, she had a female chaperone at all times. Therefore, she was never alone with any men in her room.

When she was in a good mood, she often referred to me affectionately as "Gayatri Mummy." One day a devotee relayed to me the following statement in Amma's words: "Gayatri is like a mother to me, and it would be difficult without her. Only Gayatri knows my character well. She has been with me for so many years, has received only scolding and abuse, yet she can't live without me."

Hearing such a profound declaration touched me deeply. (Back then I didn't note the narcissism.) At the same time, her words made me nervous and uncomfortable. I feared that if I took her words to heart, my ego would inflate. This was an alarming thought to one who believed that the major goal of spirituality was to shrink and destroy the ego. Such praise directed at me was a little hard for some of my spiritual siblings to swallow as well. It gave them great opportunity to poke fun of me.

One night after an evening program we were traveling back to the ashram in the van when, out of the blue, Amma said, "Gayatri is an avatar."

I squirmed in my skin and replied, "Yeah, right. An avatar of Moo Devi!" (Moo Devi is goddess of misfortune, also a term given to women when they're in a bad mood or sulking)."

Amma sweetly replied, "No, you're an avatar of Lakshmi Devi"—goddess of wealth and prosperity.

Immediately someone started to chuckle. Even though I had trouble taking Amma's words seriously, I felt a bit annoyed that someone else did, too. I looked around. Balu was doubled over, holding his ribs in a feeble attempt to contain his amusement. His eyes twinkled with glee. In between his cackling and snorting, he chimed in: "She's an avatar of Surpanakha"— the ugly and wicked sister of Ravana, the king of demons in the Hindu epic, the Ramayana.

My razor-sharp wit rarely let me down. I instantly rejoined with, "Well, if I'm Surpanakha, then you're Ravana himself." Everyone in the van, Amma included, laughed their heads off. I was touched by Balu's innocent, brother-like behavior, and the attention felt good.

The day would come, though, after many years of such playful interaction, that I would sense a shift, out of the blue, in Balu's behavior. Then I would begin to wonder if he still viewed me as a sister, or if he were developing feelings a little more personal in nature.

Numerous devotees considered me lucky and privileged to be Amma's attendant. They didn't realize that such closeness had its disadvantages. I was indeed uniquely privileged to witness Amma's human side and her array of emotions—pretty standard ones, most of them, for non-gurus—that were highly contradictory to what she taught and displayed in public. I have seen her cry and wail when she heard her brother was ill in hospital. Yet, she preached and strictly enforced complete emotional detachment and disassociation toward family members. She would get upset if a couple of her closer "sons" didn't enquire after her every few days. With tears in her eyes, she would pout and give them the silent treatment when they eventually came to her room. After witnessing such conflicting and confusing behavior, I found it extremely hard to maintain the same level of reverence as someone who only worshiped her from a distance.

I possessed deep love, devotion, and awe toward Amma, but reverence never came easy. It was hard for me to make huge, public displays of respect and humble supplication. As the saying goes, "familiarity breeds contempt," and I was guilty.

Over the years I began developing a relationship with what I called my "inner Amma," for the external one was becoming too confusing. I always handled Amma's clothing and possessions with the utmost love, for they embodied who I envisioned her to be on the inside. I always cooked her food with care, concentration, and (once again) love. One of my greatest joys was to watch Amma relish the food I prepared for her. I'd grin from ear to ear on the days she ate everything then ran her finger around the bowl scraping up every morsel. I took great pride in keeping her belongings in order, making sure she had everything she needed. I always strived for perfection. My service to her was my meditation. It was my offering unto God.

Among some of my cherished memories are moments when Amma was in her childlike—or what I sometimes called her "girlfriend"—mood. One afternoon in November of 1989 Amma awoke from a brief nap, turned to me, and said, "I'm going for a swim in the river. Call all the girls, and let the madamas know, too."

I rushed to the phone and dialed the Indian girls' wing. "Amma is going for a swim in the river, please——," and suddenly the girl on the line began screaming and shouting with excitement. I hung up and called the Indian householders' wing, then the Westerners' office. Meanwhile an impatient Amma rummaged through her cupboard looking for a swimming dress, tossing hither and thither everything she laid her hands upon. My heart sank when I saw my hours of labor evaporating before my eyes, all the lovingly laundered and ironed clothes landing in a heap on the floor.

"Amma, it's not in that cupboard," I pleaded, hoping she would stop. I hurried to the other side of the room and retrieved her swimming dress for her.

After snatching it from my hands, she slipped on the bright-red, knee-length, baggy, strapped dress, wrapped a towel around her bare shoulders, and flew out the door. I dashed upstairs, got into my similar dress, and flung a towel over my shoulders as I hurried toward the river. There had recently been a lot of rain, so the normally brackish river was sufficiently diluted and pleasant enough to swim in. By the way, this occurred well before the ashram began dumping into the river tons of raw sewage from the multiple skyscrapers, hundreds of residents, and thousands of guests. You only had to watch out for the occasional floater from the outhouses upstream.

A mad frenzy erupted at the ashram. More than forty women representing every age bracket, height, weight, and skin color came running. An innocent bystander could have easily thought these hysterical women were being chased by a horde of infuriated wasps.

There was desperation among the ashram residents to get physically close to Amma. The women used to play what I called "asana wars." Everyone had a little meditation rug, called asana, which they would use to reserve themselves a spot for the evening bhajans, or for the following day's public gathering. All those asanas made the floor look as though it was covered with a gigantic patchwork quilt. The more frantic and needy women ashram residents owned two such rugs. They would strategically position their spare rugs, sometimes up to two days in advance, for a prime spot in the coveted weekly gatherings that took place on the roof of the temple building exclusively for residents. When they checked a few hours later, sometimes they found that their rugs had been moved. Frequently there were squabbles, and a couple of times fistfights. Even in front of Amma the women didn't hesitate to sit one on top of the other, pinch and push. Amma never seemed to mind. She always looked rather enamored and would giggle watching them fight to be close to her. I frequently had Western women complaining about the few Indian girls who were quite aggressive. And Indian girls complained about the handful of Western women who were so obsessive that they acted like stalkers.

One day I had heard enough. I stormed to the kitchen and grabbed a couple of rice sacks, went to the temple hall, loaded the first few rows of asanas inside and dumped them over the railing—to no avail.

Why should these women reconsider their behavior when it made Amma smile and giggle? I could never understand why, instead of teaching her followers to become independent and mature spiritual seekers, Amma nurtured infantile emotional dependence and attachment to her physical form.

Some of that energy infected our girlish swim that day.

By the time I got to the river, Amma was already floating on her back, squirting water into the air. She always seemed right at home in the water, and it was fun to watch her dogpaddle to and fro. I waded into the river, but as soon as the water was up to my thighs, I sprang off my feet and dove out as far as I could. In fact I never got used to the slimy mud that oozed up between my toes. It always made me shudder.

Amma played pranks by swimming underwater and popping up unexpectedly. When she ducked under, all the women giggled and frantically looked around with anticipation, hoping she would surface near them. Separating from the group, she swam away. So I followed closely. When she went to stand, she couldn't touch bottom. She clutched onto me like a child to its mother, then climbed on my back and wrapped her legs around my waist. Fortunately I was a strong swimmer and able to tread water and stay afloat. After a minute or so, she let go and swam closer to shore. As I approached, she linked her arms around my neck, and I supported her as though I was carrying a child. All the women's eyes sparkled with love, and their hearts overflowed with joy to witness Amma in such a playful mood. Many envied my close relationship with her, and I was frequently met with the phrase, "You're so lucky."

These bouts of affection always took me by surprise and filled my heart with warmth, but they also added to my confusion. One minute Amma was my guru to be treated with the utmost respect; next minute I was giving her a piggy-back ride. Instances like these made my guard drop. They contributed to a familiar and free behavior that some might have considered disrespectful.

Occasionally when Amma was in her room, she would suffer from what she called "viprati" or restlessness. Then she would act in a crazy yet endearing manner. Sometimes she would be lying bare-bottom on the floor, rolling all over the place and needing to be massaged. Other times she would nibble on any food in sight, then raid the refrigerator. One day she sat on the floor in front of the fridge and had me remove nearly everything inside. She ate half a tomato, bit into a baby mango, drank some lime juice, played with yoghurt, drank a little buttermilk, floated roasted chic peas in milk, and then scooped them off the top with a spoon. I watched with amusement her peculiar behavior. She reminded me of images I had seen of baby Krishna sitting on the floor with his hand in a clay pot stealing butter.

After a while she would turn, look at me, begin laughing, and say, "What to do? I suffer from the karma I took from the people this morning. I have to wear it off somehow." Saying thus, she once got up, lay on her bed, propped her feet up on the windowsill, and began reading a Malayalam version of *The Adventures of Huckleberry Finn*. Within a few minutes the book dropped from her hands, and she was sound asleep.

Another fond memory is the time when Amma ran away from the ashram with Saumya, Ramakrishna, and me. On the evening of March 7, 1991, as Amma was leaving her room for Devi Bhava, she looked at me with a mischievous grin and signaled me to come close.

Into my ear she whispered, "Tell Ramakrishna to get the car ready and bring it this side of the river. Pack a few things, as we're going away for a couple of days. But don't let anybody else know, okay?"

She told me to let Saumya in on the secret. I was thrilled to be part of this top-secret assignment. I packed the necessary items and hid the bags on her balcony so as not to arouse any suspicion. Around eight p.m. Ramakrishna came and reported that the car was in position behind the ashram on the beach road. As inconspicuously as possible I snuck off with some of the luggage and placed it in the trunk. For quite some time Amma had been threatening to run away from the ashram, complaining that she was getting no peace, that she was tired of chastising certain individuals to do their spiritual practices. I don't think anyone believed she would act upon her threat, so I feared it would be a huge shock the following morning when her absence was discovered. I also harbored a little doubt as to whether she would actually follow through. But sure enough, after Devi Bhava, she ate her dinner, changed her clothes, and said, "Let's go."

I gently opened her front door and closed it using the key, to avoid the loud click it usually made. I placed the remaining luggage in the entryway, looked at Amma with a grin on my face, put my finger over my lips, and went, "Ssshhh."

"Wait here," I whispered. I tippy-toed down the stairs. At the bottom I surveyed the surroundings, determined that the coast was clear, ran back to tell Amma, and we made a dash for it. It was quite unbelievable that, even though Amma was with me and I was carrying luggage, nobody saw us come down the stairs or head out the far side of the ashram toward the beach. As we snuck by the string of huts where the young Indian men lived, I could see through the bamboo slats of the windows that they were retiring for the night. Suddenly I felt bad, as if I were betraying them by running off with Amma. But it was her wish, so I pushed aside any feelings of guilt.

We successfully made it out the gate to see Saumya and Ramakrishna anxiously waiting by the car with huge grins on their faces. At one-thirty a.m., with Ramakrishna behind the wheel, we headed south to Kanvashram, an estate in Varkala we had visited many times in the past. The place was originally owned by a Dutch man who had been a spiritual mentor to Ganga prior to his meeting Amma. However, it had been at least seven years since we'd been there. The owner had since passed away, and the place was now held in trust. We arrived around three a.m. We had trouble finding the entry because the property was now completely surrounded by a brick wall. Eventually we found a side gate, but it was locked. Ramakrishna honked the horn several times. Alas, nobody responded. Looking back, I think, why should they? Nobody was expecting us. We were not invited guests, and don't forget, it was three in the morning.

The brazen honking shattered the tranquility of the night, arousing a neighboring woman from the depth of slumber. Standing in the threshold of her home, she draped the sari across her chest and flung it over her shoulder as she sleepily gazed toward our car. From inside the vehicle, Ramakrishna loudly explained our plight. Without any sense of irritation the lady graciously gave us directions to the main gate, but alas, it was also locked. Finally, a couple of men from the local tea shop stirred, and with surprising conviction they informed us that the only person living on the estate was an old swami, and that he lacked the authority to let anybody in. Upon further investigation we learned that a lawyer in town was in charge. We needed written permission from him to get inside.

Long story short, after waking up nearly everyone in the neighborhood and dragging a prominent lawyer out of bed to write us a note, we gained access at five fifteen in the morning. Only in a place like India could you get away with such inconsiderate behavior. I think the bulk of our audacity came from the fact we had Amma on board. She was our universe, so we didn't hesitate or even stop to think that perhaps not everyone shared the same sentiments.

The next problem was accommodation. The tiny bungalows we had once stayed in were also locked. Fortunately we remembered there was a covered picnic area. At least we had a roof over our heads in case it rained.

The estate was huge, sprawling several acres down a steep hillside and covered in thick, lush jungle. Back at the teashop one of the men had warned us to be careful because the property was rumored to have wild cats that sometimes attacked people. With this worry in the back of my mind, I spread a thin blanket down on the concrete floor, and Saumya and I lay on either side of Amma.

As soon as we turned off the flashlight, we heard an eerie noise. Amma jumped up shouting, "Put on the light, put on the light, I hear a poocha (cat)."

Ramakrishna courageously volunteered, "Amma, you go to sleep. I will stand guard." Armed with a flimsy straw broom, he stood peering into the darkness, hoping to ward off any stray animal that might dare approach.

Amma turned her head and mischievously whispered into my ear, "Let's play a trick on him." A few minutes later, with panic in her voice, she shouted, "Poocha! Poocha!"

Ramakrishna's limbs flew every which way as he jerked with fright, sending the three of us into hysterical fits of laughter.

"Did you see him jump?"

Amma roared, as she pinched me and Saumya. (I don't know why, but when she was in a good mood and in the thick of laughter, she had this weird habit of pinching anyone nearby. Even though these pinches hurt like hell, the recipient always managed to crack a smile because the attention felt good.) After this little bit of fun Amma settled down, and we dozed for a couple of hours until daybreak was upon us.

We ladies discreetly changed into our swim dresses. Then we all headed down the steep and narrow path to the pond at the base of the hill, which was filled with natural spring water. Along the way my heart was singing, for the only sounds were those of birds chirping and trees rustling in the wind. Compared to the ashram this place was so calm, quiet and peaceful, and I especially loved the fact there was not a soul in sight. We were only going for a bath. But I always took advantage of such an opportunity, and couldn't help but break out into freestyle swimming, butterfly strokes, and many a backwards somersault. No matter how subdued and submissive I tried to behave, water always managed to resurface a bit of the good old Aussie spirit in me.

After bathing Amma told us she wanted to meditate for a while at Vishnu Tirtham. It was a tranquil site at the top of the property, nestled amid acres of cashew trees. There a mysterious shallow pool of water cupped in the center of a large rock formation. We had been shown this sacred place years before on our first visit. Legend had it that many great yogis and seers had meditated there over the ages.

The climb was steep. Ramakrishna suggested that he drive us to the top.

While they all headed toward the car, I rushed to grab a few things for Amma. I heard the doors slam, and even though I felt certain they were waiting, I hurried just the same. But I was wrong. Suddenly the engine started, and they drove off without me.

"What, they can't even wait one second?" I grumbled out loud. "How can they take off like that, leaving me with all this stuff to carry?"

I felt upset. It was a long walk up the hill, and I wasn't sure I remembered the way anymore. With Amma's meditation rug rolled and tucked under one arm, and her basket of drinks and snacks in hand, I looked around to ensure I hadn't forgotten anything. That's when I noticed Amma's shoes reverently sprinkled with flower petals sitting on the makeshift altar. *Oh no, she's gone off without her shoes. Hang on a sec, where are mine? Oh great, she's gone off wearing them. She simply grabbed the first pair in sight.* Letting out a huff, I placed her shoes in the basket then trudged barefoot up the rocky path. Eventually, with a little trial and error, I found the spot. Amma and Saumya were peacefully meditating on the water's edge under the shade of a small tree as a gentle breeze rippled across the pond. The serenity of the place had an immediate calming effect, so I let go of my cranky thoughts and decided to take a seat and meditate. Looking around, I soon realized there was no shade left. Ramakrishna had the only other spot. So I gave up that idea and plopped down on a hot rock in the sun.

After a couple of minutes, I saw Ramakrishna coming toward me. *Should I let him know I'm mad?* I wondered. *Should I ask why he couldn't have waited one second while I grabbed Amma's things?*

Before I could decide, he crouched down and whispered, "Amma has told me to go back to the ashram. She doesn't want Balu, Rao, and the others to feel she is favoring me."

"But how will we get back?" I asked.

"Amma said Saumya has her license, so she can drive. First though, I need to take the car into town to fill it with gas. Should I bring back some food and drink?"

He was good like that. He always had Amma's well-being in mind. So I forgave him about the other stuff. Besides, he may have just been following orders. I whispered my request list and handed him a thermos to bring back some hot tea.

After our meditation, the old swami who lived on the estate came to greet Amma and apologetically gave us a key to one of the bungalows. We made our way back down to the hut, snacked on some nuts, and then took a nap. When I awoke, it was one p.m. Still no sign of Ramakrishna. I became worried Amma would be hungry when she awoke. But he finally showed at about one-thirty, explaining he had accidentally locked the keys in the car. After lunch Ramakrishna took leave of Amma and headed off to catch a bus back to the ashram.

We were on our own, just Amma, Saumya, and I. This was quite out of the ordinary and, I must admit, slightly unnerving. Around five p.m. we went for another swim. I was so enjoying the peace and quiet away from the chaotic and noisy ashram—no relentless phone calls, no questions, no problems to solve, just pure peace.

Nevertheless, I felt certain that once night fell Amma would become restless and want to return to the ashram. Sure enough, after our evening meditation, Amma asked me to pack up. By seven forty-five we were off. Saumya was the driver. I was the co-pilot and Amma was the lone passenger on the back seat. Slowly and cautiously we were making our way when a car rashly overtook us. Even though this had happened several times already, this wild car-driving was different. Someone in the passing car was precariously dangling halfway out the window waving a flashlight, signaling us to pull over. The car looked like an ashram vehicle, so we did. Once we stopped, I could see it was Rao.

He sprang out of the car, jumped in the back seat with Amma, and wildly slammed the door. He was—well, let's just say that he was upset. It seems he and a driver had been cruising around for hours. He complained that the whole ashram was in shock from the guru's highly unexpected disappearance.

In an hour we were back at the ashram. As soon as we drove through the gate, the car was swarmed with teary-eyed, hysterical devotees. Many had been fasting, meditating, crying, and praying for her return. Within an instant the word spread. People came running from every direction.

Amma seemed moved by their display of emotion. She called out, "My children, my children, my children."

Now all of them had their beloved mother back. Everything was back to normal for them, and for me, too. Although it had been short and sweet, this secret getaway became a cherished memory for me, an often longed-for image of retreat.

But that was it.

There would no longer be any external peace. Somehow I would have to find peace within myself and be satisfied with it.

EIGHTEEN

GROWING PAINS

"Five, four, three, two, one, Happy New Year" are the words people shout as the first seconds of January roll into existence each year. Carefully tucked away in the hearts of those making the declaration is hope that the upcoming year will be kind and that many of their dreams will come true.

For the somewhat superstitious folk, this day holds even more importance. They believe that whatever the first day of the year brings indicates how the forthcoming year will shape up.

In Kerala this belief is taken very much to heart on the special day called "Vishu." Usually falling on April 14th, this date marks the beginning of the Malayalam year and signifies the sun's transit into the first zodiac sign in Indian astrology.

The most important event on this day is the Vishukkani, or "the first to be seen on Vishu." Traditionally, on the night before, families decorate their shrine room elaborately with auspicious items such as rice, fruits, vegetables, gold jewelry, yellow flowers, and a holy text. Then they light a brass oil lamp. The following morning at dawn, without opening their eyes, they shuffle their way to the shrine, thus making this holy display their first vision for the year. Some even sleep blindfolded in fear of unintentionally opening their eyes and viewing something less auspicious.

It is also considered favorable to read verses from the Hindu epic Ramayanam. The contents of the random page selected, it is believed, will predict the course that your life will take in the coming year.

Vishu was celebrated in the ashram as well. It attracted many devotees who believed that to spend this holy day in Amma's presence would bring great fortune to their lives.

In 1989, the night before this supposedly fate-determining day, I too made elaborate plans to launch the new year with a fabulous start. I was going to wake even earlier than usual, meditate until Amma woke, then fast and keep silence the entire day. I wanted to get off to a good start with Amma. I desperately wanted to have a smooth and peaceful year. I imagined how pleased she would be to open her eyes and see me meditating.

Unfortunately, as most of us have experienced some time or another in our lives, even the best-laid plans don't always pan out as we had hoped. From the depths of a distant and peaceful dream, I was jolted awake by the familiar sound of Amma's irritated voice.

"Hey! Wake up! It's Vishu!" she bellowed. "A true disciple would have gotten up early morning, bathed, lit a lamp before Devi (a white marble goddess statue in her room), and placed some adornments on her. Oh my God, what am I doing with this madama who has absolutely no culture? Go find yourself a book, and read up a little on today's significance," she grumbled in disgust.

I had overslept. I couldn't believe it. My vow had gone down the toilet, and I was knee-high in trouble once again.

As I was trying to figure out how on earth this could have happened, I remembered that Amma had been terribly restless the night before. I had spent hours massaging her.

Instantly, like a feisty little boxer jumping all over the ring just raring for a fight, my mind reacted. *Oh, and by the way, I am not a cultureless madama, thank you very much. I do know the meaning of Vishu.* I wasn't happy about my reaction. *Oh shit, here we go again. I don't want to start this new year engaged in battle. Give it up already. You should have set an alarm clock,* I told myself.

Amma hastily bathed, got dressed, and without drinking anything headed to the temple to give a brief talk and lead bhajans before the hundreds of devotees gathered that morning. I scurried behind her, frantically struggling to twist my hair into a bun and my sari into some sense of order before facing the crowd as I dropped her off at the stage. I was careful not to engage in eye contact with anyone, lest they too discover I had slept in and was not yet bathed—a big no-no before entering the temple. I did, however, take a quick peek into the shrine and absorbed the dazzling array of items that lay beautifully arranged around the flickering golden hue of oil lamps. Immediately my mind turned submissive and fell in tune with my heart. Once again I was at peace and basking in the incredible spiritual vibrations emulating from the temple.

Because this event wasn't the normal occurrence, I had no clue when Amma would return to her room. So I went about my usual business. An hour or so later I was taken by surprise when she came back and sat down on the floor to eat breakfast. Suddenly I was in a quandary. I was in the middle of scrubbing her bathroom floor and didn't want her to slip and fall if she went inside, but I knew she would ask for something to drink. Compromising, I hurriedly threw a few mugs of water across the floor, washed my hands, and dashed upstairs to make her tea.

The water was almost boiled when I heard her screaming, "Hurry, bring me something to drink."

She sounded in distress, so I peeked down from the top of the staircase to see her holding her hand on her chest with an angry look on her face. I knew it would take too long for the tea to brew, so in a state of panic I ran down with a cup of hot milk. I knew tea was her drink of choice, but I thought this way at least she had something to drink. She snatched the steel tumbler from my hand. I felt relieved and went to rush back upstairs to make the tea.

Upon seeing the contents she exclaimed, "Since when have I drunk milk?" She hurled the cup across the room.

I stood transfixed and watched it noisily bounce and skid across the floor, leaving a trail of milk in its path before crashing into the wall, where it spun to a stop. In a fit of rage she grabbed my sari by the pleats and began trying to rip it apart with her teeth. After she released me from her grip, with rather dampened spirits I continued with my plan to make her a cup of tea. After all, she hadn't thrown me out yet, so I had to at least try.

A few minutes later, apprehensively, I re-entered the lion's den with my humble cup of tea. And it was on again. Ding, ding, ding sounded the bells, and round two began.

"If you come near me, I'll stab you to death. I'm just dying to do that." Saying this, she hit herself three times on the head and told me to get out.

Ignoring her command, I stood there. In the past I had gotten into trouble for leaving right away. You know, the whole dog and master thing—even if you are beaten, you are to remain faithful and stay put. She told me once more, then twice more, but I was still confused as to whether I should stick to my guns or run for my life. It was a damned if you do, damned if you don't situation.

Clarity dawned when she screamed at the top of her lungs, "If you don't leave the room, I will cut off my hands and feet."

Okay, I guess she is serious.

I gracefully slid out the front door, closing it behind me, slumped down on the narrow entry way, and hugged my knees to my chest, into which I buried my head. *Happy New Year! Boy, does she get carried away. All over a stupid cup of tea?* There I sat once again with tears in my eyes, wrestling with my mind to try and make sense out of yet another traumatic incident. I knew that if I fled the scene I would be criticized and labeled arrogant. So I stayed put in front of her door, trying my best to do the right thing on this important New Year's Day.

Almost an hour later, my body was attacked by a rush of adrenaline when I heard the metallic click of her door opening. My body sprang to attention, but I barely had time to stand up halfway when it slammed shut again. The words "Ughh, I don't want you in here" bounced off the concrete hallway.

I felt certain that it wouldn't be long before she'd head back to the temple to begin hugging everyone. So I decided to stick it out, consoling myself with, *After all, what else could possibly happen?*

Ten minutes later the door opened once more, but this time it stayed open. This was Amma's way of implying, "You have my permission to enter." It seems she had cooled off—it was the calm after the storm. I stepped back into her room, and we lived happily ever after for a few more months until the next episode.

All said and done, I remember thinking how well I had fared that day. *Wow*, I thought to myself. *It seems I'm actually making progress. Maybe I can become the perfect disciple after all.*

A couple of years later, once again I was feeling frustrated with my lack of spiritual zeal. We had just returned from a grueling forty-one day tour of India, Mauritius, and Reunion Island, which had left very little time for meditation and diary writing. I wanted to get my routine going again, and I planned to utilize my arrival-anniversary day of January 15th to give myself a jump-start. Despite my determination, though, I was feeling a little discouraged. All my previous attempts had started off great then fizzled out as I got swept away by the round-the-clock hustle and bustle that was becoming the norm at the ashram. I feared that this resolution would wind up being just another futile attempt, another failure.

I was sitting outside on the balcony of Amma's kitchen feeling rather glum, lamenting the good old days, when Vidya came out and joined me.

Turning to her I asked, "Don't you miss the old days?"

Even though she was slender in build, her cheeks were puffy, accentuating her slightly buck teeth. So with even the minutest facial movement she was able to make the most comical and expressive of faces.

With such a look in place, she nodded in absolute agreement. "Of course I do," she exclaimed. "It felt so much more spiritual back then. I used to meditate from three until eight in the morning. But nowadays?"

Giving her a loving nudge, I teased, "Yeah, you little bitch. You were quite the yogini. I often envied you as I headed to the kitchen each morning." I chuckled and jumped back in with, "But I tried. I meditated as long as I was able and have a few pieces of poetry to show for my rare moments of bliss."

"Oh Gayatri Akka," she sighed. "Where are we even supposed to meditate? We're not allowed on the rooftop anymore. We're crammed into tiny rooms with two other people, so no solitude or peace there. Plus the ashram is so busy and crowded nowadays."

"Do you remember when Amma told us to meditate at night?"

"How could I forget? Some of my best meditations were at night on the roof of the temple building."

"Mine too," I concurred. "No matter how tired or sleepy I felt, after gazing at the sparkly sky with the occasional cool breeze drifting by, somehow I would feel energized. And my mind became clear and focused."

Vidya sighed. "Then Amma put a stop to that. She didn't want boys and girls up there together."

"Oh yeah. We don't want any hanky-panky going on, now do we?" Suddenly I felt more sarcastic. "That's why she recently told the girls not to use the narrow spiral staircase. She's afraid if a sari as much as brushes up against one of her boys, they will fall prey to lust."

Vidya blushed and chuckled at my remark, but she added no comment. Instead she grumbled, "Nowadays it's virtually impossible to find anywhere to sit in peace and quiet."

"Well, at least you get time to sit," I retorted. "You don't have to do all the traveling like I do. When Amma's away, the ashram becomes somewhat peaceful, doesn't it?"

"You mean to say you don't enjoy flying around the world like a big shot, to America and all those cool places?"

"Smart ass, that's not what I'm saying. It's not that I want to stay back. It's just that I wish I had more time to meditate, reflect, and feel inspired like I used to, that's all."

I spun around and folded my arms across the balcony railing, then sank my chin into that cradle. Vidya followed suit. Saying nothing, we glanced across at the ladies' side of the ashram. With sympathy and disgust I stared at the newly constructed three-story dwelling where the Indian female ashramites lived, crammed together like sardines in a can.

This building served as the backdrop to the kitchen, where steam and smoke were billowing, pots and pans were clanging, grinders whirled, and intense activity went on day and night. Huge baskets brimming with cooked rice and curry-filled steel buckets were perpetually whisked off to the dining hall, where hundreds sat cross-legged on the sandy concrete floor waiting for their meal. From inside the temple, loudspeakers blared the devotional singing of ashram residents as they watched Amma shower her blessings upon the hot, tired, sweaty, sticky, yet hopeful devotees who had been standing in line for hours—standing in line all for a split-second touch, for a glance if they were lucky, for a tiny packet of sacred ash and a candy that Amma placed in their hands as attendants yanked them away before they knew what had happened. The outside air was hot and humid enough, but the steamy conglomeration of odor generated from all those bodies packed inside the temple was overwhelming. I was constantly amazed at the faith and determination of these people, and I was surprised that so few of them passed out.

Even though I felt free in this way to vent with Vidya a little, I couldn't neglect my role as wise big sister. So I concluded our discussion with, "Amma's on a mission to touch as many people's hearts and lives as she can. So it's only going to get crazier. I guess we just have to do the best we can and trust that, whatever the outcome, it's Amma's will, and she's looking out for us."

Not so convincingly I added, "I guess this is our spiritual path now."

As the years went by, we were on the road so much that six weeks became the longest stretch we stayed put in any one place. For that six weeks we returned to the ashram headquarters in south India. It was festival season. Amma's birthday, Onam (similar to Thanksgiving), and Vijayadasami (Tenth day after the Navaratri Festival or Nine Nights of the Goddess) were the key holidays, and the place was always swarming.

My role in the ashram was changing. I was spending less time with menial tasks—laundry, cooking, housecleaning—and becoming more of a CEO, a liaison for the centers overseas, and mother superior to the many young Indian women residents. In 1987, when we went abroad for the first time, there were only four women in the ashram. By 1991, just four years later, there were fifty-two, and by the time I left at the end of 1999, there were two hundred and eight. This number didn't include the many young Indian men, Indian household families, or Westerners who had also given up their comfortable lives to reside at the ashram. It was not like in the past, when Amma was quite selective about whom she permitted to join, and based her decision upon their apparent spiritual qualities. The doors were now wide open. All people (even those with slight mental illness), as long as they paid their way or worked for the ashram, were welcome. The majority of devotees did both. Any Manoj, Kumar, or Hari could join now.

Amma didn't care if families were torn apart, marriages and partnerships destroyed, if individuals became estranged from their relatives, or if the fate of many of these young Indian women's lives were sealed.

In traditional India, once a woman turns thirty she is no longer a desirable match for marriage. So if these Indian women ever wished to leave the ashram, there was a good chance they would not be accepted back by their families. They would be hard to marry off. They would become a financial burden. Unless they had previously acquired some good education and possessed street smarts, or came from a rich family, they would have no meaningful way to support themselves. Even if they had a dowry to offer, their only option would be to marry someone much older than themselves, most likely a widower—a person also shunned by traditional Indian culture.

This makes me wonder if many of these poor Indian women are still living in the ashram by choice, or because they have no choice.

To me, the place no longer felt like an ashram. It was more like a cross between a theme park and a business park. It attracted masses of visitors, and it had become the home of many dedicated and extremely hard-working individuals.

Some of the departments run by the residents were soap, incense, and ayurvedic medicinals. The ashram included an ayurvedic treatment center, a medical dispensary, tailor shop, kitchen, canteen, Western canteen, laundry service, desktop publishing, printing press, and accounting. Off-site there was a computer institute and hostel, AIMS (the super specialty hospital), engineering college, orphanage, and many schools and branch ashrams. I often wondered what some of these educational institutes had to do with spirituality, especially when they weren't charities. Yet I felt a sense of pride that so many people were inspired and willing to work in Amma's name.

On days when we were at home base, when it wasn't chaotic from Devi Bhava or some other festival, the ashram embraced for moments a serene and peaceful atmosphere. There was a time of day when almost everyone stopped working and offered himself or herself in song and prayer. This was my favorite time of day, and most often when my heart experienced peace and solace. As the sun made its descent in the cloudy sky above the grayish blue waters of the Arabian Sea, the heat of the day would become one with its soulmate, and together they would disappear beneath the horizon. With the golden rays of the sun out of sight, the ashram would be graced with a refreshingly cool, moist, and salty sea breeze that swept in from across the expansive ocean. The usual hubbub of people faded into quiet murmurs as though someone from up above was turning the volume down. No longer drowned in human noise, I could hear the crackling and rustling of the giant coconut palms swaying in the wind, as if dancing to some divine melody that only they could hear. The chirping of mynah birds and sparrows brought a serene smile to my face, and even the abrasive cawing of crows resonated more favorably to my ears. From the nearby prayer hall, the sublimating, musky aroma of incense came to me on the breeze and enveloped me in its soft embrace.

At dusk I would sit in meditation on the tiny bridge that linked Amma's building to the second story of the prayer hall. I would lock the doors on either end and surrender unto my safe haven. This one-and-a-half-hour time span, during the evening bhajans, was pretty much the only time in the day I could be assured of no disturbance. Already swimming in feelings of peace and serenity, once the heavenly sounds of the music and singing commenced, I would fervently dive deep within myself, into a blissful heart space, into communion with God. Over the years, it was during this time of day that I received my greatest moments of inspiration and brief glimpses into states of bliss I had only read about.

On one such day, as I was feeling increasingly enraptured by the music and lyrics, I felt my body spontaneously sitting more erect. As though being pulled tall by an invisible string, my spine and rib cage began lifting. My jaw locked tight, and my tongue was pushing firmly against the roof of my mouth. My breathing slowed down, and my heart began to race. No longer consciously listening to the music, my mind became extremely one pointed and my sole sense of being. As the sensation grew stronger, I observed myself becoming smaller and smaller, disappearing into this enormous, brilliant, and ecstatic state. My awareness continued to expand to the point that all that remained between me and nothingness was the minutest sheath.

Just as I was about to slip between the veil, I gasped in panic. My eyes sprang wide open. I was afraid to disappear into oneness. As blissful and enticing as the experience felt, I wasn't ready. I did, though, feel blessed and privileged to have received this utterly magnificent preview of a state that can be mine, when I am ready.

The bridge where I sat in the evenings doubled as my office. It was where I met with anyone who needed to speak with me. Female residents, both

Indian and Western, came to me with various matters to discuss. Sometimes this involved a desperate need for more staff for an ever-growing department. Sometimes, it was personal matters. I offered everything from spiritual advice, practical advice, and personal counseling to conflict mediation and resolution. I always tried my best to be there for the women in my role of "akka" or elder sister. This role meant the world to me.

Despite the fact that Amma, the head of the ashram, was a woman, the ashram was very patriarchal. Male hierarchy was firmly set into place by Amma herself. Although I was head of the women's side, and I was Amma's personal attendant, I often found myself up against resistance from members of the opposite sex. In times like these, I was glad to be a "madama," thereby able to speak my mind and stand my ground for what I felt was right.

Naturally, this didn't go over too well with some of the Indian men. They were used to being bowed down to by one and all. My outspoken approach and unwillingness to display humility before these fellows resulted in resentment, but I didn't care. Someone needed to stick up for the Indian women, because their culture trained them to be silent and subservient to men.

Not only would I stand on the bridge. Metaphorically, I was a bridge. I was a bridge between the two radically different cultures of East and West. Although I was raised in Australia and a thoroughbred madama, I knew the Indian culture well, with all its idiosyncrasies, and by now I spoke the language fluently. As Amma became increasingly busy and less accessible, for many, I was the only link for them to her. It was a role I took very seriously, always trying to oblige anyone who wished to speak with me and striving to conduct myself with sincerity and fairness. This function helped me rise above my ongoing tumultuous life with Amma and gave me a sense of purpose, caring, and belonging.

But nowhere was I safe from Amma. Inevitably she began undermining and attacking any sense of well-being that I was struggling to acquire and hold onto in my new role.

It was September 1992. This was not long after we had returned from what I considered a horrible three-month world tour. Before the tour the ashram astrologer had warned me that I was entering an extremely difficult period and could also suffer health problems. After we returned from the tour, he confessed that this period was so intense he saw a chance of suicide and a break in the relationship between guru and disciple!

Neither happened. But during the entire tour Amma was incredibly severe toward me. I tried to accept her treatment as the outcome of my malefic astrological period, but that didn't help much.

When we hit Europe, unimaginably, she got even nastier. Most of the time I was either kicked out of service or sick with cough, cold, fever and strep throat. If I did go near her, immediately she would become enraged and, for no apparent reason, begin throwing harsh words and various objects at me.

I began counting the days until the end of the tour, hoping that once her feet touched holy Indian soil, she would cool off and leave me alone.

In Munich, one evening after Devi Bhava, as we were returning in the car to our residence, she began ripping me to pieces in a new fashion. Out of the blue she began: "You useless wretch. You've got no skill at giving speeches or singing. You have no love for me anymore and are only hanging around for power and position. When we return to India, I am going to throw you out of service indefinitely, cut off every iota of position you hold, and publicly humiliate you."

Blankly staring out the window of the Mercedes, I watched the world whiz by as we picked up speed along the autobahn. The night was dark and gloomy, and I became mesmerized by the rain drizzling under the bright street lamps. The wet road accentuated the sound of the tires as they licked their way home, and I prayed they would deliver me swiftly so that I could escape this metal torture chamber.

With venomous scorn, Amma continued.

"Nowadays you've got a hundred people to love you. But just you wait and see. Not one of them will even look at you once you lose your position.

They'll find someone else. It's not because of you they feel any love. It's because of your association with *me* that anybody even looks at you."

In the midst of my shock and numbness, I somehow managed to wonder what the driver was thinking. The lady who was our chauffeur and host couldn't understand the language, but any fool could sense the mood. She must have felt that I was the recipient of Amma's harsh tone.

Wrapping up her tirade, Amma said, "She thinks that whatever I say, I will change my mind later and take her back. This time, she's in for a real surprise."

Sensing it would soon be over, my body began to unwind from its state of suspended existence, when the final and usual piercing words came.

"I don't need anybody to serve me."

After we made it home, I staggered out of the car, feeling like a useless wretch, a cheat, an imposter. *Was I really only hanging around for my position?* I worried. *Was I really that useless and worthless? How could I possibly come before Amma and serve her wholeheartedly when she thinks I'm a fraud?*

Now I was even dreading getting back to India, something I had been clinging onto as my only source of hope. *How can I face the Indian girls who look up to me with such admiration, when Amma views me with such contempt?* I was clueless as to how I could possibly live up to her expectations. Or please her, for that matter. In moments like these, I turned to God for consolation.

THE FIREFLY

Sitting alone in the dark, silently weeping to myself I wonder, "Is nobody hearing these cries?"

Roaring of the ocean ahead, and occasional lightning above makes the scene even more grim.

Off in the distance I see a light through the swaying coconut trees, reminding me of the journey left to travel.

No consolation, except for the sparse ocean breeze saying, "I am with you; don't be sad."

Not a star in sight, only the gray storm clouds hovering above.

The moon doesn't even want to show her face.

Holy Hell

Even the little firefly rushing by seems to know where he is going.
I have been lost too long.
Please give me your hand.
Show me once again you are there.
Are there any coals left? If so, please fan them.
I have to feel their warmth again.
I have been too long in the cold, feeling weary and desperate.
All I can do is cry for your Love and Guidance.

After this tour it crossed my mind for the very first time: *I don't know if I can do this anymore.*

I don't know if I will ever live up to Amma's expectations.

Little did I know, but I was about to get my big break. I was about to receive a strong gust of encouragement and acknowledgement that would keep me sailing for a few more years.

It seems all was not lost.

Not yet, anyway.

NINETEEN

TO BE OR NOT TO BE?

It was the 30th of October, 1989, and Amma was seated on the floor of her room having her usual meal of rice and fish curry. I was seated nearby, intrigued as usual watching her remove the heads and strings of tender bones from the sardines, chew them to a pulp, and then release the goop from her mouth onto the floor. I watched her squish the rice and curry between her fingers as she simultaneously converted the food into balls, then popped them into her mouth. This fine afternoon a conversation occurred which took me rather by surprise.

Without looking at me, Amma aloofly asked, "This morning when I called a brahmacharin to my room, you know what he asked me?"

"Why, no," I replied, as a rush of inquisitiveness overtook my body.

"He asked why I never gave you yellow robes," she said popping another fish ball into her mouth.

It had been a few years since Balu was initiated into brahmacharya and received his yellow robes. The remainder of Amma's senior Indian men, along with Madhu and Ganga, had also received their initiation. I was accustomed to women being considered second-rate, so it didn't even cross my mind that I would be worthy of such an honor. I was a little disturbed that Nealu had never been considered. He was now stationed permanently at the California center, which was probably a good thing considering his fragile health.

I became nervous. I couldn't quite grasp where she was going with this. Was she angry at the brahmacharin for having the nerve to ask such a question? Was she wondering that maybe she should have given me yellow robes? I panicked. *Do I even want yellow robes?*

If it meant having to leave the ashram to propagate on her behalf, then my answer was no.

But I dared not say so.

With a firm gaze she turned to me and asked the very same question that had just run through my mind, "Do you want yellow robes? Should I give you?"

I was shocked and momentarily speechless, for the question caught me completely off guard. "It's up to you Mother," I murmured. Secretly I hoped she wouldn't offer. I didn't want to be sent away to preach.

To my relief, that was the last I heard on the subject.

A few more years passed. I was rolling with everything. But then it came time for the men to drop their intermediary yellow robes and receive the highest initiation into ochre robes, becoming swamis. A swami is a monk who has taken the oath of renunciation and abandoned his (or her) social and worldly status in order to spend the remainder of his (or her) life in spiritual contemplation. The ochre color symbolizes that the swami has died in the fire of knowledge.

This time I felt extremely dejected. Overlooked. Unappreciated. I began to wonder if Amma valued me at all. Was I just a workhorse and punching bag to her? I began to question—what *were* the criteria for her decision-making? Seniority, surely, wasn't one. If it were, I had arrived long before the place was even an ashram and long before most of the men who had been initiated. My original understanding that it meant you'd be sent away had proved to be false, as one yellow-clad fellow never moved an inch from the place. Spirituality was my life, and I was as serious and dedicated as any of the men. So I couldn't understand why I wasn't being considered.

The only conclusion I could come up with was gender. They were getting their robes because they were men and so Amma held them in higher esteem.

I couldn't come to grips with this new situation. I found myself brooding, struggling to accept Amma's ways.

The men retreated into solitary confinement and began the customary forty-eight-hour vow of silence and fasting. The initiation ceremony was to take place in the wee hours of the morning of Vijayadasami, a day which signifies the victory of righteousness after the Nine Nights of the Goddess Festival. Later that evening Amma was in her room talking to Balu about the upcoming event, and going over some of the details. He had been ordained into swamihood the previous year, and he'd received initiation in accord with ancient tradition by a swami of the Ramakrishna order. I was sitting in the corner of the room, not paying much attention to the discussion—too busy nursing my heart and stewing in self-pity. Of course, I was careful not to let too much show on my face.

Then out of the blue I heard my name.

"What about Gayatri and Leela?" Amma queried.

Suddenly I was all eyes and ears, inquisitively tracking their discussion. *What about me and Leela?* I wondered.

That's when Amma looked at me and asked, "Have you chosen a name yet?"

I jumped up and mumbled, "What do you mean? A name for what?" As it began to dawn on me what she was inferring, a grin spread across my face, my spirits lifted, and my heart raced with excitement.

"For becoming a swamini, you dodo. What do you think I'm talking about?" she teased.

My mouth gaped, my eyes filled with tears, and my mind was whirling. For the first time in many, many years I felt acknowledged.

Coming back down to planet earth, I immediately knew what name I wanted. Swamini Amritaprana was the name that sprang forth from my heart—amrita meaning nectar of immortality, prana meaning life breath.

Amma turned to Balu and asked, "What do you think?"

He bobbled his head in agreement but deferred the decision to Amma. All of a sudden, Amma cast me a look of love and nodded in approval.

I felt as though the entire universe had just graced me with a smile and nodded in approval as well.

The following afternoon, Dr. Leela and I headed to the seashore where the ashram astrologer and master of ceremonies was about to perform the first of many rituals. When we arrived, the male initiates were already seated crossed-legged in the sand before oil lamps that were struggling to stay lit in the sea breeze. Engulfed with profound feelings of love and honor, I took my seat and glanced over at the men, smiling at them warmly. Like daggers plunging into my heart, their faces reflected my smile with varying degrees of indifference, shock, and downright rage. I knew that a couple of the fellows didn't care much for me. But I thought to myself, *Surely under these holy circumstances you could put your grudges aside.*

Only then did it cross my mind that perhaps things were playing out according to Amma's calculations. Maybe she knew there would be opposition. So she waited until these chaps were locked away and bound to silence before announcing that Leela and I would also be getting robes. Perhaps on some level the chaps felt betrayed or tricked by her.

A simpler explanation—it was just their male chauvinism acting out. It was hard for them to accept the fact that two women were being initiated during the same ceremony.

Because I had only twenty-fours to go until the ceremony, I immediately began fasting and observed silence as best I could. Amma didn't seem too concerned about it, though. She was constantly conversing with me.

By the following evening, I was feeling faint from not eating. Much to my amazement, Amma noticed.

"You look terrible. What the hell are you fasting for? Go eat something instead of walking around looking like death," she insisted.

Sensing this rare moment of compassion, I seized the opportunity to share a concern.

"Amma, shouldn't I shave my head? That is part of the custom, isn't it?" I meekly asked.

Naturally, I was nervous and knew I'd look like a freak for a while. But I was serious about following the tradition to a tee.

"Yuck," screeched Amma with a look of horror on her face. "No, no, no. Ladies don't need to shave their heads."

"Okay," I replied with instant surrender and relief.

Later that night I lay on my bed in Amma's kitchen, hoping to catch a couple hours of sleep. With so much excitement darting through my veins, I doubted I would actually drop off. But I set my alarm for three a.m. just in case. On this historic day there would be no sleeping in.

What felt like minutes later, my eyes sprang open as the first sounds of my alarm disrupted the still of the night. Before the third chime I was sitting upright, yawning and rubbing my burning eyes, realizing I must have nodded off after all. Quietly I shuffled out of my room and onto the balcony by my bathroom, where I was greeted by the scent of wood-smoke drifting through the air. At once my excitement reignited. I knew the fragrance was coming from the temple. Preparations were already underway. Now, I was wide-awake and my mind was as clear and crisp as the magnificent morning air ushering forth this new day.

By three-thirty a.m. I was bathed, dressed, and ready for the life-changing event. I stepped out of my room, pausing for a moment to glance at the night sky where a multitude of stars were sparkling and winking at me. With a serene smile I headed across the little bridge, along the corridor, then down the spiral steps that led to the temple. Through the doorway I caught my first glimpse of the circular fire pit, which heightened my anticipation of the upcoming ceremony. Calming myself with a deep breath, I entered and took my seat by the fire.

I sat in reverence listening to the Vedic chanting and the snapping and crackling of the fire. Various items were offered to the mesmerizing golden flames. This was the Ganapati Homam, a fire sacrifice performed before the supplicants embark upon some great undertaking. Its rituals invoke the blessings of Lord Ganesha, the remover of obstacles.

The priest handed each of us a small bundle of twigs, which we offered one by one into the fire after repeating various Sanskrit mantras. Toward the end of the ceremony, much to our delight, Amma entered. Even though she wasn't able to present us with the robes, due to the orthodox tradition (sannyas can only be transmitted by a sannyasin), we desired her presence and especially her blessings.

Once the fire ceremony was complete, Leela and I were asked to step outside so the men could have some privacy. The curtains were drawn and the door closed. The reason being: the next phase of the ceremony involved removing one's clothing and stepping forward naked (literally) to receive one's robes.

Patiently we waited outside while the men continued with the ritual. I was thankful for the fact we were in silence because it removed any awkwardness from not having much to say to Leela. Even in the best of times, I avoided where possible talking to her. One of the first statements she made to me after joining the ashram was, "I can't believe Amma has someone who is not a virgin serving her." I was speechless and stood there with my mouth ajar. *How dare you,* I thought. *First of all, how do you know I am not a virgin? Secondly, what does the status of my vagina have to do with anything?* That was no way to start off any relationship, and I pretty much decided then and there, *I don't like you.*

With spare time on my hands, I began to worry how this segment would play out for the women. At least one man was going to be present—would we have to strip naked in front of him? My stomach twisted into knots of anxiety, and I cringed with embarrassment as I pictured myself standing in the buff, then waddling forward in all my glory. I took a sideways glance at Leela to see if she was showing any sign of worry. But she was far, far away in her own little world, with her eyes closed, humming a tune in her customary off-key fashion.

Eventually the door reopened and we were asked to enter. Stepping inside, I quickly noted that only Amma and Balu were present. The remainder of the men were cloistered on the opposite side of the thick curtain.

Much to my delight, Amma told us we only needed to remove our saris and blouse and to tie our ankle-length underskirt up over our breasts.

My mind at ease now, I began focusing once more on the grandeur of the event. Bare-shouldered and dressed in my simple white underskirt, I prostrated before Amma and moved toward Balu who was holding in the palms of his hands the robes with which I was to be adorned. With an unusual amount of humility, I prostrated to him as well, and then accepted, with honor, my orange robes and the title Swamini Amritaprana. After I was dressed in my new garments, Amma came over, pulled the sari off my shoulder, drew it up over my head and gently tucked it behind my ears. She then smeared a generous amount of sacred ash across my forehead and cast me a loving smile. I was now an ordained swamini.

My cup was overflowing with love and gratitude.

Once Leela received her robes, the curtain was pulled across. I saw for the first time the six men who'd also just become swamis. I studied them intently and without warning let out a tiny giggle. Some looked so different that they were barely recognizable. Not only had they shaved their heads—all their facial hair was gone.

Amma was beaming with delight and seemed immensely proud of her children who were all grown up, so to speak. We stepped onto the stage. As the temple bells rang loudly, the main doors were drawn open, revealing us to the hundreds of people congregated outside in the hall. One by one, we stepped forward as our new names were announced to the crowd, which they shouted back in unison. In grand pomp and style the men began stepping down from the stage, and I watched as they were garlanded and disappeared into the mass of frenzied devotees.

I then stepped off the stage and made my way around the crowd in my usual uncomfortable fashion—cringing as people fell to the floor and began touching my feet. This was a part of the culture I never got used to. I held the tail of my sari out in front like a basket, into which people placed offerings of money, tiny pieces of gold, and rice, which would later be cooked and served as our first meal. Traditionally, swamis were to go out and beg for their food. Instead, we symbolically received offerings from the devotees for our sustainment.

The excitement gradually subsided and devotees began dispersing as breakfast was being served. I retreated to my room, elated but exhausted. I sorted through my little pile of offerings and sent the rice to the kitchen. There were a few hundred rupees in total, a gold ring that one lady had ripped off her finger in an outburst of emotion, and an envelope from a long-time devotee who was visiting from California.

I was impressed that this American benefactor was eager and knowledgeable enough to follow such a custom. I tore the envelope open, wherein a fifty-dollar note was revealed. I thought, *That was very generous of him*, and set it aside with a smile on my face. I was beat. So I lay down for a while to rest and settle into the fact that I was now a swamini.

Periodically I found myself opening one eye, peeping at my orange robes, and bursting into a big smile.

A couple of hours later I was summoned to the hall, for it was time to partake in our first meal. Upon arriving, I noticed straw mats had been laid out on one side, presumably for the swamis and swaminis to sit on. I began counting out the number of spaces required for the men, and was planning to sit farther down the row of mats. My concentration was disrupted when I heard a noise.

"Ppssst," came the hissing sound, which I sensed was directed at me.

Looking up, I saw Rao glaring at me, vehemently pointing to the opposite side. Seemingly, I didn't know my place after all. In his mind, it wasn't enough that I sit after them—I shouldn't be seen sitting anywhere near them.

I wasn't about to make a fuss. So with an extremely heavy heart I moved to the opposite side and sat on the cold, tile floor by myself amid a bunch of Indian householder men. Now this was a time I actually would have liked Leela to be around, but she was nowhere in sight. I ate my food as fast as I could and fled the scene. My bubble of elation now had a hole jabbed in it. The air was leaking; it was deflating, and fast. Back in my room, I had a tiny, therapeutic release and mumbled, "Screw him, rotten bastard, pompous, arrogant, son-of-a-bitch." *Aaahhh, that feels better*, I kidded myself, and swiftly succumbed to a catnap.

Later that afternoon, one by one, the offerings collected by the various swamis were delivered to my room for sorting before handing over to Amma. I opened the first of the many envelopes from the Californian expecting to see a fifty-dollar bill, but was shocked to see a hundred-dollar note sitting inside.

Temporarily postponing the individual sorting and accounting, I grabbed the other envelopes and began ripping them open out of curiosity. Hundred dollars, hundred dollars, hundred dollars.... *You've got to be kidding. What a rat bag. Now hang on a sec, maybe he ran out of money. Don't go jumping to conclusions; just wait to see what he gave Leela.*

Eventually her bundle arrived. So with edgy anticipation and slight annoyance, I ripped open her envelope. There it was, in broad daylight. Fifty dollars. *Wow, is there a hidden message in this? All the men get a hundred dollars and the two women fifty. Seems he's adopted more of the culture than I was aware of.* I knew women weren't as valuable as men, but now I had a figure. It was fifty bucks, or fifty percent to be more precise.

I will probably never know if this apparently sexist insult was intentional, or how he truly felt, or if he in fact had run out of money. But does it even matter? In the grand scheme of things, no. Not a bit. Unfortunately, back then I paid heed to such occurrences, for it was a constant uphill battle against the men in India. And this was just another slap in the face—worse still, by an American.

All said and done, I was overjoyed to finally feel Amma's love and acknowledgement. I tried to push all the petty nonsense aside. I truly believed I had entered a new chapter of my life, and that the fourteen-year rough patch I'd just been through was merely a passing phase. I believed that my past was just a string of tests I'd had to pass in order to prove my determination and worth. I trusted that from hereon things were going to be different. With this newfound sense of hope and inspiration, I vowed to make Amma proud.

There was something else. A more specific liberation.

For many years I had been suffering a life of sexual abuse.

Now that I was a swamini, I naively felt a sense of protection in the robes. I felt certain Balu would never force himself upon a swamini and continue to use her for the disposal of his uncontrolled lust. Certain I was now unchained from the utter denial of my freedom to decide for myself.

At last I could start afresh and lead the life of honesty that I yearned for. Above all I would recover my dignity as a woman and my integrity as a human being.

TWENTY

MAN IN HEAT

One night in the depth of slumber I had a dream. I saw thousands of people with tear-stained faces screaming, "Why, why?" as they looked at Amma and clawed from outside the pearly gates.

"Out of devotion for you, we sacrificed our right to sacred human pleasure and slept with no man or woman. Wasn't that the agreement? Wasn't that what you asked of us?" they wailed. "Oh Amma, how could you betray us and not practice what you preach?"

My face was not among those crying and screaming. For I was holding her many secrets.

And, much to my utmost dismay and deepest loathing, I had secrets of my own. One secret, that is. One I had been carrying for many years, and one that was killing me from the inside out.

In a perverse way I had become "the other woman."

Not that I was cheating on a married woman or trying to steal the love of anyone's life. Nor was I having a torrid love affair. No. I was manipulated, forced actually, in some kind of ménage à trois. The first (the all-knowing guru woman) did not know that the second (the disciple and personal attendant woman) was being regularly abused and raped under her very nose, sometimes right beside her bed while she was asleep—at any rate, in her divine and sacred abode and under her all-knowing protection.

Upon joining the ashram, all I wanted was love and illumination. I possessed the purest ideals and highest intentions. Little did I know that within five years and completely out of the blue I would have a sobbing mess sitting before me professing his love. Little did I know that I would succumb to his pressure and wind up being owned by it for years. Due to my innocent and soft-hearted nature, and one moment of weakness, I became a captive object for Balu's sexual gratification. To put it more bluntly, I became the victim of his manipulation and ongoing rape.

It was an average afternoon in the mid 1980s. I was walking across the sandy compound minding my own business when from behind someone ran up and bumped into me. Hastily I turned around. It was Balu, with a cheesy grin on his face.

"Out of my way," he said in jest as he pushed me on the shoulder. He continued looking back at me with an out-of-the-ordinary smile on his face.

My heart flinched for a second. I thought, *Oh my god, was he just flirting with me?* I pushed the crazy thought aside, telling myself to stop being stupid, that I was merely imagining things. These were my spiritual brothers with whom I had been living for the past five years without even a trace of inappropriateness.

Later that day during the evening bhajans he glanced across at me with a look of longing and what seemed to be tears in his eyes. He did this a couple times. Straightaway I sensed these were not tears of devotion. So I shut my eyes immediately and kept them that way for the duration of the singing.

Now I was worried. Perhaps, that I wasn't imagining things after all.

His odd behavior continued for a few more days until one evening he was standing before me in Amma's room pouring his heart out. To a backdrop of sobbing and sniffling he blurted out, "Gayatri, I am so in love with you."

Nervously looking around the room to ensure nobody else was hearing this conversation, I rejoined with, "What are you talking about? This is not right. You need to pull yourself together."

Reaching out to grab hold of me, he pathetically said, "I need to see you. I need to see you alone."

Stepping backwards, I stood my ground, and said, "You'd better go now."

Like a child reprimanded by his mother, he left the room sniffling and pouting. I began to feel ill. I worried where this was heading. That night I cried myself to sleep. My heart palpitated with fear of the consequences of such a situation.

Human love was not part of the equation in my quest for God. A couple of years prior, when I noticed the faintest hint of a crush developing toward Venu, I nipped it right in the bud. Years earlier, after I arrived in Tiruvannamalai, I chose the path of chastity. Ever since then, I never looked once at a man with any longing. I only desired God.

Yet somewhere deep down in my humanness Balu's unrelenting attention made me feel flattered. I began to feel vulnerable.

The following morning I lay asleep on the verandah of Amma's room when I was rudely awoken. Opening my eyes, I saw a stick prodding me through the gaps in the railing. In shock, I sat up to see Balu standing on top of the water tank with a large branch in hand and tears streaming down his face.

"Go away," I mouthed silently and shooed him away in a state of panic.

He left. But later that evening he was back. Sitting at the top of the inner staircase to Amma's kitchen he said, "I can't live without you. I need to see you alone," he begged.

"What for? You can talk here," I stressed.

My head was spinning, and my heart jolted in trepidation. Amma condemned any form of emotional attachment, let alone between her disciples.

Suddenly he leaned forward, grabbed me round the knees, and began weeping profusely.

Holy Hell

This behavior went on for a few more days. Then it happened. My resolve weakened, and I agreed to meet him early the following morning in his room. I could have run to Amma and shared the recent events, which may have shielded me from him—but I chose not to. I was already so wounded and worn out from her harsh ways that I felt touched and weakened by someone showing he cared for me. When I agreed to meet him, sex was the last thing on my mind. At that stage I was still quite naive and innocent and couldn't even imagine that these spiritual brothers possessed lust. I believed their relationship with Amma was pure and I had no idea that Balu was already sexually involved with her. I believe I went to receive some emotional relief and a bit of a boost from the love he supposedly possessed. Looking back I think that a part of me, stupidly, was also feeling responsible or manipulated into feeling responsible for his anguish, and that it was up to me to ease his pain.

That night I had trouble sleeping, for I was in a state of absolute panic. *Doesn't Amma know what is going on? She's supposed to know our every thought, so why hasn't she intervened by now? Is she perhaps allowing this to happen?* I was confused and a nervous wreck.

Early the next morning I proceeded to the library to talk with him. He immediately locked the door and wrapped his arms around me. Before I knew it, I was lying on the floor and he was forcing himself upon me. It all happened so fast. I felt powerless. I flinched as his initial entry came with a sting. I was no virgin, but it had been six years since I had allowed any man inside me. There I lay, motionless, staring at the wall, but this time the tears were in *my* eyes. There was not a drop of sexual excitement running through my body, only terror and shock. I couldn't believe what was happening. But it was too late.

Anyway, within one minute it was all over. He quickly ejaculated into a wash cloth he had kept ready.

I wondered about his technique. After all, I couldn't get pregnant—not after an eighteen-pound tumor had taken over my womb, resulting in a complete hysterectomy. My mind flashed to seeing similar washcloths partially washed and soaking in Amma's bathroom after Balu had been alone with her.

I started putting two and two together. I couldn't get pregnant, but Amma could. In that moment I suspected he was having sex with her, too. Now I was really disgusted—not only with myself, but with him, and even more with Amma.

Getting up off the floor, I straightened my sari. In a state of absolute terror and repulsion, I declared: "This can never happen again!" I made a dash for the bathroom to wash away my error. That's when I noticed blood on my skirt. I was horrified. For a split second I wondered if my hymen had grown back, or if some scar tissue remained from the surgery. But my number-one concern was that nobody see the evidence. I hurriedly ripped my skirt off, rinsed its stains, wrung it out as hard as I could, and put it back on wet.

The blood washed off, but the inward stain from what had just happened would haunt me for many, many years.

A few weeks later he was back. "I need to see you," he said in his sick voice.

I tried to argue and plead my way out, but he was obsessed and relentless. I felt trapped. If I didn't oblige, he would start sulking and acting weird. People would begin to wonder what was going on. If this ever came to light, I would be the one to suffer. I would be the one punished—not Balu. Amma had never shown any leniency to me before, so I had no reason to believe this time would be any different. The common notion in India is that Western women possess loose morals. I believed I would be blamed, possibly kicked out of the ashram, and most definitely no longer allowed to serve Amma. I knew I couldn't live with such consequences. I felt I had no other choice but to succumb to his demands—to his manipulation.

As though placing an order, he would inform me that he needed to see me, and I was supposed to find a way to make that happen. I was expected to let him know when an opportunity revealed itself. He only approached me a few times a year, but they were a few times too many. I did my best to dodge him and delay the inevitable. But the longer I delayed, the angrier he became.

At night my phone would ring. "I need to see you," he would say in a deep and breathy voice.

"No," I'd cry, slamming the phone down as my heart did backward summersaults. My guts would wrench. It killed me to live such a lie. Immediately the phone would ring again.

"You always say no! You have to oblige me! I will be up shortly."

Sure enough, when Amma left the room to go elsewhere in the ashram, I would hear the click of her door downstairs. Seconds later, standing before me would be the disheveled, dark figure of a man in heat. His eyes no longer radiated love but overflowed with rage. His face was no longer gentle but intense and disturbed.

With his now grossly overweight body and his shoulder-length hair shading his face, he would rush toward me and shout, "Why do you always say no?"

One night, holding my arm in a tight grip, (it later turned black and blue), he raised his fist and began beating me in the back. In fear and disgust I moved toward the cold, dirty bathroom floor and lay down. I lifted my sari, clenched my teeth, and waited for the current episode to pass. I would scream in anguish without making a sound. I would sob uncontrollably without shedding a tear.

As the Indian ashram became busier and more crowded, Balu had less opportunity to violate me. He began relying on overseas travel to gain access, so to speak. When we visited Europe, he never went to the morning programs but stayed at the house in order to write the next book of Amma's "teachings." His free time was bad news for me. While I was busy in the kitchen trying to prepare lunch for Amma and the group, Balu would harass me to come to his room. Until I found the time to discreetly step away from the stove and the girl who was my sous-chef for the day, he would periodically appear in the hallway. Lurking like an evil spirit, he would get darker and angrier the more time that elapsed. It was this type of disturbed behavior—eyes that mirrored a pent-up rage—that made me feel trapped, not so much from fear of him but the constant terror that his unsettled state would arouse suspicions. If that happened, I would be persecuted.

After such intense persistence, in order to gain some peace and be rid of this fellow's torment, I would resentfully go to his room. In haste he would mount me like a clumsy animal, relieve himself, then get back to work on Amma's teachings.

One year, on a Reunion Island and Mauritius tour, I succeeded in dodging him. I was so relieved and pleased to have outsmarted him by ignoring his repeated requests. It was time to leave for the airport, to head back to India, and Amma was already seated in the car. I was grabbing the last pieces of luggage and ensuring nothing was left behind when suddenly in the doorway—there he was. Like a dark demon from hell he barged into the room. In a flurry of wrath he raised his fist to beat me, to punish me. I swiftly extended my arm to block his punch. Unfortunately my thumb took the brunt of the blow and bent backwards. I hunched over in pain. By the time I looked up, he was gone.

With no time to waste, I took a deep breath, firmly clamped off the tears that so desperately wanted to gush forth, grabbed the bags, and headed for the car. My heart exploded with anger when I saw him seated in the front seat, looking straight ahead with a dead gaze.

There was nothing I could do or say, so I placed the luggage in the trunk and hopped in the car next to Amma. My hand was hurting like hell, but I dared not show any sign of pain lest Amma ask what was wrong. How would I explain what had just happened, and worse still, why? My aggravated mind would have loved to tell her, "Oh, my hand is sprained because your darling son just punched me because I failed to find him an opportunity to have sex with me. Does that answer your question?"

Alas, no such words were ever spoken. I just sat there and suffered in silence. A couple of hours later on the plane, my hand began swelling like a balloon. I did my best to keep it discreetly tucked by my side. I think at one point Amma noticed, but she never bothered to ask. This was the one time I actually felt glad that she cared so little for my physical well-being.

Eventually, I began taking Balu's exploitive and abusive treatment for granted. Even though I felt trapped, it never once crossed my mind that I was a victim. Like many who suffer from sexual abuse, I felt it was somehow my fault.

There was only one instance where I succeeded in beating off this rapist. We were on the north Indian tour, and we had arrived at our destination in the early hours of the morning after being on the road all day. I was utterly exhausted and more than just sound asleep; it was as though I had passed out. Suddenly I was awakened by a pair of hands groping me. I don't know when or how, but he had come through Amma's room and found me lying alone outside on the verandah. From a state of deep sleep and near-delirium, I began thrashing my limbs, beating him and shouting at him to go away. In a flash he vanished. I fell right back to sleep. In that moment I didn't care if Amma heard the racket. My instincts were to protect myself.

The next morning after waking and remembering, I felt a sense of panic. *Surely Amma heard me fighting with him?* I worried. But I was never questioned about the incident.

There were other times when we were on tour in the West that Balu came to Amma's room at night and sat by her bedside rubbing her legs till she fell asleep. My heart would sink, for I knew that shortly afterwards I would hear him crawling across the carpet toward me. Right there on the floor at the foot of her bed, right under Amma's nose, I would be raped. It was useless to fight against the abuse. So I lay there passively. While every cell of my body and soul cried in disgust and anger, I let him misuse me and walk off.

In all the years, not once did I ever approach him. I was not interested in the least. My mind was on other things. I was completely engaged in my spiritual life and my hard work as Amma's personal attendant. I didn't have the time to sit around with idle sexual fantasies. Besides, not once was I even slightly aroused by him. Not once did I receive any sexual gratification. He never tried to kiss me. There wasn't any time for that. As soon as he was in my presence, he would whip out his penis, lie on top, ram himself inside, thrust and grunt four or five times, then it was all over. I was merely an object of his primitive desire—someone used to discharge his load and relieve himself of his pent-up sexual frustration.

This fellow, Amma's head swami, behaved like someone in abysmal ignorance, someone who possessed no self-awareness or compassion—not to mention empathy, sympathy, or even basic human kindness and respect. A part of me wonders if it wasn't Amma herself who set this precedent in motion by not practicing what she preached. In Balu's sick mind, had she granted him permission for such insensitive and lewd behavior?

Deep down in my soul the ongoing sexual abuse was also eroding my faith in Amma. In my mind there were only two possibilities—either she knew, or she didn't. If she knew, then why was she was allowing him to abuse me? If she didn't know, then I could see a huge flaw in the theory that she was omniscient, an incarnation of the Divine Mother, and so on.

After I was initiated and got my robes, I believed this unfortunate phase of my life was over, that I'd gotten my lucky break. I saw the ceremony as an opportunity to forget the past and start anew. I so desperately wanted to be able to look people in the eye and feel good about myself. I so desperately wanted to be able to look in the mirror and not hate myself. Everything was going well for a few months. I finally felt safe. I truly believed it was all over.

Then one day he was back, begging and pleading.

"No," I screamed from the depths of my soul. "You cannot have me. You need to free me from this curse and allow me to live in honor. Go find someone else," I begged.

"But I only love you. I don't want to be with anyone else," he whimpered.

"You call this love! How dare you call it love when you force yourself upon me like this? It's sexual blackmail. It's manipulation!" I exploded in a tempest of rage.

It took me years to call a spade a spade and use the word "rape."

Holy Hell

Alas, my words fell on deaf ears. I couldn't free myself from this sick fellow's grip.

There were many, many reasons why I had to leave the ashram, and this sexual abuse was certainly one of them. A few months before I left, Balu began spiraling into severe depression and was put on medication. He was on suicide watch—an utter mess. He had probably had the condition for a very long time. That could explain his uncontrollable emotions. But nothing could excuse his abusive treatment of me.

I did care for him, but not in the way he supposedly cared for me. I wanted him as a friend, as a brother, not a lover—if one could even call it that. Oftentimes he was my only ally among the senior men, *but what a price to pay!*

I tucked the memory of these experiences into the dark recesses of my soul. Even after I left the ashram, I thought I would take them to my grave. Little did I realize, though, the crippling effect that these experiences were still having on my life, the guilt and shame that I was still carrying.

A few years after leaving the ashram I began seeking intuitive counseling. One day during a healing session the lady counselor exclaimed, "Oh, you have been sexually abused."

My body shuddered at the words and I became tense. I repelled the trauma of the memory. After all, it was buried so deep it could never be found.

The lady immediately reassured, "We don't need to deal with this now."

I breathed a sigh of relief. But I began to ponder the word "abuse."

Up until then I had been carrying the belief that the Balu mess was my fault. I never imagined I would refer to myself as a "victim." I began to see some light from this new perspective, but still I couldn't shake the overwhelming feelings of guilt and shame. Despite those feelings, I paid attention to the words "not deal with this now"—meaning that the mess had to be dealt with at some point.

I see now that no matter how deep we try to bury our secrets, they stand out like a dark stain on pure white linen. They blemish our souls. The stains will only fade if they are exposed to the light. The truth might hurt, but it should never be feared. Truth needs to be looked square in the face with love and compassion.

I became exhausted from holding my silence, as though sitting alone in a dark closet terrified of the boogieman. I realized it was time to step out into the light and see there was nothing to fear. It was time to face the fact that I was traumatized. I had been a victim of sexual abuse. Not only that, I was carrying a ton of shame, guilt and blame, and I had to let that go.

Around the same time I realized that Amma's secrets were not my responsibility to be lugging around for the rest of my life, either.

Internally I was a mess. Yet I hung in there for five more years after getting my robes. For the most part I numbed myself to the horror and cruised through on autopilot. In order to survive I kept a firm grip on the aspirations of the life I wanted, of the guru I wanted, not yet ready to face the fact that perhaps I wasn't living out my dream, but a nightmare instead.

TWENTY-ONE

THE DAWN OF DOUBT

Now that I was officially entitled Swamini Amritaprana and energized by the love and acknowledgement I felt from the recently acquired robes, I was moving full steam ahead. My heart overflowed with joy. I truly believed that my trials were over and that things between Amma and me were going to be different.

And they were, for a while. But who was I kidding? As if a pattern so deeply set could change overnight—despite what kind of clothing I was wearing.

Within a few months of getting my robes, history began repeating itself. Once more I was being hit, kicked, slapped, and thrown out of her room. She even invented a new form of punishment for me when she was really angry. Grabbing me by the throat with one hand, she would dig her nails in and rip towards the center, scraping the skin as she went. I was then left with bright red scratch marks across my throat, and sometimes blood.

The first couple of times this happened, I did my best to conceal the deep scratches with my sari. If anyone asked what happened, I concocted a pathetic explanation. "Oh well, you see, I was up in the attic trying to grab a couple of oil lamps and something was sticking out from one of the sacks and scratched me." I feared if I told the truth, rumor would spread, and inevitably reach Amma's ears. Then I'd be in even more trouble.

I went on creating excuses. But after a while some of my closer friends confronted me. "Did Amma do that?" I'm sure plenty more had an inkling, just never dared to verbalize their suspicion. Eventually I ran out of explanations and excuses for Amma's behavior. My fear transformed into anger. I began sarcastically telling those closely connected to me, when they asked, that the marks were guru prasadam (blessings from the guru). To a certain degree, I didn't care anymore what people thought or if I got into trouble. What she was doing wasn't right. One time in a fit of rage she twisted my ear so hard I couldn't sleep on it for days.

The battle wounds and scars healed in time, but far more damaging than having hair ripped out of my head or skin scraped off my neck was her emotional abuse.

Healing from that was going to take a lot more time and effort.

My life in the Indian ashram had become laden with responsibility. I was constantly on the phone with the various departments, and I needed to be available when problems arose. Therefore, it was no longer practical for me to spend hours on end during the daytime locked away with Amma in her room. I needed help, a babysitter so to speak—someone to mind, wait on, and massage Amma while she was resting.

In a way I was happy about this. I no longer had the physical strength nor, to be honest, the inclination. My heart had been rubbed raw by Amma's incessant abuse. It was getting hard for me to be around her.

In order to have close and constant proximity to Amma, one needs to be innocent, pure-hearted, physically strong, and above everything else, naive. The perfect candidate for this new position was Lakshmi. She had all the necessary qualities, especially when it came to being naive. So Amma drew her in. Hailing from Holland, Lakshmi was physically quite hardy, nearly six feet tall, big-hearted, slightly clumsy and goofy. She was honest to a fault and frequently confessed to Amma her latest sexual and boyfriend fantasy with tears and slobber running down her face. She began taking some of the blows that had been previously dished out to me. I felt sorry for her, but she didn't seem to mind. I guess she was just so excited to have the privilege and honor of being in Amma's private quarters.

One afternoon when we were in London, I was resting in the room adjacent to Amma's along with several other women. Amma had just returned from the morning program, and I lay there picturing in my mind the usual chain of events. All of a sudden, through the walls, I could hear Amma's voice escalating to the top of her lungs. Then, wham! A large crashing noise, and I could tell Lakshmi was getting knocked around. I took a peek around the room to see if anyone else was focusing on the racket next door.

With a look of dire concern Mira, a comrade of Lakshmi's, came over to me and meekly said, "Poor Lakshmi. But I'm sure Amma is just removing some bad karma from her."

"Bullshit," I blurted out. I sprang up from the floor.

Mira's eyes almost popped out of her head. She sat stunned and speechless before me. I was fuming at both Amma's cruelty and Mira's denial. It was the same old story. People rationalized anything and everything that Amma did, no matter what. This was something I could no longer do or tolerate.

"Do you think only me and Lakshmi have sins to be destroyed? Surely the swamis have sins to be rid of as well. So why doesn't Amma start knocking them around, if that's the case? Do you think she's only concerned about saving me and Lakshmi?"

Having ranted, I plopped back down on the carpet and jerked my sari up over my face. I was boiling with anger and frustration. *I'm so sick to death of this unfairness and ill treatment,* I repeated over and over in my mind until I dozed off.

Where there is mind control, manipulation, and abuse of power, there is normally malpractice around money. I'm sorry to say, but in this regard Amma was no different from all the other pedestal-mounters. She drew money and golden jewelry like a magnet, and her pot always overflowed. For years I noticed that rich and generous devotees received royal treatment, the red carpet rolled out before them. For the most part, I justified this behavior as Amma's way of taking from the rich to give to the poor—a modern-day Robin Hood, if you will.

Later I realized that a large chunk of the offerings placed directly in Amma's hands in India went right to her family. These offerings had been given by devotees in the belief that the money would support Amma's charitable work. Initially I was okay with this. I considered it Amma's duty to provide her parents a comfortable home and the dowry to marry off her sisters, especially in a culture that places such emphasis on family values. But Amma went way above and beyond the call of duty. Her parents, three brothers, and three sisters each received large sums of money and gold.

Here's what made me mad. Ashram residents who had dedicated their lives to Amma, who had given most or all their money to Amma, and who worked around the clock sacrificing their health for her—these devotees were living in impoverished conditions with no decent nutrition or care.

Amma was extremely conscious of the fact that numerous sets of eyes watched who came and went from her room. Some ashram residents would stake out her joint twenty-four hours a day, hoping for an unexpected glimpse of Amma or to be the first by her side if she left her room. This type of scrutiny, no matter how innocent, had Amma so concerned that she ordered her staircase be torn down and reconstructed on the rear side of her building. As an added precaution to avoid suspicion, she insisted that her family members never actually carry anything when they left her room. Instead she needed a way to convey her treasure over to the family without arousing speculation.

So for many years, I was her mule. It was a daily occurrence for me to be seen going to her parents' house carrying a little ice chest to collect fish curry for her lunch and evening meals. Unbeknown to the ashram residents, this little ice chest was often full to the brim with bundles of rupees and large amounts of gold jewelry. It was the perfect cover—one nobody would ever suspect.

At one stage a couple of outside devotees became rather vocal about Amma's family's sudden wealth. While they were making their way to the ashram, they had seen a large mansion being constructed by her brother on newly purchased land.

As soon as these accusations reached Amma's ears, she went into damage control. She dictated a sermon to Balu and had him summon a meeting for the entire ashram. Like a fool Balu stood before hundreds of devotees adamantly insisting that this newfound wealth of Amma's family had nothing to do with her, but with the extraordinary success of her father's fishing business. I cringed when I heard this, for it was a flat-out lie, and even more because I knew people were not that gullible

Well, not all of them anyhow.

In order to keep up her facade of innocence and purity, Amma had a small team of trusted individuals doing her dirty work, and I was one of them. In the couple of years Vidya also stayed in Amma's room, she made a few such deliveries. Later on it was Lakshmi who fulfilled the role of mule.

Another matter that saddened my heart was to see Amma give preferential treatment to Western residents who donated large sums of money, then judge those who were less fortunate. One particular incident remains fresh in my mind. It was during a retreat off the coast from Seattle at Fort Flagler, an antique military base that is now part of the Washington State Park. It was mid-morning. Amma was in the nearby hall greeting her devotees while I cooked up a storm in the century-old, quaint, colonial-style home. From my kitchen window, I could see the grayish-blue, wind-whipped waters of Puget Sound, and the white forms of seagulls with their graceful wings spread wide across the clear blue sky. The air was cool and crisp with a friendly and comforting seaside scent to it. I heard the front door open and the floorboards creak as feet hurriedly shuffled over them. I turned around to see Priya standing before me, puffing and panting. She was a beautiful, well-educated, young Indian woman who traveled with us on tour. Her almond-shaped eyes were like that of a goddess, and her skin was slightly dark yet emitted a wonderful luminous glow. She had been born in India but raised in the United States, so her reserved demeanor had the pleasing blend of confidence and assertiveness of a Western woman.

Catching her breath, she said, "Amma wants to know how much money Kripa gave when she joined the Indian ashram."

"What on earth for?" I asked, unable to conceal my annoyance.

Priya explained, "Kripa is sitting by Amma's chair crying and begging forgiveness, and wants permission to come back to the ashram."

I knew Kripa's situation, and that she had been told to leave a few months prior. She had been working on a project for the upcoming US tour, alone in a room with a young Indian brahmacharin. The unfortunate part was that she and this young man got entangled in a little romance. I don't know and frankly don't care what base they got to, or if they hit a home run, but I do know she was the only one punished.

"All right then," I said, letting out a groan of disgust. I wiped my hands on my apron and ran to get my little black book. I kept a secret log of the money Westerners gave when they became permanent residents in India. The reason I kept it secret was because I refused to give the information to the newly established Westerners' office and risk subjecting those who gave less money to unfair treatment. Scanning the pages, I found Kripa's name and the figure: $3,623. Quite an insignificant amount compared with many of the other donations which went as high as $108,000, but still, I didn't see why it should be a factor in the decision as to whether Kripa could return to the ashram or not.

Later that afternoon Amma was up in her room resting. I asked Priya, "So, what did Amma decide? What's Kripa's fate?"

I felt empathy for this woman. She had been living for many years at the ashram, and I knew she would be devastated if she weren't allowed to return.

With a look of pity Priya replied, "At first Amma said no, she can't come back to India."

"She can't come back to India! What's that supposed to mean? Amma doesn't own the goddamn country."

Calming me down, Priya whispered, "I presume she meant the Indian ashram."

"Yeah, you're probably right. So, then what happened? What made Amma change her mind?"

With obvious compassion Priya replied, "When Kripa heard the word no, she began sobbing uncontrollably. This I think made Amma soften a little. Finally Kripa was given permission to work at the hospital in Cochin. But she's not allowed back at the ashram."

"Whatever," I muttered, shaking my head in disapproval. I felt knots of anger forming in my belly. If the woman had donated more money, she would have received a more favorable response. I felt sick to my stomach knowing that so many people were eagerly dedicating their lives to Amma oblivious of the fact they were being judged and treated in accordance with the thickness of their wallet.

Over the years, from living so closely with Amma, I got to hear all kinds of juicy tidbits of people's personal lives. Disciples and devotees unburdened their souls by sharing very private and intimate details with Amma. They held the belief that she would keep such information confidential.

Unfortunately, such was not the case.

Soon after those sessions, I would overhear Amma gossiping these tidbits to some of the senior men. I was privy to the numerous scandals occurring in the ashram and got to witness the different ways Amma dealt with these matters. I saw some people's private details get splattered publicly across the ashram and the persons involved crucified. On the other hand, I saw some matters kept top-secret, discreetly swept under the rug.

For instance, the same young Indian man who became involved with Kripa, a couple of years later was engaged in homosexual relations with a young lad who eventually confessed his misdeeds to Amma. Once again, there was no sign of any punishment for Kripa's former lover. He remained unscathed.

But a few years later, when he fell in love with a female computer student living in the ashram hostel, Amma turned on him. He fell head-over-heels for this young woman and declared he wanted to leave the ashram and marry her. Amma's claws came out. Overnight he became a bad, bad person, and she began spewing his many secrets to everyone. I found it curious that she didn't seem to mind his sexual escapades. What upset her was the realization that his heart was going to someone else. Was it because she was no longer number one?

Despite Amma's condemnation he stood firm. He left the ashram and married the girl.

Having to witness such erratic, manipulative, and unjust behavior began taking its toll on me. I was also becoming tired of the special treatment Amma dished out to her senior men. Balu wasn't the only one intimately involved with Amma. Late at night Rao would frequently sneak into her room using the key she gave him. I'd hear the door to the room where I slept gently close and the bolt slip into place. His quarters were conveniently just a few yards behind Amma's building, so nobody could see him coming or going. I never personally witnessed these two having sex, but I saw plenty of evidence. Bedding spotted with semen, the usual hand towel soaking in the bathroom, a pornographic magazine that had been confiscated from a computer student and given to Amma was frequently out of its hiding place after they had been alone together.

One day local laborers who were digging up the plumbing around Rao's quarters started yelling to each other, "Look, there are fish bones and condoms in this swami's drain!"

I know Amma gave her leftover fish curry to this fellow, so that would explain the bones. As for the condoms....

A young Indian lady overheard the laborers' conversation and brought it to Amma's attention. Amma explained that the condoms most likely belonged to a married Indian couple who had recently confessed that they were having trouble abstaining from sex. When I heard this, I struggled with all my might to conceal my reaction. Amma's excuse was pitiful. This couple, who she named, lived in the main temple building, and all that plumbing drained straight into the river, not in the opposite direction to a tiny, single pipe connected to Rao's dwelling.

A few of the other senior men would occasionally spend time in Amma's room alone behind locked doors. When I entered her room an hour or so later, several times I noticed that her petticoat was on inside out. Meaning it had been removed while these men were in her presence.

Apparently Amma has also been intimate with at least one Western man. This man has openly shared his story with me. Knowing him to be an honest and loyal person, I felt his words ring true in my heart.

Balu traveled a lot. Before heading out he always wanted some alone time with Amma. She was afraid to turn the light out in her room in case Rao noticed. Instead she'd leave me and Lakshmi in her room and go with Balu to the upper-level kitchen where she could turn the light out, lock the door, and not arouse suspicion. A short while later they would come back downstairs. Balu would promptly exit her room with a towel strategically draped over his shoulder and a sheepish grin on his face.

I silently witnessed her carefully juggling these fellows, trying to make sure each of them felt they were the nearest and dearest. I'd hear her gossip against Rao to Balu, then against Balu to Rao. Meanwhile Ramakrishna got to hear gossip about both of them. He needed less attention though, for he was secure in his relationship with Amma. He knew she trusted him the most. I draw this conclusion based on the fact that I know he holds secrets that none of the other men are aware of.

Despite the ongoing evidence I was faced with, I chose to block it all out. My only recourse as long as I wished to stay in the ashram, was to somehow accept the behavior.

Even though I was beginning to form rather strong opinions about Amma's character, I fought with all my might to suppress them. I didn't want anything to rock my boat or challenge the very foundation of everything I believed in—Amma, that is. I continued to try to accept her ways as being somehow "divine." But I was failing miserably. I was starting to notice distinct human weaknesses in her. These weaknesses made me question the belief that had been drummed into me from day one. That she was one with God.

I began floundering in doubt, especially when I saw Amma turn insecure and dare I say jealous when another female Indian guru appeared on the scene.

Up to that point Amma had cornered the Divine Mother market. So when some of her followers began flocking to this new woman named Karunamayi, she and some in the community felt a lot of unrest.

I thought if someone wants to go check out another guru, then let them. But Amma dissuaded her followers from going elsewhere and frequently served up this classic story: "A farmer desperately in need of water started digging a well. Day after day he kept digging new holes without success. One day, a neighbor asked, "What on earth are you doing? You'll never find water from digging multiple shallow holes! You need to choose one spot and stick to it."

Some of Amma's more zealous Western devotees began mocking and accusing this new guru of being a charlatan, saying she was imitating Amma. There was so much effort put into preventing people from straying elsewhere. In fact, talk about or promotion of any other spiritual teacher within the ashram was strongly condemned, and there was a task force of fanatics ready to crush and pounce on anyone who dared try.

One afternoon a few months later Amma was relaxing in her room when Ramakrishna entered saying he had an urgent matter to discuss with her. My curiosity was tweaked, and I couldn't wait to hear what had so twisted his knickers.

With a note of panic in his voice, he began telling Amma, "I was just having a chat with Steve, and he mentioned in passing that some of your American devotees are also attending the weekly gatherings in honor of Karunamayi."

Steve was a long-time devotee and held gatherings for Amma followers throughout the year in his East Coast home. This new piece of information devoured Amma's attention. In a flash she was seated upright. Her relaxed demeanor turned tense. She was bouncing up and down on her bed having a temper tantrum.

"What!" she screeched. "How many? Who are they?"

Ramakrishna looked distressed. I don't think he was expecting such an intense reaction. "I don't know," he said nervously. "I didn't ask such details. I just thought I had better report it."

"You did the right thing, my son. Now go find out how many people and try to get their names," she commanded.

Just as he was about to leave the room, she screamed, "Forget it. Forget it. Just tell Steve that if any of *my* devotees dare go to those other meetings, he shouldn't let them back into mine."

I couldn't believe what I was hearing. I was in absolute shock. My heart sank as I watched Ramakrishna bobble his head in compliance like a brass-lamp genie, "Your wish is my command." And off he went.

Fortunately he chose to leave via my upstairs room. So as calmly as possible I followed him.

Once out of Amma's sight, I stopped him dead in his tracks. "Ramakrishna, surely you're not going to tell him that?"

He stood still and silent with a blank stare on his face.

In a fit of disgust I blurted out, "What's Amma so afraid of?"

Now he became animated. His raven-like eyes, already intense from the dark circles beneath them and the contrasting head of silver hair, grew wide. "She's not afraid of anything. How dare you make such an accusation!"

Realizing what I had just said, I thought, *Oh crap. I wonder how long it'll take for that comment to reach Amma's ears.* I had my enemies, and they rarely missed an opportunity to get me into trouble.

In that moment though I didn't care, for I was so passionate about my belief. Maybe I was turning into a bit of a rebel. But I had Amma's best interests at heart, despite my mounting inner turmoil and doubt.

"Ramakrishna," I stated solemnly. "Do you know how bad that is going to make Amma look? Do you realize that making such a rule will turn people away? There will be rumors, you can just bet on it. Is that what you want?"

I was wasting my breath, for his only concern was to obey Amma. He gave me a dirty look, hastily turned on his heel, and poof! He and his pigeon toes were gone.

Deep within my soul I began to sense that I was on a sinking ship. I had to choose whether to go down with it or to grab a life jacket and swim for safety. This realization was both terrifying and gut-wrenching. I wasn't at all ready to look at it, let alone accept it. My heart knew the truth, but my mind just wasn't ready to face the facts. I wasn't ready to abandon the only life I had known for nearly nineteen years.

So war was declared.

I became engaged in mighty inner battles, panic attacks, and many nights howling into my pillow, not wanting to leave, but somehow knowing I needed to get out. The emotional pain was enormous.

I knew I could not leave until I was one hundred percent clear. So I continued to suppress and delay the inevitable and knuckled down for another year.

For one very long year filled with anxiety, anger, tears, sorrow, illness and utter exhaustion, I was so torn inside that I began coming apart at the seams. Yet I wasn't quite ready to throw in the towel. Amazingly, I still wasn't ready to put my own health and happiness before others.

That was all about to change, though. It had to. For I was living a slow and painful death that I could no longer endure.

TWENTY-TWO

THE MELTDOWN

By early 1999, the final year of my stay in the ashram, I was so depleted that my nervous system began collapsing. I had been working and serving around the clock for almost twenty years without one healthy break. The days of journal writing, inspiration, contemplation, and rejuvenating spiritual experiences were long gone. I was trapped in a never-ending whirlpool of travel, activities, and responsibilities with no hope for relief. To top it off, my faith dangled like a loose tooth ready to give way at the slightest provocation. The only peaceful and quiet places in the entire ashram were the rooftops. But if I as much as put one foot out my door, I would get mobbed. It became impossible for me to get from point A to point B without being stopped every few feet by people requesting to talk, or by Indian devotees as they reverently prostrated themselves at my feet. I was a celebrity in this little kingdom, a swamini and Amma's personal attendant, so I had to keep on smiling no matter how I was feeling inside.

Up until that point I had been very much a "yes" person. I tried to accept every situation that came my way as God's will. That is, Amma's will.

"No" was a dirty word in the ashram, and I hadn't uttered that syllable in a very long time.

But that was all about to change. "No" and I were about to become the best of friends. Through my courtship with this new word I began to see the light. I entered a whole new realm of thought. *Here I am, sitting all alone in my little rowboat, getting knocked around incessantly by waves, and calling my condition 'self-surrender.' What if I am fooling myself? The oars are here for a reason, aren't they? Maybe it's 'God's will' that I grab hold of them and paddle to calmer waters by saying no for a change?* What a marvelous and liberating thought! I rejoiced at it. I was excited to think that I *did* actually have a choice in the matter, something that had never before crossed my mind.

I implemented this new strategy at once, and I was amazed at how powerful it felt. Of course I had to wrestle with my old battered self—who kept sticking her nose in, trying to convince me I was being selfish. But I held strong. When people fell at my feet, I gently touched them on the shoulder, acknowledging their gesture and the divinity within them, gave them a smile, then kept walking. When requested an interview, I'd smile and say, "I'm sorry, but I'm just too busy at this time."

I used to spend hours trying to resolve the numerous squabbles that occurred between the young Indian women. As big sister I always made myself available to hear their grievances, and I would call for whoever else was involved to get the other side. I would then summon a meeting between the two parties and mediate until an amicable resolution was achieved.

But now I had zero tolerance for such petty matters. I decided it was time that they grew up and learned how to cope. I was tired of feeling like a hamster, puffing and panting, frantically running nowhere in my little wheel. And I was tired of working myself to near death and neglecting my body to prove to the world how great my devotion and dedication was. Thanks to my budding romance with "No," I began to see that I didn't have to perpetuate this fanatical ashram way of life.

A door revealing new opportunities began creaking open, and I just needed the courage and faith to take a peep and walk through.

Holy Hell

Withdrawing in this way helped somewhat, but travel was once again bashing on my door. With frail body and raw nerves I had to pull it together and trudge forward.

The trips that really pushed me over the edge were the five-day programs at the various branch ashrams with temples, called Brahmastanams. At six a.m. the loudspeakers would erupt, blaring the recitation of the thousand names of the Divine Mother, adding recorded bhajans at intervals. This racket would continue non-stop until at least two the next morning, or whenever Amma finished greeting the thousands who had come to see her. There was no escape from the din. Inside the hall, loudspeakers stacked in tall boxes screamed at me, an assault from every angle. If I tried to escape by wandering around the property, there were speakers strapped to coconut trees that shouted after me to ensure my captivity. The overwhelming crowds, with their pushing and shoving and endless chatter, didn't help either. To be honest, I hated those programs. Even if it *was* God's name blaring at me around the clock, I couldn't help feeling that the Lord's name was being taken in vain. Nowadays I use the memory of those events as a source of inspiration to motivate and encourage myself through difficult situations. I remind myself, "Hey, if you can survive five days at a Brahmastanam, you can survive anything."

At the third of these events just a week or so apart, my nervous system began to verge on collapse. I felt a debilitating electrical current running through my body, which left me with barely the strength to stand. The back of my head hurt, and my jaw locked tight. So much heat was pouring off the top of my head that I had to keep a damp towel on it for relief.

Finally I thought, this is crazy. I mustered the courage to ask Amma for permission to go back to the ashram. As the morning program drew to a close, I made my way to Amma's room and waited along with Lakshmi for her return. I was feeling rather nervous, for this was something I had never done before. When we heard Amma coming toward her room, Lakshmi turned and gave me a sympathetic smile. Neither of us knew how Amma would react, and we both feared the worst. But I didn't see any choice in the matter.

When Amma stepped into the room and saw me, she acted surprised. She poked a funny face at me. But she said nothing. Lakshmi closed the door. Amma unpinned her half-sari that was stained with dirt, grime, and vermilion from the foreheads of hundreds of devotees. As it dropped to the floor, she grabbed the hem of her dress, raised it up over her head, and tossed it across the room. Dressed in just her petticoat, she sat down to have her meal.

She looked tired. Her lips were chalky, her skin dull, and her right cheek by now permanently bruised from hugging hundreds of people for hours on end. She no longer had the radiant and vibrant glow of those days when I first met her. The wavy, dark locks that framed her face were showing the first signs of gray. Her two slightly buck front teeth now had a large gap between them. Her arms and legs remained quite sturdy, but her always slightly oversized belly was now huge. The belly, she always joked, was from having so many children.

When Amma finished her meal, I poured water over her hands as she washed them into a steel bowl. Then I apprehensively popped my question.

"Amma, I'm really not well. My body is so weak I can barely stand. Is there any way I could go back to the ashram?"

Glancing at my face and studying me intently she asked, "How will you get back?"

"There's a train in a couple of hours. I'd just need a ride to the station. Oh, and I'll prepare a complete list for Lakshmi so she knows how to pack for your return journey."

"Okay," she replied in a somewhat detached tone.

Then much to my surprise she asked me to come close. She straightened my hair and tucked the loose ends behind my ears. Then she neatly pleated the tail of my sari, pulled me close, and rubbed her nose back and forth across my cheek giving me a big sniff—the Indian equivalent of a kiss.

Holy Hell

I prostrated before Amma. Then I left the room so that she could rest and I could pack.

As I stepped outside—I couldn't believe it—I actually had butterflies in my tummy. I was about to go somewhere by myself. This coming excursion would be only the second time I had ever traveled separately from Amma. And it would be the first time I had ever left her behind in the middle of a program.

My entire world was slowly but surely crumbling to pieces, and yet this fragment of distance made me realize that I still loved her. I loved her even if what I loved was more like the person I originally believed her to be. This realization added a new element of torment to my growing desire to flee the ashram.

The car that took me to the station pulled away from the drowning noise and frantic madness of the devotees. Out the rear window I watched that reality fade like a bad dream. Finally we passed the last loudspeaker-harnessed coconut tree—the one that just wouldn't let *anyone* forget that Amma was in town. Then everything went quiet. I faced forward, let out a sigh of relief, and settled back into my feelings of exhaustion and inner turmoil.

On the six-hour train journey I soaked up the beauty of Kerala with its lush vegetation, coconut jungles, and myriad rivers and streams. Whenever we passed a cool body of water or a pungent forest, I inhaled deeply. I was thoroughly enjoying my little taste of freedom. Yet all the while, something was nagging at me—something one of the brahmacharinis had said to me the day before.

I had been resting in my room, which as usual doubled as Amma's kitchen, when a girl peeped through the curtain.

"Gayatri, can I have a word with you? There's something I really need to tell you."

Even though I really didn't have the energy, I was curious to hear what she had to say.

Bubbling over she said, "Yesterday I went with my mother to talk with Shakti (the ashram astrologer) about my brother, for he's entering a really bad period. Shakti advised us on a few remedies, then afterwards—you won't believe what he said."

I knew that Shakti spent a lot of time studying the astrological charts of us senior disciples. Sometimes his work felt like an invasion of privacy. Now my heart began to beat fast, for I worried where this conversation was going.

Sitting up, I snapped. "Will you please stop beating around the bush. What did he say?"

With wide eyes and mouth gasping for air she whispered, "Shakti is predicting that one of Amma's senior-most brahmacharinis, and someone you would never expect, is going to leave the ashram this year."

My heart skipped a beat. Then like a lightning bolt the very idea of the prediction struck my mind.

"Gayatri, I'm really worried," she continued. "Who could he be referring to?"

I brushed it aside. "Who knows, who cares. Maybe it won't even happen."

I knew fully well that I was lying. Shakti was an extremely accurate and profound astrologer.

After she left the room, I lay stunned, my mind whirling. *Maybe he meant me. Maybe it's going to happen after all. Will I really find the strength to break loose and leap to freedom? But wait, he said brahmacharini, and I'm a swamini. So maybe it is someone else.*

Concluding thus, I let out a disappointed moan. Yet felt relieved at the same time.

Sitting in the train, my mind swirling with ideas that my drained body lacked the strength to entertain, I closed the door on further speculation. For now. After all, where would I go, what would I do? I had lived in India since the tender age of nineteen, and I would soon be turning forty-one. I had no money, no career, no friends or identity outside the ashram, minimal ties with family, and I hadn't lived in the West for twenty-two years. The outlook was horribly dismal.

From the station I took a taxi to the ashram. When I walked through the front gate, heads were turning left and right. Residents came running up asking if Amma had returned. This was a natural question, after all, to ask the woman known as Amma's shadow.

Much to their dismay, I told them no, she was still in Tellichery. I had returned because I wasn't feeling well. Inside I chuckled. *Boy, that was the understatement of a lifetime.*

As I made my way across the compound, I was surprised at how serene the place felt. It had been years since I had experienced the ashram without the presence of hundreds and sometimes thousands of outsiders roaming around. I staggered up the three flights of stairs to Amma's kitchen and turned the ceiling fan on full blast. It began whirling like a helicopter, stirring up the thick, sultry air. I unplugged the phone and plopped onto my narrow bed, squeezed my hand through the bars of my bedside window, unhooked the wooden shutter, and gave it a mighty push. I gazed out at the evening sky, then peered around my room, taking it all in. I noted how dismayed I was with my living conditions. I lived amid shelves of steel dishes, pots and pans, and an attic stuffed with rice sacks full of old brass lamps.

Against Amma's wishes I also kept a tiny room in the main temple building that I used to do my administrative work, to prepare speeches, or sometimes just to be alone. Even though the room was only eight feet wide with a pillar in the middle, it was big enough for a skinny camping mattress and a small desk where I put my laptop. This was my sanctuary. I could escape there with relative ease—just zip across the bridge, dash through the Western women's dorm, run up one flight of the spiral staircase, then it was second room on the right.

I got that key when I needed somewhere to stay during one of my "kicked out of service" episodes. Once I had been reinstated, Amma told me to return the room for guest accommodation. This caused me much grief, and I couldn't understand why I wasn't allowed my own space. Trying to focus or get any work done in Amma's kitchen was impossible. When Amma was in the temple greeting devotees, the kitchen became Grand Central Station with a constant stream of helpers dropping off the mountains of fruit and offerings she received. I desperately needed a place where I could close a door and know I would not be disturbed. So I disobeyed Amma and kept the room.

Now that I had returned to the ashram by myself, I knew I could rest in the kitchen for a few days. But once Amma showed up, I'd have to find an alternative. I was reluctant to ask for special consideration, but I had a compelling urge to completely isolate myself for a week. I began toying with the idea of moving temporarily into one of the flats in the two skyscrapers on the far side of the ashram, as neither of my so-called rooms would provide that isolation.

Three days later Amma arrived in the wee hours of the morning. I felt it best to wait a day before approaching her about my request. I knew from experience that timing was everything. Just as fishermen check the weather forecast before heading out to sea, I had learned to gauge Amma's mood before opening my mouth.

Later that morning, reluctantly, I plugged the cord back into my phone. I knew if I didn't there would be complaints, for I was the gateway to Amma and played a crucial role in the running of the ashram. Sure enough, within minutes the phone rang, sending a tremor through my body.

I let out a sigh, grabbed the annoying hunk of plastic, and uttered, "Namah Sivaya," the standard ashram greeting that means, "I bow to Lord Shiva." This mantra was used by one and all with various ranges of inflection, depending on the circumstance. It was used politely to say hello or goodbye, excitedly to catch someone's attention, and rudely to infer get out of the damn way.

Through the receiver I heard, in the most charming accent, "Gayatri, this is Kamala from Singapore. I'm here in the ashram visiting for a few days. May I come see you?"

The very thought of seeing anyone made my body go limp. But this was one lady I should oblige. Only weeks before this her teenage son, studying abroad, had died unexpectedly without any medical explanation.

Dutifully I replied, "Certainly. When Amma leaves her room, come up to the bridge. I will see you then."

A while later there was a knock at the door. I compassionately rounded up whatever energy I could and summoned a smile to my face. I liked the woman. She was quite motherly and always took great care of us when we stayed with her family. I braced myself, though. I felt certain that she would start sobbing about the loss of her son. Instead, right off the bat after barely saying hello, she began feverishly complaining about her husband. This usually calm and gentle woman was fuming about matters over which I had no control, and I had to take it.

I quickly grabbed hold of the railing and maneuvered myself against the wall for support. I felt attacked. I realized that I no longer had the strength to shield myself from another person's raw emotion. After she left, I collapsed onto my bed with a screaming headache, and I remained there for the rest of the day. It was now evident—I had no choice but to go into isolation. I knew then that I wasn't overreacting or being lazy. I was on the verge of a nervous breakdown.

Later that evening I could hear Lakshmi in Amma's room awkwardly trying to converse in Malayalam, and Amma in twists of laughter. Malayalam was by no means an easy language to master, especially because many of the words sounded alike. For example, the only difference in the spelling of the word "fever" and the word "pig" was a single to a double "n." So it was very easy to say, "I think I am coming down with a pig." Lakshmi was full of such side-splitting statements.

Sensing that the mood downstairs was light, I knew this was the perfect moment to ask my question. Nervously but gracefully I made my way down the stairs to Amma's room, where I was met with a smile left over from Lakshmi's accidental comedy show.

"How are you feeling?" Amma inquired sweetly.

"Not so good. I'm still really weak. In fact, I think I need to rest in one of the flats for a week or so," I blurted out.

I sat there anxiously observing Amma's face, trying to predict her reaction. At the same time I imagined patting myself on the back. *There, you said it. You came right out and expressed your needs. That wasn't so hard, now was it?*

In a reluctant tone Amma replied, "If that's what you feel you need, then okay."

"Just for a week or two. Then I should be fine."

I left her room and went back upstairs to lie down. I couldn't believe how kindly she was treating me. Immediately I got on the phone, called the Westerners' office, and arranged a flat to stay in. I gave the lady strict instructions to keep the room number confidential, for I was going into isolation.

In the morning I asked one of my friends to set up the flat with essentials—some drinking water, a mattress to sleep on, and a bucket and mug so I could bathe. Food would be delivered three times a day. Other than that, I was on my own.

For the first couple of days all I did was sleep, eat, and fall back to sleep. I was suffering from years of exhaustion. Even though the sleep helped somewhat, I could tell that my system was still in overdrive. Whenever I heard footsteps coming down the hallway, I panicked, fearing someone was coming to talk to me. The sharp echo of metallic door bolts opening and closing in the stark, concrete corridor sent tremors through my body. The only time I left my room was at sundown, after the evening prayers commenced. Stealthily I'd unbolt my door, peep into the corridor to ensure nobody was around, then like a fearful animal creep out of my hole and sit on the verandah of the ten-story building for an hour or so. As though in a dream, I watched the flood of activity in the ashram, people darting around like ants. From my seat towering high in the sky, I could see the Arabian Sea to my right, the wide brackish river to my left, and this weird maze of gaudy concrete buildings plopped right in the middle. The ashram looked like something out of a science fiction movie, as though a metropolis had fallen out of the sky and landed by accident in the middle of a coconut jungle. The ashram looked so out of place that I began to wonder whether I, too, weren't out of place. I felt so peaceful and detached where I sat. *How on earth can I ever put myself back into the thick of that madness?*

Then the temple bells began to signal the end of prayer. Alas, it was time to scurry back to my cave before anyone spotted me.

Over the course of my isolation my body slowly regained strength. My nervous system settled somewhat. However, my mind was running rampant. Free time had opened the floodgates of reflection. *Why does spirituality have to be so hard? Can this life I've been living even be called spirituality? Is it possible to lead a nurtured and self-caring life and still know God? If a person leads a balanced life with relaxing walks, healthy food, and time to rest, can she still be considered spiritual?*

I remembered when we were in Byron Bay, a gorgeous town on the east coast of Australia, I had to go buy some fish to cook for Amma's lunch. As I headed out the door, Amma gravely warned, "If you go swimming in the ocean, I will kill you." I had no intention of swimming. Heaven forbid! But why should I be threatened with death if I did?

This memory angered me.

Another question had been coming into focus for some time—why the lack of personal empowerment? Anything good that happened in your life was supposed to be purely a result of Amma's love, Amma's blessings. Anything bad that happened suddenly had nothing to do with her but was solely due to your bad karma. This little notion, which the devotees themselves perpetuated, made no sense and completely contradicted itself. *Can we not take any credit for the blessings in our lives? Can we not rely on our own intelligence and intuition to guide us?* It was almost as though Amma wanted her "children" to remain crippled and needy, to have no independent thoughts, to believe that they were worthless and would perish without her. I seriously questioned—is this humility or enslavement?

Before I knew it, my two-week vacation was drawing to a close. Fortunately my energy had replenished just enough to enable me to face the world again. My mind was already kicking into gear, excited about the upcoming U.S. tour and the challenge of packing for Amma. I carefully tucked my doubts away, for there were no easy answers. I had enough love and attachment to keep me going for a while longer, so I knuckled down and forged ahead.

I discovered that my batteries had recharged just enough to see me through the six-week tour. Shortly after returning to India, though, alarms began sounding once more. My tolerance was running thin. I had to face the facts. I was no longer able to put up with things the way I used to.

One evening at the end of an outdoor program in Bangalore, Amma was leaving the stage and walking down a wooden ramp when her foot skidded slightly. As usual I was right behind her with my arm linked through hers, keeping her stable as feverish devotees grabbed hold of her. I was relieved she didn't fall and thankful it was only a minor mishap. After safely seating Amma inside her car, I closed the door, pressed my body tight against the vehicle and did my usual side-steps to get through the crowd to the opposite side, and jumped in. Amma's window was down, and she was smiling, calling out, "makkale!" (children!) and graciously letting people touch her hand as the car slowly drove off. Once out of view of her adoring fans, she raised the window and exploded.

"A true disciple would have checked the ramp before allowing their guru to walk on it. What are you doing here in the car with me?" Saying thus, she swung her arm to hit me.

For the first time ever, spontaneously I turned my head, ducked, and shielded myself from her blow.

"Did you see that?" she growled to those seated in front.

Through the rearview mirror I caught the driver sneaking a quick glance. I could tell he was listening, but he kept his gaze on the road. Balu turned his head slightly to reassure Amma he was listening, but he remained aloof. He was quite immune to her outbursts.

"Did you see that? Today she raises her arm to shield herself, tomorrow she will be striking me back. I'm going to need protection soon."

Normally she would have laid right into me, both physically and verbally, but this evening she resisted. Instead she did something quite out of character—she sat there stewing in silence. Through the corner of my eye, I could see she was seething with anger and immersed in deep thought. I imagined she was in shock because I had never reacted in this way before. Perhaps she saw it as a sign that I was no longer afraid of her, that I was escaping from under her thumb, and that perhaps she was losing control. Of course, one can never truly know what is going on in someone else's mind. But when you've lived with the person for twenty years, you know them well enough to have a pretty good idea.

A week or so later upon return from another venue, we stopped at the house of a devotee Amma had promised to visit. Even though it was four a.m. and devotees had been requested not to publicize the visit, there were over one hundred people waiting for her. (This always happened, by the way. Devotees always leaked the news of her house calls, perhaps for the bragging rights, perhaps from sheer excitement.) Amma got out of the car, was greeted by the husband and wife who were shaking with emotion, then was surrounded by a group of men to shield her from the crowd as she made her way into the house. Many a time, as I struggled in these situations to catch up to Amma, I found myself being shoved and elbowed in the gut by well-meaning people. On one occasion I had to karate-chop a man's arm to get near Amma and break the human chain surrounding her. But this night, or early morning, or whatever you want to call it, I gave up. No longer could I put up with the heat, the crowds, the hysteria, the exhaustion, and the bodily punishment. I let out a shriek, threw my arms into the air, broke free from the crowd that was pushing its way into the house, and returned to the car.

I was just about to lose it when Amma's driver curtly asked, "What are you doing here? Who's with Amma?"

Rather than divulge my list of reasons, I lied and said, "I couldn't get into the house." By that point my claim was true.

On the remainder of the journey back to the ashram I was forlorn, barely holding it together. I kept a steady gaze out the window. In my mind I composed a letter to Amma, telling her all about my state of affairs and how I was crumbling to pieces. I wasn't sure if I would actually write such a thing, but I was desperately seeking any form of consolation.

The following day as I was standing by my kitchen window, a few women huddled outside on the spiral staircase began waving at me. That was it—I snapped and fell to the floor. I began wailing and lamenting that not only did I have no freedom to move around in the ashram, but I didn't even have privacy in my so-called room. There was nowhere to escape. In my state of overwhelm, I made a beeline for Amma's room. Without restraint I told her everything that was on my mind.

"I hate this place. I feel like a caged animal. I can't even look out my window. I can't move freely anywhere without getting mobbed. There is nowhere peaceful in this damn place anymore, and I hate the crowds."

Amma was relaxing on the bare floor with a pillow under her head. She lay there stunned and speechless but listening intently. She had never, ever heard or seen me like this before. Her ever-so-controlled and dedicated servant had finally lost it. Amma's mouth dropped and her eyes widened as I ranted on:

"There is so much hypocrisy, unfairness, and inequality in this place. I am sickened by it. Before we went on tour, Saumya asked that a tiny hunk of wood be made into a stool for her to kneel on when she waits on you for ten hours during Devi Bhava, and she was denied. Yet Rao's stylish little pad now has an intricately carved teak door that took two months to make. Was that done with your permission? If not, what are you going to do about it? I have to beg here to get a glass of milk for girls when they are sick, and yet he can spend tens of thousands of rupees on a door?" I couldn't contain the explosion. "And you! You are constantly demeaning and humiliating me in public and undermining everything I do."

Amma spoke for the first time. "Oh, my darling daughter Gayatri, I may not always show it but I have so much love in my heart for you."

"Stick it," I retaliated. "Aren't you the one who professes that love should be expressed and not kept inside, otherwise it's like trying to get honey out of a stone?"

Amma was in shock, but hearing me out. "What do you want? What can I do to make your life easier?" she pleaded.

Taking a deep breath and letting out a huge sigh as tears formed in my eyes, I said, "Well for starters, I could use a room. You've just had your room extended and there is a huge empty platform now by the kitchen. It would be easy to build one there. Besides, it will keep your apartment cooler."

"Fine, I will tell them to build you a room. They can do it when we leave for Europe next month."

Amma wrapped her arms around my neck, pulled my head forward, rubbed her nose back and forth across my cheek and gave me a big sniff. "Now go lie down, go take some rest."

I think she needed to be alone to digest what had just happened. Frankly so did I. I couldn't believe that I had spoken like that. I was surprised she had heard me out. I was even more surprised that she had granted my wish.

But it completely slipped my radar that she had dodged my very legitimate concerns about ethics and fairness in the ashram. Instead she cleverly maneuvered the conversation off topic by professing her deep love and by bribing me with a room to make me more personally comfortable—and quiet perhaps?

She must have been aware of the astrologer's prediction. I suspect that she feared a defection by her most capable female servant—the one who was carrying all of her dirty little secrets. She had to do something to remedy the situation.

In my confusion, exhaustion, and anguish, I took the bait. I felt ecstatic to know that finally, after all these years, I was going to have a room of my own. With a huge grin on my face I thought, *Better late than never*.

Unfortunately that old cliché bore no relevance to my situation. No room could possibly cure my ailments. It was time for me to move on, and the walls would continue to close in on me until I accepted that fact.

TWENTY-THREE

SHATTERED DREAMS

The sweet after-effects of what I perceived as Amma's unexpected bout of compassion lingered for a couple of weeks, and I was bathing in delight. I wanted to believe that this upward swing was permanent—that way I could avoid shaking hands with reality and moving into unknown realms. This wishful thinking was a combination of both denial and fear. Deep down I knew it wouldn't last. It never did. My life was in constant flux—a yoyo being spun, hurled, and tossed up and down.

A few days later Lakshmi came up to the kitchen saying that Amma was calling. Unsuspecting, I made my way down the stairs thinking she probably just wanted to ask me something—which was correct.

In a rather cold tone, without looking at me, she asked, "Why isn't the money from the canteen sales being brought to my room anymore?"

I was caught off guard. For an instant I panicked, thinking I was in trouble. Then I brushed that feeling aside knowing I had done nothing wrong. "I don't know. Would you like me to ask the fellow in charge?"

As though a match had fallen into a massive barrel of gasoline, her eyes burst into flames. Nastily glaring at me, she shouted, "I already have! And he said *you* told him to stop bringing the money here and to take it to the office instead."

My mind went blank. I was frozen in shock and couldn't believe the accusation. I knew I would never do something like that on my own whim, but I had no recollection of the event.

I pleaded, "But I never said such a thing."

"Lakshmi! Go call Prakash. Get him here at once. I will show this liar!" Repeatedly flicking her hand in the air, and with a look of disgust on her face, Amma muttered, "Step aside. I can't even bear the sight of you."

I did as I was told and leaned against the wall with my eyes glued to the door awaiting Lakshmi's return with the key witness to my alleged crime. Minutes later the young Indian man was reverently bowing before Amma.

"Go on, now. Tell her what you told me," she snapped.

He turned to me and said, "A couple of months ago, you phoned and told me not to bring the money to you anymore, but to give it to the office instead."

It felt as though I were on trial and the verdict had already been cast—guilty on all counts. A death sentence. I honestly couldn't remember saying such a thing. I knew there had to be an explanation. My head was spinning and my body shaking. I had no defending argument.

"Thank you, my son. You may go now," said Amma with a defiant look of satisfaction upon her face. Once he left the room, she started up again. "I know why you told him not to bring the proceeds here anymore. It's because you don't like me giving money to my family!"

"What?" I blurted in utter disbelief. "I would never tell him to do something like that on my own!"

"Get out of my room, you disgusting madama, you rotten bitch. And if you ever lie to me like that again, I will strip you of your robes and throw you out of the ashram."

Like a lifeless ghost I staggered up the stairs, but I continued out through the door, across the bridge, and up to my little hideaway. Once inside I fell onto my slender mattress, rammed my face into the pillow, held the sides up around my head, and let out a few visceral screams. Then I settled into gentle sobs, which eventually ceased and transformed into rage.

How could she go behind my back and rally evidence to accuse me of such a thing? Why couldn't she have asked me first, so I at least had a chance to calmly gather my thoughts? Once again, she has belittled me, humiliated me, and worse still, made me look like a liar in front of this relative newcomer.

Now more than ever I wanted out. I lay there fuming.

An hour or so later I heard singing. This meant that Amma had left her room and was down below in the temple seated amid her throng of devotees. I took a deep breath. With downward gaze I stormed back to Amma's kitchen, grabbed some snacks, and searched for a large jar I could pee in. I was planning to stay in my cubbyhole for a few days, and I didn't want to show my face to anyone, for any reason. I felt that all the blood had been drained out me.

As I scurried around in a tempest, I sensed Lakshmi tracking my every movement. I could picture her big, dreamy eyes oozing compassion. Suddenly she broke the silence and with great trepidation asked, "Gayatri, are you okay?"

I looked up. As our eyes locked, I shouted, "No, I'm not okay." I began howling.

Lakshmi rushed over and wrapped her lanky arms around me. This unleashed a gush of emotion. "I hate her, I hate her, I hate her," I bawled, and I thumped poor Lakshmi on the back.

Pulling myself together, I gently pushed her away, reassured her that I would be all right, then fled the scene with my emergency supplies.

I spent the next two days flat on my back fantasizing about how to escape. *I will need to disguise myself in regular Western clothing. Possibly I can exit the country by flying from Trivandrum to Sri Lanka. But wait—how do I buy a ticket with no cash or credit card?*

I let out a sigh as I realized I wouldn't even make it out the front gate before being spotted.

Maybe I can secretly arrange a taxi through Vidya's sister and have them come to the back gate late at night?

I let out another sigh when I remembered that my passport photo shows me dressed in orange swami garb with the unmistakable Hindu red spot on my forehead. No matter how good my disguise, this photo would be a dead give-away. Many officials at the airport knew me and would be on the lookout.

I concluded that it was absolutely impossible for me to pull off a successful escape from anywhere inside India. Without a doubt I would get caught and coerced back to the ashram. My life would then become worse than it had ever been. I would be treated like a prisoner, under surveillance every given moment.

I was fully aware of the nasty things Amma said about those who left the ashram. I knew that the same condemnations would be hurled at me. No matter how many years you had served, no matter what position you held, once you severed your alliance, you were a traitor, an enemy, a despicable person. Amma always explained to the residents that the person who left had been overcome with materialistic and sexual desires, or else the person was mentally unstable, or the person had some major chip on his or her shoulder.

Pai, one of Amma's senior swamis, had just made his exit from the ashram. Several devotees expressed their desire to help support him. Not if Amma could help it. She went out of her way to dissuade such support by vilifying him and destroying his reputation. She didn't like anyone receiving benefit from *her* devotees once they had left *her* fold. Her frequent statement (in private) about such defectors was, "Let them suffer for a while."

Another example was Manju, who had lived at the ashram along with her brother, sister, and parents since the very early days. They had sold their family home, donated the proceeds along with most of their life savings, and dedicated their lives to Amma's service. Fourteen years later Manju's brother, who was in charge of a branch ashram, phoned Amma to discuss his desire to drop his yellow robes and lead a normal life. She had a fit. After he hung up, she immediately phoned a devotee who was a policeman. That night itself she had the lad forcibly removed. Her reasoning for such swift action was this: if he wasn't removed immediately, he might try to steal money. So the young lad's reward for being open and honest with Amma was to be stripped of his robes and dumped on the doorstep of the tiny dwelling where his father lived just outside the ashram compound. Penniless, he then went to live with relatives and eventually found a job, in order to start life over. Such ill treatment deeply wounded the family.

A few months later Manju's sister wanted out. She was permitted to remain at the ashram for the couple of weeks until Amma left for the U.S. tour. Employment was arranged for her at a devotee's company far, far away, in the middle of India—Amma didn't want the girl living in Kerala.

Shortly before that October European tour, Manju decided she had had enough, so she presented Amma a note. I was in the room at the time but had no clue as to what the letter contained. Amma turned cold and severe, and she said, "As you wish." Only after Manju left the room did I realize she had just told Amma, quite boldly, that she wanted out as well.

This time Amma showed no leniency. Many of the Indian girls looked up to Manju. She possessed leadership qualities. So her departure posed a threat. Manju had been one of the closer female disciples and had occasionally spent time in Amma's room. She too had been slapped around a few times.

Amma called Manju's closest friend to her room and gave the girl instructions to persuade Manju to change her mind. Once this persuasion proved unsuccessful, Amma phoned Manju's mother and told her to escort her daughter off the premises immediately. She was to go to her father's house and stay there. Amma then broadcast a grave warning to all of the Indian girls. "If any of you dare go visit Manju, utter a word, or as much as send a note to her, you will be kicked out of the ashram!"

It gave me comfort to fantasize about leaving. But I had to set all such thoughts aside for the time being. I knew I only had one shot, and it had to be executed with the utmost precision.

Holy Hell

After I got tired of stewing and fantasizing, my mind calmed down. Then I realized the truth behind Amma's accusation that I was diverting the canteen money to the office. Now I clearly remembered. A few months prior, when we were on the north Indian tour in Gujarat, Amma had received a phone call from the head of accounts at the ashram. He had just received a tip from a devotee who worked at the Income Tax Department. There was talk of a raid and audit at the ashram. Immediately Amma instructed Pai to catch the next flight back to Kerala, destroy any incriminating documents that might be in the Western office, and remove all the money and gold jewelry from under her bed to a secret hiding place.

Upon our return *Amma herself* told me to call Prakash and order him to send the canteen money to the office. She was afraid that a raid might take place and the authorities would discover that she was sleeping on top of massive sums of money and gold.

Now I was furious.

Given the chance, I would have remembered such details. What the hell was that all about? Sure, I've got my opinions about her giving so much money to her family, but I wouldn't dare do something like that behind her back. Has she become paranoid? Or was she feeling guilty perhaps?

I never bothered to clear my name with Amma. I knew that once her mind was made up, she wouldn't budge. Before I could finish a sentence, she would shoot me down mid-air. I couldn't tolerate being called a liar again, nor subjecting myself to such excruciating pain and despair.

A few days later, as the saying goes, I sucked it up and moved back into Amma's kitchen. But not without resentment. I did this out of self-preservation, for I had no alternative just yet.

After returning to work, my resolve to run away weakened. Once more I found myself torn between the life I knew and the life I dreamed about.

During Devi Bhava, when the soul-stirring bhajans began, I found myself sobbing and fretting. *How can I leave this place? How can I isolate myself from these devotional songs that have graced me with so many powerful spiritual experiences? I love singing. It's when I feel most at one with my heart.* I would miss the simple Indian way of life, the Indian girls, and the many Western devotees with whom I have a special bond.

In the middle of the night I would wake abruptly, submerged in panic from a recurring vision of myself floating around in outer space. I kept hearing the haunting words, *But you won't be Swamini Amritaprana anymore.* How could I leave all this behind and go back to a life in the West—a life I had condemned as empty and meaningless many, many years ago?

To top it off, my mind was ensnared in numerous beliefs that I had been force-fed over the years. Number one, it was a sin to leave the guru. Number two, only within the confines of *Amma's* ashram could one truly lead a spiritual life. Number three, if you did choose to leave, your life was doomed, and you would surely be cursed.

But that third point had already started to lose its hold on my mind.

Ganga, for example, had left the ashram six years earlier, and nothing untoward had happened to him. He actually looked brighter, happier, and healthier. Whenever we were in Europe, I studied him intently and used him as a gauge as to what life was like on the outside.

During our years together in the ashram I had never interacted with him much. However, after his departure, and after I saw how badly he'd been treated, I developed enormous empathy for him. His Indian brothers were cordial but stoic, and they gave him the politically correct cold shoulder. Their behavior appalled me. In the few years before I left, I sometimes had private conversations with Ganga—always out of sight of the inner circle so that I didn't have to worry about getting chastised by them later. I confided much in him, and he rendered invaluable insight and advice.

For Ganga, being true to the guru implied being true to oneself. He would speak of his "god" as truth and honesty. His years of spiritual search had led him to embrace the humility and the modesty of his human condition—while continuing to dedicate himself totally to Amma's service as her representative and teacher in Europe. His only crime was that, as a consequence of this inner growth and maturity, he had decided to drop his yellow robes and get married.

During his eight years of service for Amma as a yellow-clad brahmacharin, surrounded mostly by women, he had not faltered in his commitment. He stuck to his vows and ideals. On the European tour, he would spend hours the first night confiding in Amma, telling her where he thought he was weak, seeking her advice. Amma wanted all the details, and he was plain, honest, and straightforward. He was a free-thinker, not a following type. But he respected and obeyed—until obedience no longer made sense to his keen intellect.

When he told Amma he wanted to become a layman, she simply banned him. She became irate. She told him to go live in any country in the world where she was not known. She refused his service. He was shocked and disconsolate.

Upon returning to Europe he was met with sympathy and understanding from some of the broad-minded local organizers. They respected him as a person and as a seeker, and they appreciated his work. So they continued to help him conduct his talks and workshops. But his status was not so clear. To the fundamentalists he was out. Others, though, found him more worthy now that he was married—that he was one of them and shared their lives.

Amma immediately began spreading false rumors about his misuse of funds, his sexual misbehavior, and his disobedience. The same Amma he had cherished, served, obeyed, and respected turned on him. She went even further. She had U.S. lawyers accuse him of embezzlement and misappropriation of funds. The poor chap, who was honest to a fault, had to take a lawyer to protect himself from the wrath and meanness of his own guru. The transactions between lawyers dragged on for three whole years.

During his years of official service in Europe, he came to Amma regularly with drafts of associations and other structures to legalize and formalize Amma's activities. She consistently refused to legalize anything. Ganga had no alternative but to create European bank accounts in his own name. So he became, in the eyes of local administrations and tax authorities, a private party amassing large sums of money in various personal accounts and forwarding those funds straight to India. His situation was untenable, and he took enormous risks just to be obedient. Amma's accusations about his money-handling were totally unfounded. He had simply followed her advice.

Notwithstanding the cruel treatment and all the backstage stuff, he kept a positive outlook on Amma and her work. After legal matters were resolved, he came to some of Amma's European programs. They reconciled in a way. She authorized him to continue teaching in a not-so-official, discreet fashion. But Ganga met opposition from some of his fellow European coordinators. They became the watchdogs of the temple and began creating all sorts of obstructions and demands.

Frustrated, Ganga sent letters for me to read to Amma. I rarely got past the second sentence before she would start grumbling and arguing with me about the contents of his correspondence. So I would tuck the letters back in my bag and sit there and stew. I felt sickened that she was not being upfront with him. To his face she pretended to be on board with his ideas. Behind his back, though, *she* was the one stirring up opposition. She managed to effectively pollute his network and alienate him from it. She even called his closest devotee friends to tell them, "Even if he comes to you asking for a pair of dirty underwear, you are not to help him."

I never quite understood her hostility. Did she object to the precedent he set, that one could drop one's robes and marry yet continue to work in her name? Or was she just flat-out resentful that *she* was no longer the sole recipient of his adoration?

In fact, with Ganga's departure Amma's movement lost a precious asset. Amma realized this later, and she tearfully apologized to him for her mistreatment. She called him. He recorded the conversation on tape. She repeatedly invited him to come back. But he refused every time. He articulated his reasons in a letter that she would not read.

Witnessing Amma's dishonesty and her malicious treatment of Ganga only reinforced my desire to leave her, to sever all ties, and to make sure I was not dependent upon her for anything.

Holy Hell

Despite the fact I was loved by many and constantly surrounded by people, I was drowning in acute loneliness. A few friends empathized, but nothing they said or did could alleviate my pain. My heart was out of reach, for it was shrouded by the many secrets I was carrying. If I shared even a fraction of the information I possessed, I would shatter their faith in Amma—their god. Therefore, as long as I was living in the ashram, I felt I had to hold my silence. This burden compounded my pain. My closer friends worried about me. They could see I was deteriorating both physically and emotionally, but they felt helpless. Towards the end "Amma's Shadow" acquired a new label, a name that summed up my condition quite accurately— "The Walking Corpse."

For many years I gave a speech in Malayalam on September 27th as part of Amma's birthday celebration. Amma always called me beforehand and dictated a story for me to include. Most of the time her story was a complete and utter fabrication. For years I justified her lies by telling myself, "Oh well, as long as the devotees gain more faith in Amma, then I guess it's okay." I was never comfortable, but I did what was asked and chose not to give it much thought.

Below is an excerpt from my notes for one of those concocted stories that I, regrettably, included in my speeches in 1995 in Boston, in five cities in Europe, in Australia, as well as at Pallai and Chalakudy, Kerala in 1996.

> A German lad had been reading in a lot of scriptures about the power of Mahatmas (great souls) and how they can change anything in the universe by their mere will. One day he saw Mother sitting with Swamiji and some devotees outside, and he thought he would take advantage of the situation. He then told Swamiji about his doubts, and said it was impossible for him to accept such a thing. He said, "Mother, you claim to be a Mahatma. Now the sun is shining brightly. If you are such a great soul, why do you not make it rain now?" He had not even finished the sentence when it did actually start raining on the exact spot where

Mother and we were sitting. The boy then realized there was a power far beyond the understanding of the intellect, and that Mother had that power within her. He then dedicated his life to her.

Amma later modified the story slightly. It became Amma transforming into a ball of light in front of a group of men from Madras. The story was similar to that of baby Krishna giving a glimpse of his true nature to his mother Yashoda. This new "ball of light" tale became part of my speech in November 1996, at the California ashram, Sydney, Melbourne, Singapore, and Paris.

I was dreading the upcoming birthday bash and felt ill at the thought of sitting on stage in front of thousands of people lying my face off. No longer could I bear to be a pawn in her game of lies and deceit.

A few days later, Balu came up to the kitchen from Amma's room and began to say, "Oh, about the birthday speech, Amma told me to tell you—"

I swiftly cut him off and said, "What cock-and-bull story does she want me to tell this year?"

Instantly he saw red. "Don't you dare talk like that," he hissed, not wanting Amma to hear. "If anyone hears you saying such a thing, you're going to be in big trouble. Have you gone mad?"

I said, "We are leaving for Europe a couple of days after the birthday, and I need the next two weeks to pack. I don't have time to write a speech, get it translated into proper Malayalam, make the phonetic notes"—I could read but not write Malayalam— "then memorize the damn thing."

Throwing his arms up in the air, Balu stormed out of the room saying, "That's *your* problem."

Indeed it was, in more ways than one. It was my huge problem. I had been an accomplice to deception long enough. I was determined not to give a speech that year. Somehow I managed to convince Amma I just didn't have the time. That got me off the hook and extremely relieved.

Then the grand birthday arrived. At nine a.m. in front of at least ten thousand devotees Amma made her way to the stage. She sat in her stately chair, elaborately decorated with a brightly colored silk sari. Lotus blossoms surrounded her feet. She closed her eyes, cupped her hands as though in prayer, and allowed the ceremonious foot-washing to begin. Balu reverently placed her feet on an ornate silver platter. I kneeled down clasping the hem of her dress and sari out of the way. The crowd excitedly chanted "Aum Amriteshwaryai Namah" (salutations to the Goddess Amrita) as Amma's feet were bathed in milk, curd, honey, ghee, and rose water, one after the other. All the while, my stomach was churning. I felt like a charlatan on stage in front of the thousands of tear-streaked faces because I had not one drop of devotion left in my heart. How could I? My heart was broken and shattered like jagged glass—shattered along with all of my hopes and dreams.

Once the ceremony was over, each of the senior men took turns placing a garland around Amma's neck and waving a burning camphor lamp before her. Then with impressive showmanship they fell flat on their bellies, their arms stretched over their heads as though they were diving off a springboard, and lay in full prostration for a few seconds. I was dumbfounded at how some of these fellows could have sexual relations with her yet perform this seemingly sincere display of reverence and humility. *How on earth do they wrap their heads around such a contradiction? Surely they suspect that they are not the only ones? Equally baffling—how does she dare to call these fellows her "sons?"*

Standing a few feet from Amma's side, emotionally numb, I watched the hypocrisy of it all. Then I felt a sharp nudge in my buttocks. I turned around. Amma's father was sitting back in his chair angrily shooing me out of the way. Both Amma's parents were seated toward the back of the stage with a clear view of their illustrious daughter. I stepped aside a couple of feet thinking, *What's his problem?* Then I realized what it was.

Reporters had arrived on the scene. Their cameras were flashing wildly. I turned around to see the parents sitting up straight, posing for the photographers. It seems I had been blocking their chance to appear on the front page of the newspaper.

Shaking my head in disgust, I looked across the stage to see Sreekumar holding up a garland, asking if I wanted to place it around Amma's neck. I nearly puked at the thought of feigning devotion, so I politely raised my hand gesturing, "No thanks, I'm fine."

After Amma spoke a few words of inspiration and we sang a few bhajans, she began greeting the masses. I fled the stage. I headed back to my kitchen for some breakfast and a much-needed cup of tea. I felt weak and drained from the emotional torture. Shortly after, Balu came up to the room. With a strange look on his face he enquired, "What's going on? You looked absolutely ill back there on the stage."

There was no way I could explain what was really going on. So instead, as convincingly as possible, I began describing how Amma's father had poked me in the butt. Right then my phone rang. I was urgently needed in the main kitchen.

Leaving my little yarn unfinished, I guzzled my tea down. "I've got to go," I said and split.

He never followed up on the conversation.

It was the day before we were to begin yet another six-week tour. This trip included ten cities in Europe before heading onto Michigan for three days, then one week at the California ashram. Amma's two suitcases and other miscellaneous items were packed and ready for take-off. I had planned every minute detail of organization for the duties to be performed by the now two hundred Indian women residents. Their temporary accommodations during Amma's absence were now final. Whenever Amma left the country, she enforced strict segregation. That required moving these poor women from their rooms by the kitchen and cramming them into the flats on the opposite side of the ashram.

I opened my cupboard and looked at the three shelves. There lay everything I considered mine, all my worldly possessions, gazing back at me. On the top shelf was a stack of five orange saris, seven blouses, five underskirts, and a few of Amma's old bras I had dyed orange. On the second shelf were my many diaries, a couple of photo albums, and a small bundle of letters from my Mum and Dad. Seeing these items made my heart flinch, for they meant so much to me. At that point I didn't know if I was actually leaving. But I worried that if I did leave, these items would be lost forever. Even though earlier that year I had someone type all of my diaries into my laptop computer and backed up those files onto a CD, my handwritten notebooks were precious. There was no way I could take them with me because I was only allowed one small travel bag. We had to keep our personal luggage to a minimum to leave room for as much bookstall inventory as possible.

With my heart all aflutter I ran to Vidya's room. I sat on the floor next to her and whispered, "Can I give you my diaries and a few other items to hang onto?"

"I don't understand," she said. "Why would you need me to do such a thing?"

I took a deep breath. "Just in case I don't come back from tour."

Vidya's eyes went dewy and she gasped in horror, "Gayatri Akka, no. I can't. I refuse to do anything that would set in motion your not returning. I can't bear the thought of living here without you."

I, too, became teary-eyed. The thought was just as painful to me. "Okay, forget it. But promise me this. If you do hear news that I have run away, then you will somehow try to retrieve them, okay?"

Silently she nodded in agreement.

"Hey, stop worrying. It's not definite," I said, trying to lighten the mood. "I just don't know how much longer I can go on like this, that's all."

But I left the room with a heavy heart. In my bones I knew it was over. I just didn't know when or how it would end.

In the morning it was time to depart. My heart was pounding. I picked up the last piece of luggage and flung it over my shoulder. Letting out a sigh I stepped out of the kitchen and onto the bridge.

But then I paused. A voice inside told me to turn around. I went back to the doorway and looked around the room, taking it all in. The crazy kitchen that had served as my bedroom for many years, the rickety bed I'd slept on a few hours each day, the cupboard containing my few life treasures. I absorbed it all into my heart, and said goodbye. I sensed I would never see any of it again.

I hurried across the bridge, along the temple balcony, and down to Amma, who was bidding farewell to the devotees. Shaking, feeling guilty, I looked at the many faces I loved. *Will you miss me?* I asked in my heart. *Will you forgive me if I don't come back?* I tucked my anguish aside and hopped in the car next to Amma. As we drove along the beach road, I gazed at the Arabian Sea, the coconut trees swaying in the wind, and the villagers as they stopped and stared. I wondered, will they ever see me again?

Just in case, I said goodbye in my heart.

TWENTY-FOUR

THE GREAT ESCAPE

In Europe we traveled from city to city at the usual exhausting pace, two and-a-half-days in each program concluding with Devi Bhava that ran into the wee hours. Usually we would hit the road from that venue, drive to the next town, and start all over again that same evening.

Upon arrival at the new destination, the group staggered off to their beds. I staggered off to the kitchen to prepare lunch for Amma and the mandatory rice and curry for the Indian men. A few hours later, just as I lay down for a brief nap, everyone else would rise like the dead from their graves.

The crowds in Europe were astounding. We had very little down time between programs. In some locations the home of the sponsoring devotee was rather far from the hall, so the devotees would set up a room where Amma could rest at the venue. On the second evening of our program in Zurich, I couldn't tell if Amma wanted to stay at the hall or come back to the host residence. Even though the home was comfortable and private, it was an hour's drive away. And this night in Zurich looked as though it was going to be a long one.

I waited until ten p.m. to make my way through the crowd. Then I crouched by the side of Amma's chair. Between a couple of her magnanimous hugs, I leaned forward and asked, "Amma, are you staying in the hall tonight or coming back to the house?"

Casting me an irritated glance she said, "Piss off (*podi*). What difference does it make to you?"

My guts tied into a knot. But I did my best to keep a straight face and not reveal any emotion to the audience. As I made my exit, I heard Amma laugh, as she always did to cover up the scowl anyone might have seen her make. I headed back to her room. When I got to the doorway, I let out a huff as I looked at the carload of her stuff. "What difference does it make to you?" I mumbled.

Lakshmi stared at me, wondering if I had an answer. I said, "Just leave everything. We can't start packing yet because Amma is not saying where she wants to spend the night."

I waited an hour, hoping Amma would voluntarily send word about her plans. But as each minute passed, I became more and more agitated. *Doesn't Amma realize it takes several hours to cook her evening meal and set everything up as she likes?*

Despite the anger and hurt I just didn't have it in me to say, "Screw you." But in this mood I dared not go near her again. So I approached Ramakrishna, feeling he was my only hope. He said he would try. So I waited and waited. Half an hour later he came back scratching his head and saying, "She's still not answering."

A decision had to be made.

"What do you think I should do?"

With mighty apprehension and the equivalent of a disclaimer Ramakrishna said, "Don't blame me later if I'm wrong, but my hunch is she will go back to the house."

"Yeah, I think you're right. Amma will probably stay there one more night out of courtesy to the host." But I felt nervous about my decision.

Holy Hell

In a jiffy I had everything packed and headed to the house with Priya. To cover my bases, I instructed Lakshmi to stay at the hall just in case Amma did make up her mind the other way.

It was one a.m. Her room was set up perfectly. A fresh set of clothes, neatly ironed, hung ready for the morning. Her rice and her fish curry were warm on the stove. Then the phone rang. It was Lakshmi in a state of panic.

"Gayatri, Amma just said she wants to stay at the hall. A car is on its way to pick you up. But I don't think you'll make it back in time. There are only twenty people left in line."

"Shit, here we go again."

I frantically packed up her bedding, clothes, toiletries, bag of books and Hindu comics, snacks, large bowl and pitcher for her hand washing, and flask of hot cumin tea. I transferred her food into travel vessels, then wrapped them in towels to stay warm. Even though it was not my fault, and there was nothing I could have done differently, I knew we were going to get it. It was two a.m. Still no sign of the car. Priya and I dragged everything out to the street in order to save a few seconds. In the late October Swiss air we stood shivering, teeth chattering, rubbing our hands together and blowing our steamy breath over them. After what felt like forever, I saw headlights come flying around the corner and the car pulled up with a screech. The driver jumped out. We threw everything helter-skelter inside the car. Then he slammed his foot on the accelerator. The tires spun, and we burned rubber as we sped off.

At the hall I made a dash with Amma's food, instructing the driver and Priya to bring the rest as quickly as possible. As I turned the corner to Amma's room though, I stopped running. I could see Lakshmi sitting outside slumped against the wall. She put a finger across her lips, rolled her humungous eyes, and awkwardly pointed to the room. Her face was bright red with slap marks still in place. Her hair, which she normally wore slicked back and almost glued to her scalp from the tightly tied ponytail, was a wild mess.

She whispered, "Amma's angry because the room wasn't set up, and there was nothing for her to eat. So she threw me out."

I put the bag of food down. Squatting next to Lakshmi, I asked, "Is anyone inside with her?"

"Yes. I went and fetched Rao."

I rolled my eyes, shook my head, and let out a moan of disgust. The antidote for whenever Amma had a temper tantrum was to call either Balu or Rao. After twenty minutes of their sweet cajoling and loving persuasion she would cool down, then do what she was told and eat her food.

No way in hell was I going to enter Amma's room. I was in no mood to hear what she might have to say, to get roughed up, or to witness such pathetic behavior. Lakshmi had the ropes down pretty well by now. So I waited for the rest of the luggage to arrive and left everything in a huge pile outside Amma's door.

With a sincerely sympathetic smile on my face, I saluted Lakshmi. "It's all yours. Have fun."

I went back to the house in the same car, upset and livid. *Why does she have to be so difficult all the time? A simple yes or no was all I needed. Instead, she says nothing, waits until the last minute to give an answer, then beats the shit out of Lakshmi when things are not in place.*

After the conclusion of Devi Bhava the next day, Amma stepped into the small RV (camper van) that was parked out front ready to deliver her to the next location. She received a heartfelt send-off by her Zurich fans, and I closed the door to the camper. At the threshold of morning light we headed for Munich. I curled up on the floor in a tiny slot of available space by the kitchenette while Amma and Balu each lay on one of the two fold-out beds. Lakshmi was seated on the floor, struggling to stay awake as she massaged Amma's legs. A short while later I heard a crashing noise. I suspected that Lakshmi had dozed off and gone toppling into the vehicle's wall or cupboards or something.

Amma jolted awake and called out, "Balu, my son, are you okay? Did you hurt yourself?"

Before he could answer, Lakshmi confessed in a groggy voice, "It was me. I fell asleep."

Amma grunted and rolled over.

I lay there in disbelief. *Where did her compassion go, all of a sudden? Why was she only worried about Balu? Why didn't she ask if Lakshmi was okay?* I was sick of her doting on the men.

For the remainder of the European tour I was a ticking bomb. I barely showed my face at the programs. During the day I worked at various homes, cooking and taking care of everything behind the scenes. Then I would go to the evening programs. But as soon as the discourse and singing were over, I'd grab the nearest driver and split.

That same tour I had Lakshmi's buddy Mira sitting before me with a distraught face. There were tears in her eyes. With a quivering voice she whispered, "I just got a call from India. It was from the brahmacharin in charge of the ashram's publications. He said that he had been confronted recently by an angry devotee of Osho." This fellow claimed that several paragraphs in Amma's latest book of "teachings" had been lifted word for word from Osho's books.

When I heard this, I shook my head and let out a huge sigh. This series, which Mira had helped edit, was written by Balu. Supposedly. It consisted of conversations between Amma and her devotees that he had faithfully recorded. Supposedly.

I asked, "Did you inform Balu?"

"Yes. I told him immediately. He became so angry that he pushed me backwards out of his room and slammed the door in my face." Mira started sobbing. "I am really afraid Amma will be accused of plagiarism."

I do know that Balu had an extensive collection of Osho's works under lock and key in his private library. I know this because shortly before we left for that European tour Amma ordered me once again to read up on the guru/disciple relationship, in which, according to her, I was failing miserably. So I went to the library and asked Balu for a book. He grabbed a key out of his desk drawer and unlocked a cupboard. Before my very eyes were shelves of Osho books. He selected the book titled *Just Like That*. He wrapped the cover in white paper and gave me strict instructions not to show it to *anybody*!

No longer could I put on a smiling face for the devotees. No longer could I pretend everything was all right. My mind was ready to blow its stack any second. I needed warning signs hung around my neck. Danger—Highly Flammable. Caution—High Voltage. Beware of Dog. I couldn't believe the rage I was swimming in.

I used to ask our traveling jyotish, our astrologer, for a reading whenever I was having a rough time. He had incredible insight. Some of his descriptions— "this planet is in conjunction with that planet, and due to your being in this period with that sub period"—went over my head. But I'd gain relief from knowing he could see how long the difficult phase would last. So I went to him. This time all he could see was fire, fire, and more fire. Every single aspect, whether it was planetary or geographic, was ablaze. He predicted that once we left Europe and landed in America things would cool down. This news gave me tremendous relief and helped me hold it together. I hoped to God he was right, for I was beginning to find myself intolerable.

We made it to California. As soon as we turned off Crow Canyon road and drove through the neighboring horse corrals, I noticed an immediate shift in my mental state. A grin spontaneously spread across my face. After a couple of bends on the tree-lined gravel road, the car bounced its way over the rickety wooden bridge. Instead of turning right and heading to the main gate of the San Ramon ashram, we took a sharp left toward the adjacent hill and headed up the mile-long private road that snaked its way to what was referred to as Ron's House.

The home sat alone on the private hill, a massive, two-level, grayish wooden structure built by Nealu's relative, Ron. The building reminded me of a giant moth with wings spread. The ground level had a slate-floored foyer, a finely crafted wooden staircase, a gourmet kitchen and dining room, plus four bedrooms. The upper level had three bedrooms at one end, a circular Great Room in the middle, and the master wing where, of course, Amma stayed—office, spacious bedroom, and luxurious bathroom. Wide decks on both levels overlooked the valley, large pond, and surrounding green hills.

In the mornings after Amma had gone to the massive barn-style program hall located about half a mile away at the base of the adjacent hill—I would sit by the pond and think about my life. Some days I would follow the path that led across the hills through a small forest over to the main ashram, where Nealu resided. There I would track down my spiritual "big bro" and spend some time with him. It made my heart happy to see that he too was now clothed in sacred ochre robes. Through our little chats, despite the fact I never divulged any specifics, I think Nealu could tell I was suffering and perhaps on my way out.

I felt sorry for him, though I never said so. For years he had been spiritual leader at the California center, and during that time several women had projected their infatuation upon him. When the rumors reached Amma's ears, she was livid. I was sickened to hear what cruel things she said behind Nealu's back and one day to him directly over the phone.

Truth be told, I was angry that she showed so little kindness to the fellow who, constantly ill, held steadfast in his devotion and integrity. All the while she pampered, doted on, and was having sex with some of these other fellows. The hypocrisy and unfairness was driving me mad. But I bit my tongue.

One day upon my return through the little forest, nature graced me with a newfound sense of serenity. It also gave me an idea. What if I stayed here for a few weeks? I could get much-needed rest, nutrition, and, most of all, some distance. I could evaluate my life and see if there was anything left to salvage.

I knew there were no trips planned back in India for at least six weeks, so the ashram could manage without me. Checking with the airlines, I learned that my ticket could be changed without penalty. This was the perfect window of opportunity, and I intended to seize it.

I wrote Amma a note—something I had never done before:

I have come to a point in my life where I am desperately mentally, physically, and emotionally worn out. I feel I need to be here for four to six weeks to gain some peace of mind and to reflect on my life a little in the hope of re-kindling some love and devotion toward you and the path. I therefore humbly request that you allow me to stay back. Please give me a straight answer.

I handed the paper to Lakshmi and asked her to give it to Amma after she finished her lunch.

The morning program ended. I waited anxiously in the circular Great Room that was serving as a dormitory for the female tour staff. An hour or so later I heard the door to Amma's wing open. Lakshmi entered carrying a tray with Amma's leftover food. After setting down the tray, she proceeded to leave, intentionally not looking at me.

I jumped up. "Did Amma read my note?"

Lakshmi's face turned crimson. Her hesitancy was eloquent.

"Lakshmi," I insisted. "You need to tell me whatever it was she said. I must know her answer."

Squirming in her skin she said, "Amma crumpled your note, threw it across the room, then said, 'Who can I trust?' She said that you just want to have it easy."

I ignited with rage. But I didn't utter a word, for the room was full of women sprawled out all over the floor on sleeping bags.

Lakshmi scurried back to Amma's room before she got into trouble for being gone too long. I went back to the linen closet where I was staying. *That's it. I'm done. I've tried my best. I can't take it anymore. I have to leave. I just have to leave*, I muttered to myself with almost one hundred percent conviction.

The following morning I awoke with a heavy heart and not so happily greeted the new day. It was my birthday, November 17, 1999, and it was going to become a very significant day.

That morning Balu, who had been speaking to Amma, summoned me to the office to render some advice. The normally well-groomed fellow's shoulder-length hair was awry, and the dark circles under his eyes were pronounced with worry. Gravely looking at me, he said, "Even if Amma agrees for you to stay back, I warn you, don't do it. You're just asking for trouble."

"Why, what did she say?"

"None of your business."

"None of my business? It is absolutely my business. I have a right to know what she's saying behind my back," I spewed in frustration.

"Let me just say this. Even if she does agree, she doesn't mean it. All right?"

"Whatever. Anyhow, she didn't agree. So why the hell are you even talking about it?"

I stormed off.

The afternoon turned cold and wet. The sun had already packed it in for the day. I was resting in the ladies' dorm feeling as gloomy as the weather. Amma had returned from the morning program and Lakshmi was attending, so I knew I had a couple of hours to rest. All I could hear were a few whispers, some faint snoring, and the creaking of an ironing board as Shanti moved the iron to and fro. Daily she would stand in that spot for hours on end, dutifully and solemnly ironing Amma's clothes with amazing perfection. Shanti had come bouncing into the ashram about nine years before as a sun-kissed Californian with a solid meditation practice and a zeal for life. But her healthy frame had taken a beating over the years. She too had developed the ashram look—ashy skin, sunken eyes, slumped posture, and thinning hair. She too got hooked on the notion that the more you neglect and punish your body, the greater your devotion for Amma. Her face carried a constant look of deep sorrow, and I often teased her by asking, "So Shanti, who died today?" She wasn't the only one who wore such a glum countenance. Many suffered from the same intense longing for Amma's love, which turned into a form of despair.

I was just about to close my weary eyes when the privacy curtain moved and some light crept into the room along with Lakshmi, who announced, "Priya, Amma is calling."

The girl sprang off the floor, rubbed her eyes, straightened her sari, and then rushed out. I dozed off. I wasn't needed or concerned. Priya was often summoned to Amma's room to assist with the preparation of Amma's evening talks.

Some twenty minutes later I was jolted awake by a horrendous, blood-curdling noise that made me curl into fetal position.

It was Amma in the hallway outside her room screaming, "Priya, what's taking you so long? How long does it take to boil some water?"

Through the door I heard a slapping noise. Then I heard Amma say, "Give me that hot water bottle, and get out of here."

Seconds later Priya entered the dorm, came to my side, and in the dim light I could see blood trickling down the corner of her mouth.

I sat up in horror. "What happened?"

Still shaking and with tears in her beautiful eyes, she whispered, "Amma was interrogating me about you. It felt creepy and evil almost. She was sitting in the dark with her hair down, and there was a heating lamp behind her casting an eerie glow. She became angry and suspicious when I didn't have any negative information to divulge about you. She then told me to go heat some water. I was barely gone a minute when she began screaming, then smacked me across the face."

I was furious that Amma had begun to take her aggression out on Priya now too. Even more infuriating was the knowledge she had begun trying to squeeze information out of my friends. I had watched her many times squeeze like this about anyone she suspected. But now she was squeezing Gayatri. She no longer trusted me. I could not bear that. Her distrust and her crumpling of my note, these were the final straws.

Something inside me clicked into place. I was centered, at peace. I no longer had to agonize or feel torn about what to do. The spell was broken. My mind was made up. And my heart was pounding with excitement. For I was about to begin my free fall into the lap of the unknown.

Holy Hell

I knew this wasn't going to be easy.

Sunday night during Devi Bhava seemed like the perfect time to sneak away, but I decided to wait until the morning to start figuring out the logistics. I was too wound up. I couldn't risk making any mistakes.

That evening at the conclusion of bhajans I got up from the stage and went out the side door to get a ride back up the hill to Ron's house. I was grabbing my shoes when two female residents of the California ashram approached and asked if I would come to the bakery tent. They needed to run something by me. The tent was right there adjacent to the program hall, so I politely obliged. When I stepped inside the tent though, I almost jumped out of my skin. Twenty women all at once yelled, "Surprise!" and began singing, "Happy birthday to you." I stood there bashfully smiling and wracked with gut-wrenching guilt. I knew the surprise was going to be on them.

"Blow out the candles and make a wish," they cried.

The candles flickered in the chilly air. The women huddled around. Before making my wish, I looked up at their smiling faces and the glowing reflection of the candles in their eyes. I took a deep breath, closed my eyes, and earnestly prayed, "Dear God, give me the strength, guidance, and protection to carry out this leap of faith."

I blew out the candles, and they all cheered and clapped. The irony was killing me. I cut the cake and distributed a slice to each of the lovely ladies. With a smile I thanked them for being so kind and thoughtful. Then I went in search of my ride.

As we drove along the gravel road before turning up the hill to Ron's house, I silently gazed out the window. Tears welled up in my eyes. I knew that what I was about to do would hit these kind-hearted people like a tidalwave. Devotees believed I was rock-solid. To them this meant I would never leave Amma. Little did they know that I was drawing on my "rock solid" in order to liberate myself from her.

Then I pulled myself together. I couldn't allow emotion to get in the way or to weaken my resolve.

For the past two years I had drenched my pillow with tears swearing I would leave, then awoken resigned to give it one more try. But things were very different now. I did not cry myself to sleep. I awoke with mental clarity. There was not an iota of doubt in my mind. It was time to escape.

Amma would never allow me to simply quit and walk out the front door. People would wonder why a swamini so close to Amma would abandon ship. She couldn't risk such a scandal, and she couldn't risk losing control of certain damaging information I would be taking with me.

To leave in secret was my only option.

I waited for Amma and the group to go to the morning program. Once the house was quiet, I snuck into the room of one of the residents to use her private phone line. I knew exactly who to call, a woman who had lived at the Indian ashram for many years and who had frequently come to me upset about the happenings there. Eventually she decided that the ashram wasn't her cup of tea and headed back to America to lead a normal life. I felt she was someone who would understand the depth of my despair and the magnitude of what I was about to ask of her. Even though she still came to the programs, her visits were really about connecting with her community of friends and the devotional atmosphere, not to gaze starry-eyed at Amma. I knew I could trust her. Most importantly, I knew she wouldn't be suspected of helping me. Nor would she be affected once the shit hit the fan.

"Maya, hi, it's me Gayatri," I hurriedly spoke through the phone.

"Namah Sivaya, what a surprise, what's up?"

There was no beating around the bush with this one. "I need you to help me escape from the ashram."

"What!" she screeched. "Oh my God.... Really? I know you've been sad for a while, but are you sure?"

"Trust me. I'm positive. Otherwise I wouldn't be talking to you."

"Okay, then tell me what you need."

"Well, first I need a ride off the property, then somewhere to hide out for a few days until they all go back to India. Of course, you know you must not tell a soul. No devotees should know a thing. You have to keep this top secret," I pleaded.

"Are you kidding? Of course. Holy shit, this is huge."

"Maya," I nervously laughed. "I can't talk long, and please don't phone me here. I know they will try to piece evidence together after I disappear, so we must not be seen talking in public either. You got that?"

"I understand," she reassured. "Tonight after the program as you are leaving the hall, I will slip you a note with what I have come up with, okay?"

"Perfect. Thanks, Maya. I had better go."

I gently hung up the phone, stealthily cracked the door open, and peeked outside. The hallway was empty, so I dashed into the bathroom as an alibi for being in that wing of the house. I gazed into the mirror, shook my head in disbelief, and grinned as I let out a gigantic sigh. My heart and mind were finally synchronized, and everything was falling into place. Even though I was about to make an incredibly drastic and traumatic change to my life, I felt encapsulated in a bubble of grace. I was being guided clearly and intuitively through each crucial step.

As promised, later that evening Maya slipped me a note as I exited the hall. Once back at the house and inside a bathroom—which was about the only place I could be assured some privacy—I read its contents.

"I have found a house for you to stay. It belongs to an old colleague, an Indian man who lives in Danville, just ten minutes away. He is not affiliated with the ashram, so don't worry, you will be safe. What next? Please advise."

I ripped the note into tiny pieces and flushed it down the toilet. I was taking no chances. That evening, I decided to inform Priya and Shanti of my plans. I was close with both women and knew I could trust them implicitly.

Even though the house was relatively quiet, I couldn't risk anyone overhearing what I was about to confess, so I asked them to come outside onto the deck with me. I closed the sliding glass door and peered over the railing to make sure nobody was down below. It was a frosty evening, so everything was closed up. The coast was clear.

In a grave voice I said, "I am about to whisper something and you have to promise not to react."

They both nodded in agreement and stared at me with confused looks.

"I am going to leave the ashram."

Simultaneously they let out gasps of horror. "When? Where will you go? What will you do? How will you pull off such an act?"

"Not telling. I am not going to divulge any more information. I cannot have you involved. You are going to be the first people questioned after I disappear. I can't risk you cracking under pressure, nor will I place you in a position where you feel you have to lie. I just wanted to let you know so you didn't feel betrayed later."

We stepped back into the living room. In the light I could see they were distraught, in shock. I thought, *Oh no, what have I done?* I cast them both an anxious smile and tried to lift the mood by saying, "Come on, let's go see what is for dinner."

The next morning, Friday, once again I discreetly phoned Maya and relayed my exit strategy.

My departure time would be Sunday night at nine, shortly after Devi Bhava commenced. I knew the house would be deserted except for maybe Lakshmi fussing around.

But I needed Maya to come earlier than that, in fact to come in the afternoon and park her car in the upper parking lot of Ron's house, then leave it and take the ashram shuttle down the hill to the program barn. Then hang around there till nine and come back on the shuttle. Here's why. I knew that once darkness fell, security would tighten. There would be a devotee standing guard at the bottom of the hill, and only authorized vehicles would be allowed up the private road. So she had to stash her car ahead of time for me and lock it, but leave a key on top of the rear left tire and also put a dark blanket on the back seat. At nine then she would shuttle back up to Ron's, get in her car, and drive away as if she had no idea that behind her seat under a blanket she was transporting a stowaway.

I chose to involve one more person. She helped me smuggle out a few items ahead of time. That person was Kusuma. After being a devotee for a few years and the original organizer of the world tours, she experienced a crisis of faith and vanished for several years. She had just started coming again to the programs. In fact, she had been given a sleeping spot in the dorm. So I felt that no suspicion would be aroused if I talked to her.

Nonchalantly, in a laundry basket I placed my laptop, sleeping bag, soft travel bag, some winter clothing, a couple of bottles of shampoo and conditioner, a set of sheets, towels, and a quilt. Inside the lining of my computer case I hid a tiny bit of survival money. Having given twenty years of my life to the organization, with no bank account or a penny to my name, I pushed aside any guilt about doing this.

Later that day Kusuma plopped a bundle of her dirty clothes on top and pretended to be going out to the Laundromat. Instead she drove to Maya's home to deliver the goods.

By Friday mid-morning my entire escape plan was in place. Now all I had to do was wait. Tick-tock, tick-tock, the minutes of my life inched forward. Sunday nine p.m., Sunday nine p.m., this was my mantra. Like a person awaiting the hour of execution, I suppose, I had trouble paying attention to daily details. But I didn't want to arouse any suspicion. I pretended to be my usual unhappy self.

Saturday morning, once the house was empty and everyone was away doing selfless service or sitting in the barn transfixed on Amma, I had a rather intense and agitated Priya and Shanti standing before me. It seems I had ignited a bundle of concerns and doubts that they too had been harboring. Priya in particular was livid. I had never seen this soft-spoken Indian woman in such a state. In her hand was a copy of Amma's biography. She flipped it open to a marked page and with trembling voice began reading, "From this day on, the little one is ever pure." Then she read the footnote: "After Krishna Bhava began, Sudhamani never had Her monthly period."

Shaking with rage Priya exclaimed, "How can they print such lies? I was in the doctor's office with you last week when Amma admitted she had her period." Angrily tossing the book onto the floor she asked, "How can I believe anything that is written here?"

I knew exactly what she was talking about. Recently in France Amma had complained of abdominal pain, so we arranged for her to see a gynecologist. Gently pushing on Amma's belly, the doctor asked, "When was her last period?"

Innocently Priya began to reply, "Oh she doesn't have her period."

Amma turned to me and interjected: "Two weeks ago."

I didn't think twice about this event at the time, for I had been carrying the secret for many, many years. Only now, seeing Priya's reaction on this day, did I suddenly admit to myself that I had been complicit in a grave deception. I was especially mortified to see in print the claim that she was "ever pure."

My mind suddenly flashed upon the numerous occasions when it was "that time of the month" and Amma called me to the hall as the gatherings were drawing to a close. She would whisper in my ear to stand right behind her when she stood up in case her dress was stained with blood. One time it was. So Amma told me what to say in case anyone asked.

Later that day I had a lady standing before me bawling her eyes out, asking if Amma was ill because when she left her chair there were bloodstains on the cover. As ordered by Amma, and to my regret, I lied. "It is nothing to worry about. Amma has a mild case of hemorrhoids."

Now Shanti, with a face more gaunt and stressed than usual, grabbed hold of the conversation. "We need you to tell us everything you know. We are going to take you high up on a mountain where nobody can hear so you can tell us the truth. What is really going on here?"

From years of being terrified to open my mouth I said, "I don't feel it appropriate to share any of the secrets I am carrying. I have had to witness and hear many things due to my close position, but that is my karma I guess. I just can't tell you."

"Stop protecting that liar of a guru," Priya retorted. "We have a right to know the truth. I read a letter Pai sent to Amma through one of his trusted followers after he left the ashram. She had me and Dr. Leela read it in her bathroom, and then burn it because she was afraid some of the other men would see it." After gasping for a breath Priya whispered, "Pai was accusing Amma of giving him a sexually transmitted disease. At the time, I did not believe it, but now I am not so sure. I am not completely naive or ignorant. I have eyes you know. Many times in Amma's room, I have seen her act really flirtatious, especially with Balu and Rao."

These dear friends were irate. They refused to give in.

"Hang on a sec," I said, getting up to look into the corridor to ensure nobody was listening.

I sat back down. Shanti said, "Okay, if you can't share, then at least tell us this. Please answer this one question. Based on everything you know, should we stay or should we leave?"

Without hesitating I answered, "You should leave."

Their faces turned rigid. I totally understood their plight. Their world now, too, was upside down, and they had a decision to make.

I said, "You know what? I don't care if Amma thinks she *is* the Divine Mother. I don't want to have a thing to do with her anymore. My service to her was out of my love for God. My love for God is not going to change. I am just removing her from the equation. I want to lead a peaceful and truthful spiritual life, and this is far from it. God knows my heart. I will be protected."

I stood up, saying I had to get to the kitchen. I felt sorry for them. But knew they would figure out what was best.

Within one week after my disappearing act, they both made their exit from the ashram.

My life crept forward in slow motion, but D-Day eventually arrived. My eyes constantly wandered to the clock on the wall just to see the hands had perhaps moved forward a minute or two. *Oh God, will this day ever end?*

Finally six p.m. arrived and Amma proceeded down the hill to the barn to conduct the afternoon ceremony, where people sat around tiny brass lamps chanting and praying for world peace. I gathered all the necessary items for Devi Bhava, which was to follow directly after, and went down the hill. I set everything up in the tiny dressing room located by the side door of the temple, and I sat waiting on the staircase nearby. My heart was pounding. I let out frequent, heavy sighs each time I remembered that in a couple of hours my life would be forever changed. A devotee came up, sat down next to me, and engaged in idle conversation. I appreciated the distraction.

Shortly afterwards the coordinator for the evening bhajans came and asked, "Is midnight until two a.m. an okay shift for you to sing?"

"Sure, that's fine," I bluffed.

I could hear the ceremony coming to a close. I knew that Amma would come out the side door and enter her dressing room very soon. Sure enough. Minutes later I heard people scurrying and the door flung open. I jumped up. Amma glanced at me as she entered the room. I chose not to go inside. It was a tiny space. More than that, to face her was painful. I sat frozen on the steps, waiting for the seconds and minutes of this phase of my life to be no more.

Suddenly the door cracked opened. Lakshmi stuck her head out saying, "Amma is calling."

"Oh, God."

I took a long, deep breath and went inside. I stood by the door rigid as a statue. Without looking up she asked me to go fetch some sacred ash. So I went into the temple and grabbed a couple of packets. She took them from me, gave me a quick once over, and that was that.

Once Amma was inside the temple and Devi Bhava was about to commence with the grand opening of the curtain, I noticed that one of her silk garlands was still in the changing room. I dashed out the side door to retrieve it and the door locked shut behind me. I stood motionless. The garland limply dangled from my hand. I was locked out. My life with Amma had officially just ended. From outside the door I could hear the curtain opening and the bells ringing. I envisioned the multi-tiered lamp brimming with golden flames being waved before her. It was over; it was all over. Now I just needed to safely complete the last couple of steps before I would be a free woman.

I gathered everything from the changing room and got a ride back up the hill along with Priya. Even though I had told her I was planning to leave, we never spoke of it again. So she had no clue that the event was just moments away.

Holy Hell

Back at the house I proceeded to my linen closet, closed the door, took out a pen and paper, and wrote the following note to Amma:

> This is the most painful, heartbreaking, devastating decision I have ever made in my life. If you knew my heart and mind, this situation could have been avoided. I sincerely tried to save the situation, but you slammed the last door in my face. I have not been happy for years, but God knows I tried. My faith is completely ruined, and you are responsible for that. Forgive me if you can. I am left with no other choice than to move on.

Signed..... ? (I did not know what to call myself)

With a broken heart, I solemnly placed the note on top of my pile of robes—my shattered hopes and dreams. Leaving the key inside, I turned the knob to the locked position, exited, and closed the door. I believed this would slow the process down, once they began looking for me. I was hoping that wouldn't be until after midnight, when I failed to show for my singing shift. I hurried back to join Priya, who was seated in the dorm having her dinner. The sight of this beautiful woman and dear friend strangled my heart—I didn't know if I would ever see her again.

Sweetly and unsuspectingly she asked, "Gayatri, can I get you something to eat?"

I had barely eaten in four days. I just couldn't. I quickly glanced at the clock, and my heart jumped when I saw it was eight fifty-eight. Time to step away from life as I knew it.

"No thanks, I'm not hungry. But I would like something to drink," I said to separate her from me.

Once she was out of sight, I tippy-toed down the stairs through the front door and out into the dark night with just the robes on my back. Somberly I proceeded up the small hill, terraced with wooden planks, to the parking lot where Maya's car was waiting. The air was still. The entire universe was holding its breath. This was a sacred and terrifying moment.

I found the bright-red two-door sedan and the key she'd left, as planned, on top of the rear tire. I cautiously looked around. The place was deserted. So I quickly opened the door and hopped into the back seat. I crouched down on the floor and covered myself with the dark blanket that had been kept ready. All I had to do now was wait. Wait for Maya to come up the hill and drive me away to safety.

It felt like a lifetime that I was lying there upside down with my face squished into the floor. Eventually I heard a car pull up in front of Amma's house, doors opening and closing, and voices saying "Namah Sivaya." My heart was pounding out of my chest. I heard a shuffle of feet coming up the steps. *Please God, let this be Maya.* My senses were screaming. I could hear every piece of bark snapping under the person's shoes and the displacement of every tiny pebble.

Suddenly the car door yanked open. My heart somersaulted when I heard a familiar voice ask, "Are you sure you want to do this?"

"Yes, I am sure. Please, let's just go," I begged through my blanket.

She closed the door and turned the key. The engine rumbled, and we went down the hill. As I lay there, I envisioned the scenery at each turn. We paused. I heard cars crossing in front of us along the narrow, unpaved road that led to the main ashram and program hall. After a brief wait, we proceeded over crunchy gravel, then drove over the bumpy little wooden bridge. I pictured Maya innocently waving at the devotees who stood by the horse corrals in the freezing cold as they guided the traffic to the various parking lots. I imagined their exchange of smiles as we exited the ashram. With a final large thump we were out of the ashram grounds and on the highway, where the vibrations of the car became smooth. My heart beat loudly the entire ride. I was praying with every ounce of my being, *Guide me. Protect me. Guide me. Protect me.*

I waited a couple of minutes until I felt we were safely out of sight, then I jumped up off the floor and let out a magnificent shriek. I could almost hear Maya's neck snap as she turned around in horror. "Are you okay? Is everything all right?"

Grabbing hold of her headrest I said, "For God's sake, keep your eyes on the damn road. The last thing I want at this point is to have an accident."

Maya knew me well enough to decide that I was okay.

I leaned back into my seat and sat there like a stunned deer watching cars zoom by as we drove toward the rest of my life. By now my vision was blurry, for my eyes were full to the brim with tears that began sliding down my face. They were tears of joy, sadness, grief, fear, pain, elation, and relief. I couldn't believe it was over. Twenty years of my ashram life was all over. I was utterly exhausted and without a clue as to what I would do next. All that mattered—I was free.

In my heart I believed, somehow, everything would be all right.

But I continued to pray to God with all my might: *Guide me. Protect me. Guide me. Protect me. Guide me. Protect me....*

EPILOGUE

MY OWN TWO FEET

On November 21, 1999, I took that deep breath and jumped ship. After a grueling swim to shore, I collapsed like a hunk of driftwood, paralyzed with grief and trauma. Eventually I found the strength to get up and live again. At first the task felt overwhelming—like poor old Humpty-Dumpty.

I shut the door on my life with Amma and hid the key for a future date. I felt too much pain to review my beliefs or to determine what had been real and what had been projection. I needed time to heal. I felt numb but also consumed with anger. Because I witnessed and experienced so much of Amma's dark side, I had been forced to give up a life that I held so dear and to divorce myself from so many wonderful people within the organization.

Adding to my anguish was the weight of all the secrets I was carrying. I feared retribution. I was not afraid of the subtle beings portrayed in Amma's biography, nor of getting struck by lightning, nor of some mighty curse at which even God would shrug his shoulders. No, I feared the harassment and character assassination that I knew would come from Amma and her followers if I disclosed even a fraction of what I knew. I wasn't strong enough yet to endure that torment. I just wanted to get on with my life and keep it as peaceful as possible.

Deep in my heart I knew that I had a moral obligation to speak out and share my experiences. I have now come forward with my story because, from the perspective of my recovered consciousness, I see how wrong it is for such information to be kept from the innocents who so readily hand over their minds, their money, and their lives. The initial sensation of euphoria from the devotional atmosphere—also from the superficial impression that this lofty team, with Amma at the helm, is doing such great work for the world—lures people with powerful force. It is not just the naive and innocent who are vulnerable. No amount of intellect or education can grant one immunity where matters of the heart and faith are concerned.

The new recruits are then informed by existing members that their absolute surrender will guarantee Amma's divine protection. She will take care of every aspect of their lives and monitor every single thought that passes through their minds. What they are not told (most likely because these devotees are blind to it themselves) is that in order to "fit in" they are going to have to give up all independent thought. They are never to ask questions. They must alienate themselves from friends and family and turn a blind eye to anything that might challenge their new found beliefs and sense of integrity and justice. They will learn to rationalize each and every event in order to keep their faith intact.

Without any thought for the future, without asking whether the ashram has any plan in place for taking care of them when they grow old or ill—not to mention, without a plan of their own in case they ever change their minds about things—these well-meaning souls dive in headfirst.

A few months after leaving the ashram, in April of 2000, I was in California visiting an Amma devotee friend. (At the time, Amma devotees were just about the only people I knew.) The phone rang and my friend said, "Yes, she is here." She handed me the receiver not revealing who was on the other end.

"Hello?"

"Gayatri, this is Stephen from Australia."

I knew Amma was in the country, so I suspected she was behind the call. I became nervous.

With excitement in his voice he continued, "They want me to tell you that they are willing to build you an ashram anywhere you like in Australia. You won't have to do anything except put your robes back on."

I was in shock. "Stephen, first, let me ask you this. Who are 'they'?"

"Amma and Ramakrishna Swami. Oh, and one more thing—if you agree, you must put it in writing. There will also be some papers for you to sign."

I could feel the anger rising. "That sounds like blackmail."

I would be nothing more than a prisoner—this time in a golden cage. I wanted nothing to do with the devious offer.

The man's voice tightened and sped up. I guess he feared that his mission was failing. "It's really important that you come back. They say it's a matter of saving face for the ashram."

His words plunged into my heart like a dagger. I began to shake inside from the insult. *Does he not realize how heartless a statement he just made? All that Amma worries about is her image. Everything picture-perfect. Not a drop of concern for the individual!*

For me!

"Gayatri," he continued, "it was our dream to have you as our Swamini here in Australia."

"Yes, it was a dream of mine too at one stage. Unfortunately it now feels like a nightmare."

"Can we call you again in a few weeks to give you time to think about it?" he begged.

"I'm sorry, but you are wasting your time. I will not change my mind. If anything, your words have only reinforced my conviction to leave."

After we hung up, I staggered to my room and spent the following day in bed physically ill with grief.

Holy Hell

It took a few years, but from much rest, nutritious food, a new circle of friends and time spent in nature, my health began to improve and my trauma softened. At night though I was haunted by a recurring dream of trying to escape, of being hunted. This made me wonder, *Am I really free? Or am I still trapped—mentally and emotionally?* Within my soul I knew I couldn't step out of the shadow of my past until I faced Amma again.

I felt a calling to go to California, but my mind refused to put two and two together. A few weeks later, a dear friend suggested I pay Amma a visit, so I took that as a sign it was time. I dreaded the thought of going back to San Ramon, but I knew it had to be done if I was ever going to heal.

At eleven a.m. on the first day of Amma's November tour in 2006, accompanied by my friend, I entered the program venue through the very same side door that had been my exit seven years earlier. The crowd parted like the Red Sea. Within minutes I was kneeling before an utterly shocked Amma. I gave her a smile, rubbed the side of her leg, and patted her on the knee. I was asked to sit beside her chair. No words were exchanged. But my unvoiced message to her was: *I am whole, I am healthy, I am happy, and you have no power over me any more.* Five hours later Amma rose from her chair, and I departed the hall. This time I gracefully walked out the front door in broad daylight.

The visit left me feeling rather drained but ever so empowered. My nightmares ceased and my relationship with myself began to heal. This change in turn healed my relationships with those around me. The spell had been broken and the final pieces of the puzzle had been set into place. At long last I was free.

Then I had another breakthrough. Suddenly I was able to distinguish the difference between my spirituality and my unique connection to God through Amma. I realized that over the course of my indoctrination these two urges had merged. Slowly it began to sink in—when I shut that door on Amma, I impulsively closed a door on my entire spirituality. So I began to reconnect with the spiritual life I had been leading long before I even knew Amma existed. This change allowed my heart to open again.

Another important part of my healing process was to turn the focus of attention to myself for a time. I had to uncover the weaknesses and flaws in my character that had attracted me to such a cultish lifestyle and ill treatment. I did this not to blame myself, but to understand why I had accepted the abuse and so willingly turned a blind eye to all the corruption I witnessed and was complicit in. Shifting the focus onto oneself does not excuse in any way the culpability of the abusers, but it does untangle one from their actions. I took responsibility for my life choices, and the shackles of victimhood broke. This shift transformed me from the victim of a guru and of a rapist to a free woman with a sense of responsibility and empowerment. It made me a disciple of life. Now that my mind was free from the sting of emotional pain, I was able to re-visit my life with Amma and begin the long process of trying to make sense out of it all.

Books also played an enormous part in my recovery process. Of all the books I read, *The Guru Papers* by Joel Kramer and Diana Alstad was by far the most insightful. It helped me wade through the myth and muck, and it shone a bright light on the guru/disciple relationship. It helped me to chisel away the ashram thought conditioning and to clearly see the underlying psychology in what I used to take for granted. I was aghast when I then read my old diaries from my years with Amma. Incidents I had viewed at the time as heart-warming, or perhaps as discipline by the guru, I now saw as narcissistic and manipulative. Whatever residual projections and rationalizations I had carried with me now dissolved. I finally had confirmation of the many doubts I had harbored, and I had answers to many of my unresolved questions. There were rather blatant and simple explanations for Amma's behavior. I began to see her as someone who exploits people's inherent desire to belong, to be loved, to find meaning in life, while she behaves like some kind of dictator claiming to be God, not requiring any learning or improvement.

Do I have all the answers? No, and I probably never will. I have come to accept the fact that Amma is a complex fusion of character and color—just like every single human being on earth. She is a person who, in her humanity, has been influenced by her upbringing, her social and economical environment, and her culture. She is a riddle I do not need to solve.

Here are some excerpts from *The Guru Papers* that I found particularly eye-opening.

The Guru Trap
"At the heart of the ultimate trap is building and becoming attached to an image of oneself as having arrived at a state where self-delusion is no longer possible. This is the most treacherous form of self-delusion and a veritable breeding ground of hypocrisy and deception. It creates a feedback-proof system where the guru always needs to be right and cannot be open to being shown wrong—which is where learning comes from."

"No matter how much evidence casts doubt on this stance of unchallengeable certainty, it is always possible to maintain that the place of such exalted knowledge is not subject to the proofs and judgments of ordinary people."

"For a guru, adulation and power are intricately connected since the disciples' surrender is the ultimate source of his power, and adulation is the prerequisite for surrender. A guru is made to feel he is the center of the universe by his disciples. It is difficult to not be 'in love' with that image of oneself."

The Disciple Trap
"Adulation has powerful emotions for the sender as well, and can be easily mistaken for love. It is likewise addicting for the sender, as it is an easy route to feelings of passion."

"There is the hope that the guru will be the perfect or idealized parent one never had—a veritable fount of unconditional love. But this so-called unconditional love is conditional upon surrendering to the guru and accepting his authority. Transference that is reinforced such that it becomes a way of life ensures the client, student, or disciple will remain fundamentally childish."

The Celibacy Trap

"Celibacy undermines coupling when presented as a higher state than sexual intimacy. This, in effect, gets people in couples to surrender to the guru rather than to each other. Gurus can exercise control over their followers in the most basic areas by decreeing whether coupling is allowed, who marries whom, how often and in what circumstances sex is permitted, whether couples can cohabit, and even whether they reproduce and how to raise the children. Some gurus actively discourage having children or separate parents from them, which is done to decrease distractions from devotion to the guru."

In the years since I left the ashram, I have gone on to make a happy life on my own. It is a simple, quiet life, but one full of nurturing. I've managed to integrate reasonably well back into Western society. I have come to understand how the tales and traditions of India and the essence of the guru/disciple relationship were misused by Amma. Instead of being based on a mutually beneficial life of respect, the relationship took on the distorted roles of submission and absolute dominance.

In fact, the Upanishads encourage an inquisitive attitude on the part of the disciple. They do not support abject and blind obedience to the guru. The latter is actually a form of perversion that has gradually developed through the centuries in Indian society.

The "Sahanavavatu mantra," so often chanted at Amma's ashram, is one of the peace mantras that has its origins in the Taittiriya Upanisad. This mantra states that the transference of mental, spiritual, and intellectual energies from the teacher to the student can be achieved through a nourishing relationship based on mutual respect, joy of giving and receiving, and absence of malice or negative thoughts.

> Let us together be protected, and let us together be nourished by God's
> blessings. Let us together join our mental forces in strength for the benefit

of humanity. Let our efforts at learning be luminous and filled with joy, endowed with the force of purpose. Let us never be poisoned with the seeds of hatred for anyone. Let there be Peace in me! Let there be Peace in my environment! Let there be Peace in the forces that act on me!

A guru/disciple relationship without underlying peace is simply not right. Amma's mode of conduct and teachings remain far from this principle. If I were seeking a guru today, I would use these guidelines to determine whether such a person is worthy of my surrender.

Nowadays, instead of seeking the love of God in a domineering guru, I find it in the goodness of all that surrounds me. I experience peace and joy in the very ordinary moments of my life. I strive to keep my mind and heart in alignment with one another, and for love to be the guiding principle of my life. I cherish the wonderful but fleeting moments of synchronicity that fill my being with reassurance in the presence of a higher power. I maintain wonderful memories from the good old days in the ashram and my twenty-one years in India. I have made mistakes and learned the hard way. These experiences have shaped who I am today.

This memoir was written as an essential part of my healing process. It is about letting go and finding peace within. It is a mere cross-section of what I witnessed and endured, a selection of details I needed to purge in order to make some sense out of it all—the good, the bad, and the ugly. If I were to reveal everything I am aware of, this book could double in size. My objective is not to harm anyone but to present a more down-to-earth and realistic image of Amma so that devotees can balance their beliefs with the hefty weight of awareness. If that weight comes down and suddenly tips the scales against a heap of featherweight rationalizations, earnest devotees can suffer the devastating effects of disillusionment.

I offer my story with the sincere hope that it will illustrate to spiritual seekers the downside of blind faith, and that surrender to a guru/teacher is sometimes mind control in disguise. Perhaps some readers will now recognize that they too have turned a blind eye to reality in order to protect their beliefs. I hope that those who doubt will feel free to question, those with questions will find answers, and those already suffering the wounds of betrayal and disillusionment will find consolation and validation.

Ultimately, I hope this book will empower those trapped in any form of abusive relationship or unhealthy situation to find the courage to step away, and to trust that an amazing life awaits them—a life full of unexpected blessings and wonderful people.

In my pursuit for God I spent years suppressing my personality, striving to be someone else and denying myself even the most basic human comforts and pleasures. I was taught and accepted the belief that this denial would bring me closer to God. Naturally, we must learn, grow and work on our flaws. But this important work should not deny us the right to embrace our own humanity, to feel empowered, and to nurture and acknowledge our gifts.

I now question: *Why on earth would God want us to suffer or to be anyone other than our own unique, authentic and wonderful selves?*

In the end, I did not find God, but I did find myself. And I thank God for that.

Made in the USA
Charleston, SC
03 June 2014